Lost Laborers in Colonial California

Lost Laborers in Colonial California

Native Americans and
the Archaeology of Rancho Petaluma

Stephen W. Silliman

The University of Arizona Press

Tucson

The University of Arizona Press
© 2004 The Arizona Board of Regents
All rights reserved

09 08 07 06 05 04   6 5 4 3 2 1

Library of Congress Cataloging-in-Publication Data
Silliman, Stephen W., 1971–
Lost laborers in colonial California : Native Americans and the
archaeology of Rancho Petaluma / Stephen W. Silliman.
p. cm.
Includes bibliographical references and index.
ISBN 0-8165-2381-9 (cloth : alk. paper)
1. Indians of North America—California—Petaluma Adobe State Historic Park (Petaluma)—
History—19th century. 2. Indians of North America—California—Petaluma Adobe State
Historic Park (Petaluma)—Antiquities. 3. Indians of North America—California—Petaluma
Adobe State Historic Park (Petaluma)—Social life and customs. 4. Excavations (Archaeology)—
California—Petaluma Adobe State Historic Park (Petaluma) 5. Petaluma Adobe State Historic
Park (Petaluma, Calif.)—History—19th century. 6. Petaluma Adobe State Historic Park
(Petaluma, Calif.)—Antiquities. I. Title.
E78.C15S57 2004
305.897'079418—dc22
2004010264

To Tracey

With love and gratitude

Contents

Illustrations

Maps

Figures

Tables

Preface

The impact of Western colonialism on indigenous people in the Americas is a topic of enduring importance for studying the past and understanding the present. The topic engages archaeologists, cultural anthropologists, historians, oral historians, sociologists, and Native scholars. From the Canadian Arctic to the tip of South America, the unique perspectives brought by each discipline have contributed greatly to our understanding of these colonial interactions and their many manifestations and outcomes. The consequences of these colonial encounters are lived daily by those whose ancestors suffered and those whose ancestors imposed colonial worlds, labor regimes, and social inequality. This legacy informs or perhaps fuels many of the politics surrounding ethnic identities, rights to human burial remains, land claims, economic development, and government power. Such contemporary relevance makes the topic all the more indispensable but, at the same time, extraordinarily complex and difficult.

I use this book to intersect these research issues via archaeology. In particular, I am intrigued by topics of labor, gender, and social agency in the study of colonialism. I am also enthusiastic about the critical role that archaeology plays in these studies, and this work feeds on my excitement and commitment. Rather than taking a broad sweep across many regions, the book grapples with Native-colonial interactions as they played out in a specific case in nineteenth-century northern California. The context is the Mexican-Californian rancho, a relatively late manifestation of the Spanish-American land grant built upon livestock and indigenous labor.[1] This is not a book about all California ranchos or an exhaustive summary of every archaeological project ever devoted to ranchos. Such a book has yet to be written. This book is, instead, a first step in foregrounding Native American experiences through the interplay of archaeological and textual sources about a particular rancho.

Because of the regional context, I engage primarily with the literature on North American colonialism and culture contact, some aspects of Spanish colonial America, and the specifics of their manifestation on the West Coast and in the Spanish Borderlands as a whole. As one might suspect, I draw much of my inspiration from archaeologists working with material culture, space, and architecture in those arenas. I also turn to the research and methodologies of historians for additional insight, often beginning a chapter with a quotation from an archival source or a twentieth-century historian. These statements are meant to reveal, to provoke, and, often, to juxtapose with archaeology or my own interpretations.

The majority of this book is about a Mexican-Californian rancho known as Rancho Petaluma. In the terminology of Latin Americanists and Mesoamericanists focused on the colonial period, this rancho was, in fact, a true hacienda. Located just north of San Francisco Bay, this rancho was owned between 1834 and 1857 by a prominent historical figure named Mariano Guadalupe Vallejo. The state of California currently preserves the core of this once vast rancho in Petaluma Adobe State Historic Park, the name of which derives from the large adobe building built by Vallejo in the 1830s. My interest in this rancho developed out of my own theoretical leanings and interests in indigenous responses to colonialism, the needs of the state park for additional interpretive material to expand its vision of the park's history, and the support of members of the local Native American community in my quest to reveal more specifics about their recent past. I wanted to write a different history of the place that did not center solely on Vallejo himself as a biographical figure prominent in historical texts and textual archives. Instead, I sought a more inclusive yet tense history that highlighted the complex relations between Native American people and the Vallejo family in the colonial world of the nineteenth century, relations that played out in the material world of everyday life. One feature of Rancho Petaluma struck a chord with me: there were hundreds of if not one or two thousand Native American people on this rancho working as field hands, cowboys, artisans, cooks, and servants during Vallejo's ownership. What were their lives like, and where did they live? How did they adjust materially and culturally to the colonial labor regime? What implications would rancho labor have for ethnic or gender identities? How would this rancho compare to other ranchos farther south in Alta California or other colonial communities in North America? There were no ready answers.

The lack of answers stemmed from three factors. First, historical documents pertaining to Rancho Petaluma revealed little about the Native American aspects of the operation. What information they did provide was provocative but incomplete. Although historians had devoted much effort to Vallejo himself (McKittrick 1944; Rosenus 1995; Tays 1937), they had not been able to probe the complexities of California Indian labor under Vallejo's control due to a paucity of relevant documents.[2] Furthermore, earlier historians' interests seem to have remained outside the issue of Native Americans in colonial California, since they, like the general public, often thought of Indian people as passive victims or perhaps even nonentities in the colonial world. However, recent trends in California historiography demarcate a radical shift in history-as-usual to one that incorporates the indigenous element (Haas 1995; Hurtado 1988; Phillips 1975, 1993; Rawls 1984). These studies provide a model for how to approach the Rancho Petaluma documentary record and examine it from new angles.

Second, archaeological research on California ranchos has a long tradition, courtesy of cultural resource management projects in southern California, but detailed information on California Indian laborers has proven elusive. Many rancho archaeological projects have focused more on rancho owners than their workers, in part due to "contract archaeology" imperatives to mitigate construction projects and to evaluate the historical significance of adobe houses. These "adobes" marked the centerpiece of rancho life for their owners and of public consciousness, but they typically represented the households of Spanish, Mexican, or American rancho owners and not those of Native Americans. Although never explicitly designing their projects to look for evidence of Native American workers, archaeologists such as William Evans Jr. (1969), Jay Frierman (1982, 1987), and Roberta Greenwood (1989) pinpointed tantalizing material evidence of the Native presence and contribution to rancho life. Despite these pioneering works and the possibilities of extending their insights, information remained incomplete and spotty for other ranchos, particularly those north of the Los Angeles region. For instance, the only sustained archaeological work at Rancho Petaluma before I began my research had taken place in the late 1950s and early 1960s, and these projects made only minimal progress toward unveiling the secrets of Native American life there in the nineteenth century.

Third, ethnographic and oral historical sources from the region north of San Francisco Bay have offered only brief insights into the rancho enterprise. These could add Native American voices to rancho history, but currently they speak in only faint whispers. Published ethnographic records for San Francisco Bay Native groups make little mention of ranchos. I suspect this omission is due to the prevailing research mode during California's anthropological heyday around the turn of the twentieth century rather than to lack of mention by Native people being interviewed. That is, anthropologists sought "informants" who could tell them about the "old days" (or times before European contact) so that they could produce ethnographic accounts of "pristine" or "traditional" Indian cultures. Consequently, the methods and end results were artificial in some respects (of course, most informants had never witnessed truly precontact lifeways), but it meant that anthropologists would frequently exclude references to the colonial period when compiling their informants' data for publication. I am optimistic that the original notes from these ethnographers may offer future insight, given the revealing comments made by a Coast Miwok woman that came to light only after the full notes taken by her interviewer were published (Collier and Thalman 1996). Similarly, contemporary California Indian communities with historical ties to North Bay ranchos harbor stories about Rancho Petaluma and neighboring ranchos.[3] During my initial research experiences, I found that those who may know stories are not always eager to relay them. These emotional accounts hint at hard, violent, and disruptive times.

In that context, I initiated an archaeological project at Rancho Petaluma. I wanted to examine the archival sources more closely to see what I could extract regarding Native American experiences of the colonial rancho. However, more than that, I wanted to turn a full array of archaeological techniques and data sets to the problem. I found the archival sources strong on the structure of Native labor but weak on the specifics of how it impacted Indian diets, tools, identities, and lives. Surprisingly, the documents also remained rather silent on the origins and identities of many of these indigenous workers. Archaeological information, despite its limitations, had the potential to fill the numerous gaps in the historical record. Like any historical archaeologist, I also anticipated that these data might call into question some of the information contained in documentary sources.

To achieve the archaeological objectives, I had to organize a project that proceeded from initial ground surveys and geophysical prospection, through full-scale excavation, to intensive laboratory analysis. Addressing a topic this complex required that I focus on the "big picture" of Native life and labor on this nineteenth-century rancho. I do not mean a big picture that swamped the fine points with a generalized image but a big picture with sharp detail that I could build up from fine-grained analyses of many types of archaeological data. For example, I could not rely solely on stone tool information or glass bead data or a list of animal remains found at the site. I needed a full arsenal that covered many kinds of material culture and environmental information. None of this is to say that I covered all possible bases, because I certainly did not. I excavated only a very small portion of Rancho Petaluma, so my interpretations are based on a restricted data set or what might be termed a judgmental sample of the available archaeological resources. This is standard practice in archaeology but a practice worth remembering.

This book does not relay all of the minutiae of the archaeological process or the material results, even though it could not have taken shape without them. Instead, I concentrate on that same big picture level that informed the research as a whole. The book takes up those bits of information from my archaeological field studies, laboratory analyses, and archival research that I found to be the most useful and discriminating and meshes them with theoretical issues of labor, gender, and social practice. Throughout the book I make efforts to define or explain some basic archaeological terminology, concepts, and disciplinary taken-for-granteds in the hopes that scholars in history, cultural anthropology, and Native American studies as well as general readers might find the material worthy of their time. In this way, I hope to offer this research as a unique contribution to California archaeology and history, Spanish Borderlands studies, and North American colonial research.

The work is an additional step toward grounding history, and this is the bigger picture that frames my research and writing. The Rancho Petaluma project is a case where archaeological data have stepped up to the challenge of studying Native American life during the historic period even when there is a shortage of written documents (see Rubertone 2000). The project has revealed the ways that Native Americans endured and adapted to colonial labor on the ground, that is, in their daily lives. The book participates in the broader project of unraveling indigenous experiences to colonialism on a global scale but from a local perspective. We cannot presume to study the global phenomenon of European expansion without examining its effects in local communities where it took root and where it may have been transformed and contested (Hall 2000). Future research will determine whether Rancho Petaluma is a representative case of Native life or colonial labor on

California's ranchos and whether my interpretations of material culture and social relations are applicable to indigenous practices in other colonial worlds. Until then I join Greenwood (1989) in offering up California ranchos as an additional venue for archaeological and historical studies of colonialism. This potential is still largely untapped.

The book's journey begins with an outline of the research problems and a summary of the state of rancho archaeology, proceeds through the historical and archaeological details of the Rancho Petaluma case, and ends with interpretations that synthesize the various strands of information gathered along the path. The interpretations speak to the particular nuances of the case at hand, but they also suggest implications for other archaeological studies of Native Americans involved in colonial labor regimes. To achieve these ends, I have organized the work into eight chapters.

Chapter 1 introduces the issues that inform the research presented throughout the book. It situates the book in the larger context of North American culture contact and colonial studies, theoretical perspectives on labor and practice, and California anthropology and history. Much of the literature reviewed here pertains to archaeology, but I draw on historical and cultural anthropological works as they inform the book's objectives.

In chapter 2 I summarize the historical background and issues that frame the anthropological problem of Native people on California's ranchos. I contextualize ranchos in eighteenth- and nineteenth-century colonial California in light of their origins, structure, and composition. The chapter spends considerable time on the multiethnic nature of ranchos by emphasizing the participation of indigenous people as laborers. The focal point is daily practice, social inequality, and labor. I conclude by discussing the state and limitations of archaeological knowledge regarding material evidence of Native people on California ranchos.

Chapter 3 undertakes the full exposition of the Rancho Petaluma study. I situate the Petaluma area within the precontact societies of the region, and I integrate standard historical accounts of the San Francisco Bay region and Rancho Petaluma with insights from my own archival analyses. This chapter details the origins, structure, and labor relations of Vallejo's Rancho Petaluma. My overriding purpose is to reveal as much as possible about indigenous experiences of the rancho, a goal facilitated by weaving together ethnohistorical and ethnographical information on Native people of the area north of San Francisco Bay. As such, I avoid detailed discussions of rancho specifics that do not inform directly on Native Americans; historians have already addressed many of these. Although the exact composition of the Native population on Rancho Petaluma is unknown, the ability to interpret indigenous responses to the rancho must be tempered with an understanding of the Native American contexts, contingencies, and histories that intersected this colonial moment. The lacunae left by the sparse historical record open the door for focused archaeological research.

I begin to fill these lacunae in chapter 4 with archaeological search and recovery for the rancho's lost laborers. The source of this information is a multiyear archaeology project that I initiated in 1996. I synthesize and explore the relevant archaeological details that have been reported on elsewhere in great length (Silliman 1999, 2000a, 2000b, 2002) and offer a comprehensive interpretation of that information. This chapter presents abbreviated details of my archaeological research design, a summary of field methods, and highlights of discoveries in different site areas. The chapter sets the backdrop for subsequent discussions of material culture and food remains.

Chapter 5 takes up the archaeological information in a more critical and specific manner, focusing on the material culture of Native American life in the nineteenth century. I summarize the wealth of artifacts in a few key categories: ground stone tools primarily in the form of mortars and pestles, chipped stone tools and associated debris, metal implements and related items, glass bottles, mass-produced colonial pottery, locally manufactured bone and shell artifacts, and glass beads. More than simply relaying empirical data, the chapter uses the artifactual information to engage with interpretive issues. Discussing the material categories separately and then in conjunction with one another opens new avenues for viewing Native American material and social practices at Rancho Petaluma.

Chapter 6 examines the food remains recovered from the rancho excavations. These plant and animal remains directly complement the information potential of the material culture, but they also offer unprecedented insights into the daily activities of Native workers. Although there is sketchy textual information on these topics, nothing but these floral and faunal remains can trace the contours of diet, environmental resource use, rancho provisioning practices, and the natural landscape.

In chapter 7 I synthesize the archaeological and archival data to explore more deeply the nature of daily practice for Native people at Rancho Petaluma. "Daily practice" does not mean a written version of a museum diorama that fixes people in a social and natural landscape. It also does not mean a neutral presentation of the things people did and the ways they acted in the past.

"Practice" may involve the mundane and seemingly innocuous events of everyday life, but these activities are not inconsequential or theoretically unimportant. Instead, daily practice refers to the constant interplay of labor, gender, and identity in the ways that Native people negotiated their position on the rancho. This negotiation was very much a material one that found its expression and struggle in foods and artifacts, and these issues can be analyzed through the intersection of archaeological and historical information. Sometimes daily practice implicated politics of resistance and subversion; at other times it demarcated individuals' attempts to live in and through the colonial rancho world and both to uphold and to make tradition.

Chapter 8 concludes by telescoping these interpretations into larger arenas of anthropology and history. I sketch, albeit briefly, the relationship of this rancho context to additional colonial venues in the region such as other ranchos, the Franciscan mission system in California, and the Russian outpost at Colony Ross. The project also has implications for studies of contact across North America, especially in the Spanish Borderlands from the Southwest to Florida. How parallel the case may be to Latin American ranchos I do not yet know, but I hope that information from the far northern frontier of what was once Spanish colonial America might offer worthwhile comparisons and contrasts.

In the end, this book presents empirical details of Native Americans on California ranchos using Rancho Petaluma as the centerpiece. It also brings a political view of history, one that seeks to expose the multiethnic nature of colonialism. The work serves to counterbalance the popular misconception of Native Americans either as nonparticipants in Mexican-Californian ranchos or as passive workers waiting for their next handout with little to contribute to nineteenth-century history. These images are not only historically false but politically disconnected. In addition, the book uses this particular case study on the West Coast to open up different ways of thinking about colonialism and indigenous people. Such thinking involves paying close attention to material culture, social agency, labor, and gender as issues that can inform particular case studies and can themselves be rethought when applied in those cases.

Acknowledgments

A book does not happen in isolation. I am responsible for my own work, words, and errors, but the book would not have reached fruition were it not for a variety of individuals and institutions. This statement is even more true with respect to the field and laboratory research that fueled my work. My utmost gratitude goes to those who read the manuscript, pored over its details, and markedly improved its content and style. In its first iteration as my dissertation at the University of California at Berkeley, this work benefited from critical commentary by Kent Lightfoot, Meg Conkey, and Genaro Padilla. Kent, in particular, left an indelible mark on this book, and I appreciate him as both a mentor and a friend. As the work transformed from dissertation to book, some sections were revamped, chapters collapsed, data removed or added, and interpretations revisited. As the book entered its final form, I benefited tremendously from the meticulous and insightful treatment of Judy Zeitlin. For that, she has my deepest gratitude. I also thank Glenn Farris and two anonymous reviewers for their sharp commentary and helpful suggestions. I express deep appreciation to Tracey Spoon for her careful copyediting of and keen insights on the final manuscript. Tracey is and has been a constant source of inspiration, assistance, patience, intellectual stimulation, devotion, and companionship, and my scholarship and life are all the better for it.

The research that led to this book was possible only through the dedication and skill of numerous people behind the scenes and in the field trenches, quite literally. I thank every one of these individuals by name elsewhere (Silliman 1999:iii–iv, 2000a:x–xvii, 2002:iii), but I must note a select few who helped this project and final book take form. I extend my deepest appreciation to the California Department of Parks and Recreation for its encouragement, support, and assistance throughout this research project. Breck Parkman deserves special recognition for his commitment to the Rancho Petaluma project and his willingness to open the park's doors to my archaeological interests, and I thank Glenn Farris, Larry Felton, and Glenn Burch for their generous assistance with material culture and archival research. I am grateful also for the considerable effort that now-retired ranger Larry Costa devoted to insuring that my archaeological field projects went smoothly at Petaluma Adobe State Historic Park. The wonderful staff at the Petaluma Adobe made my work productive and pleasurable, and I appreciate the many types of assistance that they—particularly Peggy Fontenot, Jerry Mize, and Sara Skinner—provided over the years.

I also express sincere thanks to the Federated Indians of Graton Rancheria for their support and interest. In particular, I thank Tim Campbell, who was the cultural resources officer during the field and laboratory work. I also appreciate Frank Norris, Gene Buvelot, and Rita Carrillo for their friendliness and willingness to discuss various aspects of the project. I hope that this book helps to fill gaps in recent tribal history and that my bizarre interest in old garbage has uncovered something worthwhile. The Coast Miwok do not need the archaeological data to remember that earlier generations had endured and worked Rancho Petaluma and other similar establishments in northern California, but perhaps they can use this information to help remind others of their struggles and survival.

Some of my deepest appreciation goes to those amazing people who helped me gather this information in the field and in the lab. More than 120 students and volunteers worked in the field and laboratory between 1996 and 2001. Most of the participants hailed from the University of California at Berkeley, either as undergraduates, recent graduates, doctoral students, or postdoctoral scholars, but I also had significant help from students at California State University—Hayward, Sonoma State University, San Francisco State University, and the College of Marin. I can single out here only those individuals who gave so much of their time and energy and whose lengthy commitments provided solid continuity and vitality to the project: Valerie Andrushko, Julie Bernard, Jon Goodrich, Stacey Maung, Tania Stellini, and Linda Ziegenbein. I also effusively thank members of the administrative and financial side of the Berkeley project during the research period: Sherry Parrish, Sabrina Maras, and Robin Stephenson of the Archaeological Research Facility.

Numerous other people deserve recognition for their assistance with various aspects of the book research. Tom Wake and Virginia Popper at the Institute of Archaeology at UCLA conducted the faunal and floral analyses, respectively, and Jim Quinn at Sonoma State University contributed to the fish bone analysis. Tom Origer and Kathleen Hull provided the obsidian hydration data. For multiple, diverse, and always helpful discussions along the journey, I particularly thank Rose Marie Beebe, Paul Farnsworth, Randy Milliken, Steve Shackley, Craig Skinner, Sylvia Thalman, Barb Voss, Laurie Wilkie, and Eric Wohlgemuth but also Rebecca Allen, El Casella, Ed Castillo, Bonnie Clark, Shelly Davis-King, Agustín Diez-Castillo, Ron Filion, Betty Goerke, Roberta Greenwood, Elbert "Hoppy" Hopkins, Tom Jackson, Antoinette Martinez, Martha Ann McGettigan, Deborah Meyer, Stathi Pappas, Amy Ramsay, Bill Simmons, Russ Skowronek, Rick Sprague, Dorothy Theodoratus, and Don Thieler. I also thank the staff at Bancroft Library at the University of California (particularly Emily Balmages, David Kessler, Erica Nordmeier, and Susan Snyder), Petaluma Regional Library, and the Sonoma County Library Central Annex in Santa Rosa for assisting me with my explorations of their wonderful archives and photographic records.

I would be remiss if I did not thank the multitude of people who visited the ongoing excavations and heard my various presentations on this research. I hope that this book provides some answers to their questions and keeps the spark of interest alive. I am grateful to the public for the constant reminder that they not only make this research possible but make it worthwhile and fulfilling. For similar reasons, I thank my family for their constant support and interest—you have my love and appreciation always. I hope that all of you find this book a good summary of what in the world I have been doing and thinking about for the last few years.

I could never conclude this list without acknowledging the organizations and institutions that provided funding for writing this book and conducting all of the associated research. The University of Massachusetts Boston provided a course-load reduction during the 2001–2 academic year to help bring this product to life, and for that I am sincerely grateful. Similarly, I thank my colleagues and administrators at UMass Boston for their moral and professional support. Financial sources for the original book research included the following from the University of California at Berkeley: Stahl Endowment of the Archaeological Research Facility, Lowie-Olson Funds in the Department of Anthropology, Chancellor's Dissertation-Year Fellowship, Graduate Division, and Department of Anthropology. I also thank the National

Science Foundation and the Josephine de Kármán Trust for their fellowship assistance while I was a graduate student. Last but not least, I thank the California Department of Parks and Recreation for its financial assistance with various aspects of fieldwork and laboratory analysis.

I also extend my gratitude to a variety of copyright holders for their permission to publish quotations and photographs: the Bancroft Library at the University of California at Berkeley and its agent, Susan Snyder, for quotations and citations from unpublished manuscripts; the Sonoma County Library for two in-text pictures of Vallejo; and the University of California Press and its agent, Rose Robinson, for use of extensive citations and quotations from Sherburne Cook's book. All photographs and computer-generated graphics with no attribution are by the author.

I conclude by offering my sincere thanks for the generous assistance and high editing standards provided by the University of Arizona Press. In particular, I thank Chris Szuter, Allyson Carter, Harrison Shaffer, Mary Hill, and Gilda Guerry-Aguilar.

Lost Laborers in Colonial California

Chapter 1

Native Americans and Colonialism

An Introduction

We give them [Native American servants] all they need. When they are sick we care for them as though they belonged to the family. When their children are born, we act as godfathers and godmothers, and we take charge of the education of their children. When they want to go some great distance to see their relatives, we give them animals and guards for the journey. In a word, we treat servants as friends rather than as servants.

—Francisca Benicia Carrillo de Vallejo, 1841, in Zephyrin Engelhardt, *Upper California*

The value of an Indian's life in the eye of the rulers scarcely exceeds that of one of the wild cattle. The commandant-general is frequently said to hunt them.

—Charles Wilkes, *Narrative of the United States Exploring Expedition*

Colonial worlds and indigenous practices are as entangled in contemporary interpretations as they were in past lived experiences. Colonial worlds are rife with power and inequality, and they can structure and control participants within them. This is the realm of domination, oppression, and subjugation that characterized colonial expansion into indigenous territories and societies around the world. At the same time, individuals can bend and alter structures of colonialism to mesh with other expectations, to work the system to their own benefit, to resist outright cultural imposition, or to accommodate new notions of identity and social order. Indigenous people have grappled with colonial imposition in just these ways, defying any simple categorization of people into colonizer and colonized. Stated differently, colonialism may control the settings in which everyday life occurs, but the daily and not-so-daily practices of people can chart any number of courses across the social terrain. Some of these involve staking residence and making one's way in colonial worlds; others comprise acts of resistance and subversion. Some impact only the meanings of everyday life for those involved; others can undermine the very system that confines them. The challenge for archaeologists and historians is to consider these levels simultaneously and to develop methods and approaches for studying indigenous practices in colonial worlds.

Indigenous people are sometimes difficult to see in past colonial worlds not because of a presumed passive absorption into the dominant social order but because historical representations of them are fraught with ambiguity and politics. Particularly striking in this regard are the epigraphs to this chapter, which refer to Native Americans involved in the colonial world of northern Mexican California in the 1830s and 1840s.[1] Francisca Benicia's statement about life with her husband, Mariano Guadalupe Vallejo, known as the "commandant-general" of the frontier of Mexican California north of San Francisco Bay, contrasts markedly with the observation about Vallejo's operations made by Charles Wilkes during his visit to California as a member of the 1838–42 United States Exploring Expedition. These statements encapsulate the complexities of studying colonialism and its impact on indigenous people, particularly in North America.

The quotations exude ambiguity about California's ranchos in general and Vallejo's operations in particular, but they offer insight into colonial treatment of Native Americans. Francisca Benicia believed that Native American household servants under her employ were content and loyal, and, like other colonial families in Alta California, she rationalized the use of Native American labor in these familial terms. At the same time, Wilkes witnessed rough and inhumane conditions for Indian people working for Vallejo and his neighbors in northern California and for those choosing to remain outside of colonial communities. The discrepant views stem, in part, from the types of indigenous-colonial relationships that they describe. Francisca Benicia refers to Native American domestic servants and cooks, who may have taken such positions after leaving a dismantled Catholic mission and having few other options for economic viability. Individuals in these positions may have been relatively better treated than other Native American laborers at California's ranchos and pueblos. Wilkes alludes largely to field hands and manual laborers, who were often seasonal workers or prisoners captured during armed conflicts, and to communities that actively resisted or avoided colonial intrusion. In the eyes of the colonizers, individuals working in such positions and drawn from such circumstances were more expendable and less trustworthy.

The two observations also sit in a broader political context fraught with tension and contradiction. Francisca Benicia sought to justify to others the use of Native American people as laborers, using the idiom of paternalism and compassionate care. She certainly was not alone in the practice or the justification, as these laboring relationships characterized all of Mexican California. Francisca Benicia spoke gentle words about colonial-indigenous relationships in a harsh colonial frontier fraught with military conflict, ethnic tension, and rigid labor regimes. These were sentiments offered by a lifelong resident who had a vested interest in the colonial status quo and in her family's economic fortune built on Native American labor. In contrast, Wilkes joined his fellow Anglo visitors in casting Mexican-Californians in a negative light to help build the case for U.S. acquisition of the California territory. In fact, Wilkes himself actually reported much of his information as hearsay rather than as personal observation, and he chose to represent the darker side of Alta California. Anglo writers frequently stressed the Mexican-Californian abuses of Native labor, despite the fact that U.S. ownership after 1848 ushered in more devastating and deadly policies of Indian labor and ethnic eradication (Castillo 1978; Rawls 1984).

By their ambiguity, the two accounts illustrate that divergent political views lead to particular biases in the historical record, a fact long appreciated by historians and anthropologists who rely on archival documents. The written word cannot be taken at face value, and what is and is not found in a written document does not constitute a neutral "fact." Writers emphasize certain aspects because of personal preference or political motive and exclude others for similar reasons, and they select tones for the intended audience. Therefore, we must not allow the relative absence in written documents of particular individuals or social groups such as Native Americans to channel our interpretations of the past in ways that similarly exclude their lives. In this case, the absence is political, not real. We must plumb the vast potential of historical archives, as ethnohistorians have done for decades, to illuminate indigenous experiences in post-Columbian North America, but we must be careful not to rely solely on colonial views inscribed by literate, elite, and frequently white men to create a picture of Native American life during historical periods. Native American experiences, opinions, and lifeways are often hard to distinguish reliably in these kinds of historical documents, and we need information sources that speak to indigenous practices in colonial worlds. Basing historical interpretations completely on non-Native sources locks interpretation into the histories told by the colonizers (Rubertone 2000) and, in effect, turns the history of colonization into the colonization of history. As I seek to demonstrate, archaeology provides a way out of this potential stalemate.

Returning to the earlier quotations, we can see how much these passages inform us about Native Americans living and working under colonial rule in northern California. There are many more accounts like them. Yet, are these particular statements truly about Native Americans and their experiences of colonialism, or are they more about Francisca Benicia and Charles Wilkes? As they stand, the quotations talk about Native American people, but they give no indication of Native American perspectives or experiences. They offer no Native voices. They distill colonial views of an ethnic labor class but not clear pictures of indigenous cultural practices in the nineteenth-century colonial world of California. For instance, one has to be struck by the inconsistency of Francisca Benicia's notion of "servants as friends," unless the Vallejo family acquired and kept their friends through labor regimentation, economic indebtedness, provisions rather than compensation, ethnic segregation, and military conquest. Scholars must often read between the lines for the most revealing and most realistic views of their subjects.

Part of the solution to the incomplete record of the past is archaeology. Archaeologists, particularly historical archaeologists, have made significant headway in addressing the impacts of colonialism on indigenous people in North America. The years surrounding the 1992 quincentennial anniversary of Columbus's arrival in the Americas mark the greatest flurry of activity. As with oral history, archaeological data pertaining to material culture, diets, architecture, and landscape offer a perspective on the *Native* side of colonial interactions. Archaeological studies can tap into what Native American people made, built, used, ate, lived in, and discarded while coping with new colonial worlds, and these material practices offer a direct, albeit demanding, line into cultural meanings and social relationships. Archaeological material culture can complement the information contained in written records, fill gaps therein, and even challenge the veracity of documentary claims on the past. Colonial worlds and the corresponding Native American lives inside and outside of them are inordinately complex, and only a wide range of evidence marshaled from written documents, material culture, food remains, and oral histories can restore some semblance of that complexity in our interpretations of them.

The primary objective of this book is to engage with this complexity and promise. I present an archaeological and historical study of California ranchos that foregrounds the lives of Native Americans and delve into global topics such as colonialism, social agency, labor, and gender to trace the local social contours of nineteenth-century California. The coverage is broad, as I summarize existing archaeological and historical information on the rancho phenomenon in California, but the bulk of the content emphasizes the specific case in northern California foregrounded in the chapter's epigraphs, Mariano Guadalupe Vallejo's Rancho Petaluma. Rancho Petaluma was a large livestock, agricultural, and manufacturing operation located north of San Francisco Bay. Vallejo owned the rancho between the mid-1830s until the mid-1850s, and hundreds if not thousands of California Indian people worked it. The information I present for Rancho Petaluma involves my own archival research, archaeological excavations, and material analyses, all of which were oriented from the outset to chase down the evidence that would lead to a clearer picture of Native Americans embroiled in the rancho and the broader implications for studies of colonialism and historical archaeology. Only in the local expressions and negotiations of colonialism can we begin to see the complexities of broader post-Columbian expansion into the Americas.

Colonialism, Culture Contact, and Native Americans

The proliferation of culture contact and colonial studies in the last two decades attests to the durable contributions that they offer to archaeology, anthropology, and history (see summaries in Rubertone 2000; Silliman 2004). From pioneering studies appearing in the context of the Columbian Quincentennial in 1992 (Rogers and Wilson 1993; Thomas 1989, 1990, 1991) to recent efforts to apply frameworks of identity, practice, and cultural negotiation (Deagan 1998; Lightfoot, Martinez, and Schiff 1998; Loren 2001a, 2001b; Martinez 1997; Rubertone 2001; Silliman 2001a, 2001b; Voss 2002, 2003), research on colonial-indigenous interactions in the Americas is a vital component of contemporary anthropology, archaeology, and history. These studies are crucial for understanding the anthropology and history of North America not only by interfacing the "boundary" between prehistory and history but also by marking key events and processes in the dynamic history of Native American societies and lives. By using archaeology, this research dodges the problem of relying only on the words of colonizers, frequently white men, to characterize the lives and experiences of indigenous people.

Periods of culture contact and colonialism also have serious ramifications for later ethnographic accounts. If we have not sorted out the alterations and realignments in Native societies in the post-Columbian era, we cannot rely on ethnographic accounts as valid models of past social and cultural practices. In addition, culture contact and colonialism throw into stark relief the issues that anthropologists hold dear—inequality, gender, identity, power, and material culture (Cusick 1998:5–6). These were meaningful to those involved in colonial contexts, but they also give insight into the social and cultural trajectories of groups, both indigenous and colonial, that preceded these encounters and interactions. I attempt to intersect all three of these elements in this work, focusing primarily on examining the complexities of Native American and colonial history in nineteenth-century California.

Adding the issue of labor to colonial studies turns the entanglement outlined at the outset of this chapter into a knot. Although interethnic marriage served as a locus of much cultural exchange between Europeans and Native Americans in colonial North America (Deagan 1996; Lightfoot, Martinez, and Schiff 1998; Martinez 1998), labor was a primary experience of indigenous people in many colonial settlements such as missions, ranchos, forts, and secular towns (Silliman 2001b). Unlike Native villages that experienced what might be termed nondirected contact, colonial settings engaged indigenous and European, Russian, and other individuals in sustained, daily, face-to-face interaction.[2] They were places with exaggerated social, cultural, and ethnic differences; they were localities where colonial power structured interactions and roles but where Native individuals could frequently navigate alternate courses, at least in daily practice. Native Americans typically participated in these colonial communities as workers, with involvement ranging from voluntary to forced and waged to enslaved depending on the individual, context, time period, and colonial setting. Some scholars have explicitly focused on the role of labor for Native Americans (Carrico and Shipek 1995; Hurtado 1988;Knack and Littlefield 1995; Milanich 1999;Rawls 1984; Sainsbury 1975; Silliman 2001b; Wolf 1982), but relatively few trace that issue into the knot. Yet the northern extent of New Spain is an ideal place to focus on Native labor, given the insights already garnered by anthropologists and historians working on labor policies and practices in other regions of Spanish colonial America (e.g., Salvatore 1991; Sherman 1979; Zeitlin 1989).

I take up the labor strand to begin disentangling colonial worlds and indigenous practices in the context of a nineteenth-century California rancho. The process does not presume to unravel the entirety of the colonial experience, laying bare all single strands as isolated individuals, factors, or institutions, but rather follows select strands as they wrap around each other. As an analytical device, I hold tightly to the labor strand to see not only how colonial worlds controlled indigenous bodies and practices but also how Native social agents lived through and often resisted those impositions. The premise is that individuals approached colonial labor in everyday and very material activities–tool production, food preparation, refuse disposal–and that archaeology is ideally suited for sorting them out.

Perspectives on Labor and Practice

To forge a path into indigenous experiences of colonial labor, I deploy a theoretical approach that links labor with social agency and practice. Merging labor and practice theories or considering either in culture contact or colonial contexts in North America is not common, but they offer great potential for interpreting these complex phenomena (Silliman 2001b). Concepts of agency and practice derive from a body of theory drawn heavily from the sociological writings of Pierre Bourdieu (1977, 1990) and Anthony Giddens (1979, 1984). In simple terms, these perspectives advocate studying social change and continuity through the actions of individuals nested within an array of physical and social resources, overarching rules and systems, symbolic manipulation, ideologies, and routine behavior. Intriguing insights into human social life are possible at the intersection of routine practices (those that take place with little critical reflection but continue due to their practical effectiveness) and purposive actions (ones that are put into motion to achieve an explicit end). Routine practices might be the "durable dispositions," or *habitus,* outlined by Bourdieu (1977) or the "practical consciousness" introduced by Giddens (1984). As purposive actions become routine, they become the taken-for-granteds of everyday life, often as they become a source of comfort and tradition. At the same time, these routine practices can be powerful forms of social control and compliance because individuals performing them do not regularly question these actions. In contrast, as routine practices come to express explicit goals or intentions, they can become active ways to dominate and to resist, to embody identity, and to manipulate social relations and status. The movement of cultural practices back and forth between these poles is a political one, situated within broader cultural traditions, individual backgrounds and aspirations, and mechanisms of power. This perspective has proven useful for grappling with colonial and culture contact cases (Silliman 2001a).

Uses of practice and social agency theories in archaeology have expanded rapidly in the last decade. Often, archaeologists retool these concepts to make them more applicable to the types of material data with which they typically work. For instance, Donley-Reid's (1990) classic study of the Swahili house discusses how the experience of physical household space leads to certain perceptions of order, power, and symbolism and how spatial and cultural meanings become embodied in individuals.[3] Following her lead in applying these concepts to archaeological cases with associated written documentation, North American historical archaeologists have increasingly incorporated practice and agency approaches in increasing numbers during the last five years (Lightfoot, Martinez, and Schiff 1998; Loren 2001a, 2001b; Matthews 1999; Shackel 2000; Silliman 2001a; Thomas 1998; Wilkie and Farnsworth 1999). For example, Wilkie and Farnsworth (1999) offer a pioneering interpretation of Bahamian slave plantations by combining the large-scale patterns of ceramic availability and social inequality with the small-scale actions of individuals who made choices about maintaining social and cultural identities within that setting. Lightfoot, Martinez, and Schiff (1998) advance a similar model with a contact period context in northern California. Based on notions of "practice" and its connection to cultural traditions, they use an innovative approach of comparing the material culture, foodways, and spatial layouts evidenced at the Russian colony of Ross to sort out the gender and ethnic identities of different indigenous groups (Native Alaskans, California Indians) living at the site.

Incorporating labor into daily practice provides another entry point for examining social agency, identity, and gender in archaeological studies. Archaeologists have made notable strides in analyzing the role of labor in the rise and maintenance of social inequality in prehistoric contexts (Arnold 1993, 1996; Hayden 1995; Saitta 1997; Webster 1990) and in the varieties of capitalism, identities, and class struggles in historical cases (Delle 1998; Leone and Potter 1999; Mullins 1999:127–54; Wurst 1999). Other studies also have made significant progress in situating labor within the broader context of World Systems Theory (Crowell 1997), which sees Native people as suppliers of labor on frontiers and peripheries for "core" nations such as England, Spain, and Russia. All have enabled archaeologists to recognize labor as an important element in strategies of domination at local and global scales. Using the colonial ranchos of California, I explore the ways that labor played out in the everyday lives of those performing it. I seek to understand labor as a social as much as an economic practice and as something that has definable impacts on Native American cultural patterns, gender relations, and identities in colonial periods (Silliman 2001b). The approach integrates the reality and materiality of labor into the "history of everyday life" (after Matthews 1999). For colonial cases, the approach requires knowing how labor was organized, how colonial administrators and settlers used it for economic and social gain, and how indigenous workers endured it. Endurance is a complex, multifaceted phenomenon: it involves a combination of suffering under domination and control, resisting imposition and regimentation, and staking a meaningful claim in new colonial worlds. Endurance, like most cultural and social practices, can also be very material, very physical.

The California Context

Ranchos were land grants offered to private individuals during the Spanish and Mexican periods of California and dedicated to livestock and agricultural production. Many were small family operations, but others, best thought of as haciendas, had extensive land and numerous laborers to support the economic focus of the rancho. Rancho laborers were predominantly Native Americans who had been hunter-gatherers of varying social and economic arrangements prior to European contact.[4] Therefore, ranchos frequently served as nodes of social interaction between Spanish or Mexican landowners and Native servants and workers. Not unlike many other colonial contexts around the world, labor was the nexus of interaction between indigenous people and settlers on California ranchos. However, with few exceptions (e.g., Cook 1976; Greenwood 1989; Haas 1995; Hackel 1998; Hurtado 1988; Monroy 1990; Rawls 1984), the colonial and multiethnic nature of these ranchos has not been explored in historiography, archaeology, and anthropology.[5] Several archaeologists and historians have researched Native-owned ranchos (Carlson and Parkman 1986; Shoup and Milliken 1999) and limited Native American material culture from non-Native ranchos (Frierman 1992; Greenwood 1989; see chapter 2), but most projects have focused on Spanish, Mexican, and American ranchos and their non-Native owners and residents.

The "rancho period" was a critical time for Native Americans, but they almost disappear from the documentary record (Costello and Hornbeck 1989:320). California's rancho period was born after Mexican independence in 1821 and peaked in the fifteen years following the 1834 secularization of the Catholic missions that had thrived in the region since 1769 (see chapter 2). Secularization entailed the eradication of ecclesiastical control over indigenous resources and labor in Alta California and the proliferation of private land grants and the expansion of secular towns. California Indians had worked on ranchos owned by missions and private settlers during the early years, but many more were drawn into labor pools for the flourishing private ranchos following the 1834 dismantlement of the Catholic mission system. Unfortunately, fewer historical documents that pertain to Native American life exist for the ranchos when compared to the detailed record left by Franciscan padres and the visitors to the missions. I engage that problem by using a combination of archaeological and archival information to examine the rancho period in California's colonial and Native histories. My perspective draws on historians such as Haas (1995, 2003), Hurtado (1988), Phillips (1975, 1993), and Rawls (1984) who have tackled some aspects of California Indian life outside and after the missions, but I refocus the issues through the lens of archaeology, material culture, and labor. Complementing Rawls's (1984) excellent attempt to trace the images of California Indians that were projected and manipulated by European settlers, I strive instead to reveal the realities of life for those individuals caught up in the labor system that supported those images.

I examine these issues using Vallejo's Rancho Petaluma as a case study. Vallejo owned and operated this large colonial land grant covering more than 270 square kilometers north of San Francisco Bay from 1834 until 1857, although it diminished rapidly in size and productivity after 1848 (map 1.1). Rancho Petaluma epitomizes the structure of larger California ranchos with its substantial residential center, sizeable Native workforce, and extensive production of livestock, agricultural, and manufactured products for self-sustenance and trade. Although short-lived, Rancho Petaluma encapsulated central elements of nineteenth-century colonial California. It offers an interesting case for studying the role of labor in colonialism and the social and historical nature of ranchos. Four characteristics of Rancho Petaluma frame my choice for this archaeological study.

First, Rancho Petaluma included more California Indian workers than virtually any other rancho in the region, rivaling the populations of earlier Franciscan missions and the large colonial rancho operated by John Sutter

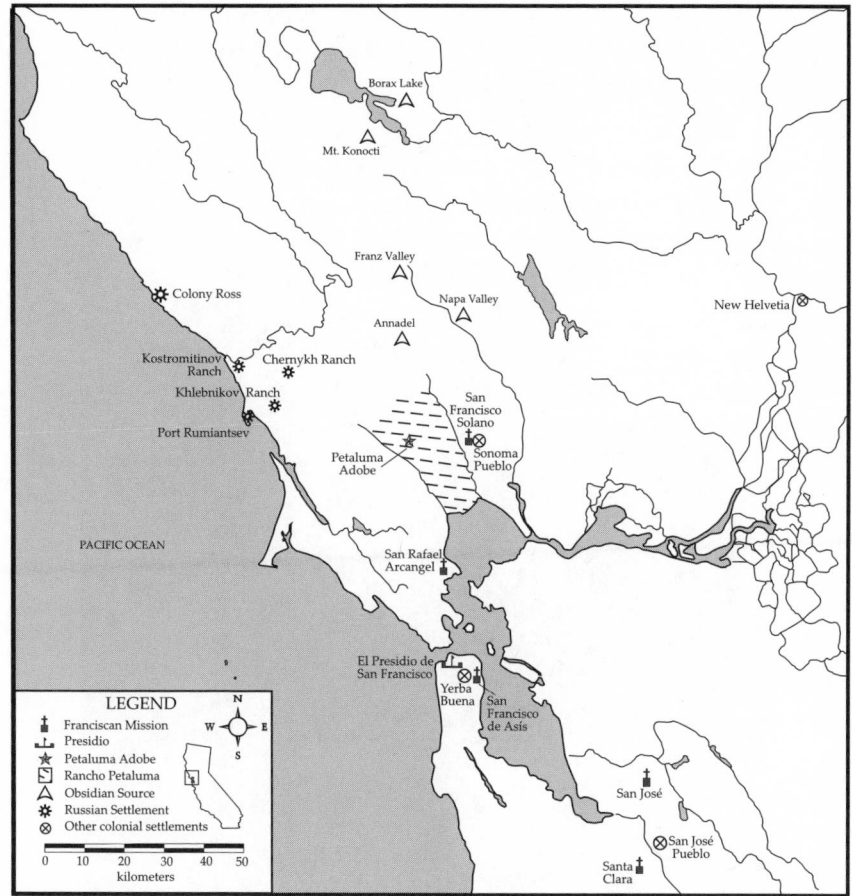

Map 1.1

Map of northern California, circa 1839.

Legend contents:

LEGEND
- Franciscan Mission
- Presidio
- Petaluma Adobe
- Rancho Petaluma
- Obsidian Source
- Russian Settlement
- Other colonial settlements

0 10 20 30 40 50
kilometers

Map labels: Borax Lake, Mt. Konocti, Franz Valley, Napa Valley, New Helvetia, Colony Ross, Annadel, Kostromitinov Ranch, Chernykh Ranch, Khlebnikov Ranch, San Francisco Solano, Port Rumiantsev, Petaluma Adobe, Sonoma Pueblo, PACIFIC OCEAN, San Rafael Arcangel, El Presidio de San Francisco, Yerba Buena, San Francisco de Asís, San José, San José Pueblo, Santa Clara

near modern-day Sacramento (Hurtado 1988:32–85). Its large labor force also exhibited a distinct diversity. Native individuals working and living on Rancho Petaluma derived from numerous villages and tribelets and at least four different ethnolinguistic groups. Native laborers also arrived under a variety of "recruitment" conditions: some joined voluntarily, but others were captured and forced to work.

Second, Rancho Petaluma was one of the largest ranchos in Alta California and a site of massive economic production in the greater San Francisco Bay region. The sheer volume of hides and tallow, agricultural products, and manufactured goods such as blankets, candles, and shoes matched that of

Figure 1.1
Mariano G. Vallejo, circa 1870. Photo courtesy of the Sonoma County Library,
Santa Rosa, California.

even the wealthiest missions of the preceding era. Indigenous people provided virtually all of the labor behind this production, and for those who worked within its parameters, rancho work was a critical variable in the scheduling and experience of daily lives. In exchange for labor, Native individuals received food and material goods.

Third, Rancho Petaluma was owned and operated by one of the most influential men in northern California's Mexican period (figure 1.1). Vallejo has been the subject of extensive research and analysis by historians (Lothrop

1926, 1932; McKittrick 1944; Rosenus 1995; Tays 1937, 1938), and his own voice is an important one in California historiography (Vallejo 1875a, 1875b, 1875c, 1875d, 1875e; see Padilla 1993). Vallejo commanded a virtual autocracy north of San Francisco Bay, as he supervised the dissolution of the two northernmost Franciscan missions, San Francisco Solano and San Rafael Arcángel, and the development of the pueblo of Sonoma that replaced Mission San Francisco Solano. Vallejo also led numerous military campaigns against Native groups on the northern frontier of Alta California (Farris 1989a; Lothrop 1932), and he promoted the political and economic well-being of the region's settlers. Even outside the North Bay, the Vallejo name carried a political weight that placed Vallejo in the upper echelons of California's Mexican-period government and society.

Fourth, Rancho Petaluma sat near the center of the geopolitical web spun by Spanish and Mexican settlement in the greater San Francisco Bay area, Russian occupation of the Sonoma County coast, American and British entry into the Central Valley to the east, and indigenous resistance and accommodation to the new arrivals (see map 1.1). This makes the area a prime candidate for investigating Native interactions with several colonial fronts and for sorting out the historical nuances of colonialism in northern California.

As the preceding four elements demonstrate and future chapters clarify, Rancho Petaluma was very much a colonial enterprise. Throughout this work, I situate this case study within the archaeological research realms of both culture contact and colonialism. In no way should my use of the phrase "culture contact" when referring to this context diminish the reality of colonial oppression, violence, and social control. In fact, I use the term very hesitantly because of its terminological baggage (Silliman 2003a). At the same time, my use of colonial terminology should not negate the possibility that some indigenous individuals could interface with the rancho in less oppressive ways. Individuals on both sides of a colonial front often made and remade themselves. Instead, I seek to integrate the interpretive and empirical value of all studies focused on the interaction of individuals of different histories and identities, whether involved in the most benign cases of first contact and material exchange or the most controlling and violent instances of cultural oppression and genocide.

Chapter 2

Native Life and Labor

A California Rancho Perspective

The Pacific Coast Indian, particularly in his [*sic*] labor relations, deserves a chapter in the social history of the United States. Although libraries have been devoted to the . . . problem of slavery, very little attention has been paid to the serfdom once in vogue throughout many parts of California.

—Sherburne Cook, *The Conflict between the California Indian and White Civilization*

From the Spanish missions along California's coastal region to Russian settlements on the North Coast and from the influx of American and British trappers into the mountains and the Central Valley to the gold rush towns of the Sierra Nevada, California's Native people have experienced a range of novel and typically oppressive social worlds for more than two centuries. Sometimes negotiation was manageable, and particular individuals could forge new identities and niches for themselves. At other times, the overwhelming weight of disease, violence, resource depletion, loss of land, and economic and social peripheralization cost individuals their rights, their heritage, and even their lives. This renders the California Native experience akin to that of other indigenous people across North America, one formed of complex strategies of survival, accommodation, and resistance. For those Native people ensnared within colonial communities, labor was a significant node of social interaction. However, as Cook aptly pointed out more than sixty years ago, few scholars have considered these laboring lives amidst colonial worlds.[1]

Frequently overlooked in California's complex history are the impacts of Spanish and Mexican ranchos on indigenous people. Even more neglected is an understanding of the larger ranchos as multiethnic communities, centers of colonialism, and significant nodes in the web of labor. Yet California Indians toiled on ranchos in great numbers, frequently nameless in written documents, striving to navigate the nineteenth-century colonial world. From the 1830s to the 1850s, ranchos were a major focus of Native American participation and work in colonial California. New trends in California anthropology (Greenwood 1989; Silliman 2000a, 2001a; Shoup and Milliken 1999) and historiography (Haas 1995, 2003; Hackel 1998; Hurtado 1988; Monroy 1990; Phillips 1993; Rawls 1984) have revealed an increasing interest in documenting Native participation in rancho history. In this chapter I summarize some of those efforts, but I also offer a new synthesis. The chapter is not a thorough exploration of primary sources, although such an endeavor is needed for the region, but rather a mixture of secondary and primary sources designed to elucidate the general character of the California rancho. This serves to ground the subsequent chapters, which delve into the richness of the Rancho Petaluma archaeological and historical case by drawing on primary archival sources and original archaeological data.

Historical Character of the Rancho

Beginning in 1769 the main thrust of Spanish colonization in California was a triad of institutions: missions, presidios, and pueblos (Costello and Hornbeck 1989). This marked the first European effort to colonize the region and the first sustained colonial contact with Native American groups outside of a few coastal landfalls in the preceding three centuries (Lightfoot and Simmons 1998). Franciscan missions provided the spiritual and economic base for transforming the indigenous residents into vassals of the Spanish Crown, presidios supplied the military backing for colonization along California's coastal region, and pueblos served as secular towns and models of "proper" citizenship for Native American converts (Costello and Hornbeck 1989). The twenty-one missions offered focal points of colonialism, from the first established in San Diego in 1769 until their final dissolution sixty-five years later in 1834, only eleven years after the last mission had been founded in Sonoma in 1823. These Franciscan missions have been the primary focus of California historical archaeologists and historians for the last half-century. We have gained a new appreciation of the reasons for Indian entry into Spanish missions and Native methods of resistance inside and outside of them (Castillo 1989a, 1989b; Coombs and Plog 1977; Jackson and Castillo 1995; Larson, Johnson, and Michaelson 1994; Milliken 1995; Phillips

1974; Shoup and Milliken 1999); cultural change and continuity in Native American material culture (Allen 1992, 1998; Deetz 1963; Farnsworth 1989, 1992; Greenwood 1975, 1976; Hoover 1989; Hoover and Costello 1985; Skowronek 1998); missionary policies of conversion, labor, and social control (Archibald 1978; Cook 1976; Guest 1979; Jackson and Castillo 1995; Silliman 2001b; Voss 2000); patterns of disease and demographic decline (Cook 1976; Jackson 1994; Jackson and Castillo 1995; Johnson 1989); and diverse patterns of mission economy and politics (Costello 1989a, 1989b, 1990, 1992; Farnsworth 1989; Hornbeck 1989). Yet other colonial settings such as ranchos have not undergone the same intensity of analysis.

Rancho History

As a colonial institution, the rancho appeared almost concurrently with the mission-presidio-pueblo triad that entered Alta California, but it held a peripheral role for many years. In California a Spanish or later Mexican land grant devoted to the raising of livestock was termed a *rancho*. Although designed originally to be ranching adjuncts to Franciscan missions and to be run primarily by Native mission residents, rancho lands were awarded to a few individuals during the earliest colonial efforts. Manuel Butron and his Native spouse received title to the first rancho in Alta California in 1775 near Mission San Carlos Borromeo in Carmel (Greenwood 1989:452). Others were granted in 1784 to Juan José Domínguez, José María Verdugo, and Manuel Pérez Nieto near Mission San Gabriel (Phillips 1980:430–31). In the next forty-six years, the Spanish colonial government granted only twenty-five other ranchos (Sánchez 1986:16).

Following Mexican independence in 1821, ranchos began to dot the landscape in growing numbers (map 2.1). More were granted again with the passage of the Colonization Act of 1824 and the Supplemental Regulations of 1828, which opened California to settlement by private individuals (Bancroft 1885:34; Hackel 1998:132). The economic focus of the rancho explains its fluorescence after 1821, as the new government relaxed the strict prohibitions on external trade that had been imposed under Spanish rule. For the earliest years of rancho operation, documentary and archaeological sources reveal that the production of hides and tallow could not compete with that of the missions and that agriculture and livestock were geared toward subsistence rather than surplus trade levels (Greenwood 1989:455–56). Not until secularization of the missions in 1834 did the ranchos approach the "zenith

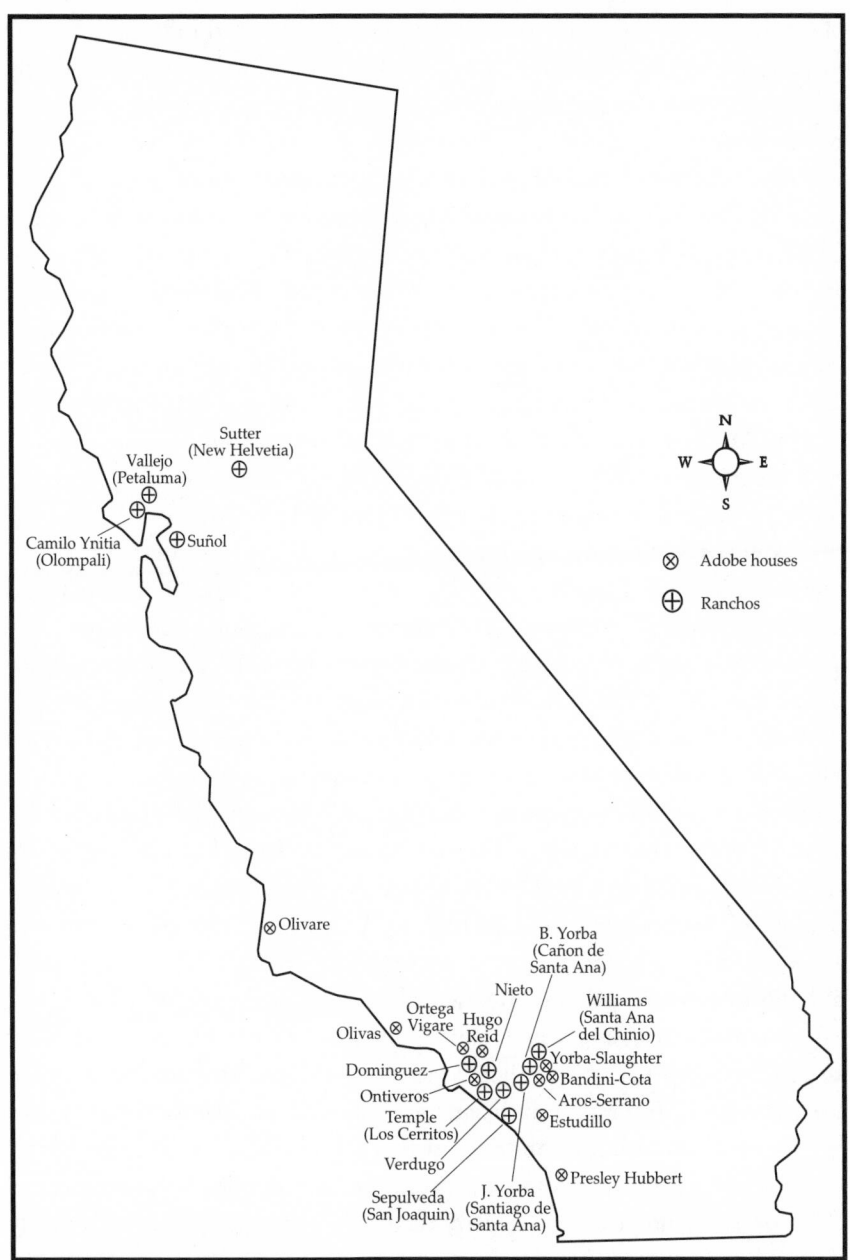

Map 2.1
Select California ranchos and adobe houses mentioned in the text.
Parenthetical names refer to ranchos; all others are individual owner names
or adobe sites.

of ranchero life and the hide and tallow trade" (Greenwood 1989:457). Higher profitability of the hide and tallow trade has been signaled archaeologically by the greater number of imported ceramics in rancho assemblages (Greenwood 1989).

Private control of land through ranchos increased by orders of magnitude when the Mexican and provincial California governments ordered the secularization of the Franciscan missions in 1833 and 1834, respectively (Costello and Hornbeck 1989:319). In the preceding decade, California politics and regional administration had increasingly separated from the Mexican seat of government, and the mission as a frontier institution was on the wane. In fact, only one mission had been established in California in the prior twelve years of Mexican rule. Secularization meant that an appointed official would turn the missions into parish churches and divide the majority of land and cattle among Indian neophytes, or mission converts. In other words, the process would make the land and resource base responsive to secular rather than religious interests. The logic of secularization was, in part, a liberal political one of the Lockean-Jeffersonian Enlightenment tradition—California Indians could be made responsible citizens of the state through ownership of private property (Hackel 1998; Monroy 1990).

Anchored in a rejection of the mission's feudal characteristics and notions of communal property rights, secularization wrested control of California's land from the padres and opened it for extensive secular settlement (Monroy 1990:122–25). The secularization decrees in California paralleled those supported by the Mexican government, but they were issued in advance of Mexican orders in an attempt to establish regional governance and to affirm a Californio identity (Haas 1995:32–38). Californios were raised in California, interested in simultaneously distancing themselves from Mexican rule and expressing a nationalistic pride in the region, and intimately attuned to California's unique landscape, economy, and bountiful world trade along its coasts. Innovative archaeological research at Spanish colonial sites has begun to unravel the subtleties of that ethnogenesis (Voss 2002, 2003). Accordingly, Californios wanted expropriated mission lands turned over to Californios and not to colonists from Mexico. The strategy proved only partly successful.

The postsecularization process of mission disintegration and rancho expansion followed two paths. First, the Mexican-Californian government granted vast tracts of private property, upon request, to influential political and military figures as repayment for their service to the government. Vallejo's acquisitions of Rancho Petaluma and Rancho Soscol north of San Francisco Bay are prime examples. Second, Californios pursued various channels to obtain land and livestock that had been previously allocated to Indian ex-neophytes as a condition of mission secularization (Sánchez 1986:19–20). Frequently, both processes converged as secular officials fought to eradicate mission control over and indigenous claims to the immense California land base. In the end, most mission property found its way into the hands of Californios and new colonists rather than indigenous people (Costello and Hornbeck 1989:319; Greenwood 1989:457; Haas 1995:38; McKittrick 1944:55; Monroy 1990:125).

Ranchos proliferated in western California throughout this period and encountered significant political resistance only with the entry of the United States into California following the Bear Flag Revolt in 1846, American annexation of California in 1848, and official U.S. statehood in 1850. Many Californios lost their rancho lands during court battles in the 1850s, but others continued with their family operations well into the third quarter of the nineteenth century. Although the rancho per se was a Spanish-Mexican phenomenon, the rancho as a lifestyle continued into the post-1848 American period of California (Monroy 1990). Similarly, the perceived role of Native American people as laborers did not change for several decades after U.S. annexation, although the intricacies of social and identity negotiation varied by locale and by colonial perceptions (Haas 1995; Rawls 1984).

Features of Rancho Life

After receiving a rancho, an individual had to build a house on the property and make "improvements" to the land (Becker 1964:xiv; Sánchez 1986:17). Landowners, known as rancheros, built these houses and other buildings of adobe, or sun-dried mud bricks made of clay-rich soil, grass, and gravel. People often referred to the structures built of these bricks as adobes (e.g., Petaluma Adobe), and they often came to represent the rancho itself. Rancheros typically constructed their houses on a high point in order to have unimpeded vision across their property (Davis 1929:45–46; Wallace 1959:18). Depending on the region, such placement afforded a clear view in case of attacks or livestock raids by California Indian groups, renegade French trappers, Mexican bandits, and Anglo American miners, settlers, and outlaws (Sánchez 1986:17). The earliest houses began as small adobes with dirt floors (Greenwood 1989:453), but later rancheros expanded them in size and complexity. This is exemplified by Vallejo's Petaluma Adobe in northern California, which was a two-story, whitewashed adobe covering 3,600 square meters with an open central courtyard and adobe mud floors (Gebhardt 1962; Treganza 1958) and by Bernardo Yorba's fifty-room adobe in San Bernardino County in southern California (Greenwood, Foster, and Duffield 1988).

Ranchos differed in size and organization. Living arrangements for ranchos varied from constant residence by the landowner, such as Yorba's permanent residence at his adobe, to seasonal residence while the landowner lived in a nearby pueblo, such as Vallejo's primary residence in Sonoma approximately 15 kilometers east of the Petaluma Adobe. In cases such as the latter, overseers and other management staff lived on-site. Smaller ranchos tended to be small, family affairs with some fields in cultivation, a moderate livestock herd, and perhaps no more than one or two Native workers; whereas larger ranchos had numerous laborers, enormous livestock herds, and extensive fields in cultivation (Greenwood 1989). Larger ones would best be termed *haciendas*, like their counterparts in Latin America.

Ranchos involved significant economic production for self-sustenance or export. Cattle hides and tallow were the most lucrative and marketable products, but rancheros also devoted considerable effort to agriculture. For large ranchos, the multitude of crops, especially wheat and barley, served not only to feed rancheros, their families, and their laborers but also to provide products for trade. For example, Vallejo's operation at Rancho Petaluma often produced surplus wheat for trade with the Russian colony on the nearby coast and British ships in San Francisco Bay (Davis 1929:136). In addition, large ranchos like Rancho Petaluma were involved in the manufacture of goods such as blankets, shoes, and candles to supply local need and to trade with Native or colonial groups. The economic aspect is crucial for considering the rancho in an anthropological light because the focus on agriculture, livestock, and manufacturing rendered many larger ranchos a scene of multiethnic interaction. With the exception of some specialized artisans or Mexican immigrants in southern California, California Indians performed virtually all rancho labor (Hackel 1998:134; Sánchez 1986:19; Rawls 1984:20–21; Rosenus 1995:41).

Native Americans and Rancho Labor Regimes

Native Americans labored on ranchos to raise and butcher livestock, grow and harvest crops, process raw materials, manufacture durable goods, and build and maintain structures in exchange for living quarters, material commodities, and food (Cook 1976:304, 458). Provided living quarters might involve a building devoted to worker housing, rooms or floor space in a ranchero household, or an informal plot of land for Native residential structures. Most Native people who worked on ranchos before and after mission secularization received payment in goods rather than coin (Mason 1986:12; Sánchez 1986:25). These goods frequently included clothing, blankets, beads, metal tools, and alcohol. In cases of large, wealthy ranchos, rancheros *reputedly* treated Native workers well, provided ample food and clothing, and paid them cash whenever possible (Cook 1976:304–5). As noted by a nineteenth-century visitor, albeit prejudiced about traditional Native American food choices, "Indians are readily employed, and, in many numbers, at the trifling expense of merely furnishing them such clothing, as a coarse tow shirt, and a pair of pantaloons of similar cloth, and with such food as meat alone, or whatever else you may feel disposed to furnish them for any thing, which you might feel disposed to provide for them, would be preferable to the crickets and grasshoppers, upon which they have formerly subsisted" (Hastings 1932:132). Rancheros provisioned most food in the form of cereals, corn, and beef (Cook 1976:458), but meat may have been the prime commodity due in large part to the rancho focus on livestock. Furthermore, some Native workers in certain areas may have tended small gardens or herds of their own (Monroy 1990:150). Those who did made a radical departure from their precontact subsistence pursuits and economic organization. Yet archaeological and archival research (see below) indicates that these workers also maintained many of their hunting, gathering, and fishing practices.

Most scholars have characterized the large California rancho as a quasi-feudal system of indebted peonage (Bancroft 1888:347; Castillo 1978:105; Cook 1976:302–4, 457–58; Heizer and Almquist 1971:19; Hornbeck 1978:385; Monroy 1990:151; Phillips 1993:107; Rawls 1984:21). Other than "compensating" workers in ways described above, most rancho products were destined for the personal or merchant interests of the ranchero. "To be sure, large groups of workers might be aggregated in a single economic unit, but the fruits of their efforts, particularly as regards capital improvements, were almost completely absorbed by the landlord himself" (Cook 1976:302). Building on Cook's work, Monroy (1990) contended that although Native American workers participated much like peons in ranchos, the system was seigneurial. Seigneurialism entailed more subtle and indirect social relations binding California Indian laborer and ranchero than those in peonage. These social relations were an outgrowth of Franciscan padres' attempts to control Native American bodies via labor and sexuality, to alter Native American relationships to their traditional cosmology, and to gain access to Native American land and resources (Monroy 1990:101, 1998:184). Therefore, Monroy perceives Indian participation on ranchos as a result of "mutual and personal dependency" rather than debt-based economic dependency, claiming that "fiestas, cloth goods, and aguardiente smoothed over the grimy bond" (1990:102, 153).[2] Although economic and social dependency structured some relations between rancheros and Native Americans, this simplified interpretation cannot accommodate the variability of Native experiences, coercive force applied by some rancheros, and Native social agency in joining or resisting rancho labor regimes. It is also problematic to assume that alcohol, clothes, and flashy gatherings could mitigate the severe inequality and oppression suffered by some California Indian people on ranchos.

In many ways, the rancho labor system mirrored that of the Franciscan missions. This similarity occurred despite the criticisms of labor practices that rancheros and padres regularly levied at each other while using the same pool of workers (Monroy 1990:116; Weber 1992:122–33). The overall political and economic form differed between ranchos and missions, but the "reasons for working"—physical enforcement, social coercion, desire for goods or food, lack of other options—were comparable and concrete in both colonial settings. Moreover, authority and supervision were as widespread and visible in ranchos as they were in the mission community (see Jackson and Castillo 1995), and rancho supervisors probably employed the same types of labor and social control. In contrast, Native families and groups had more opportunity to co-reside at ranchos than they ever had at missions (Cook 1976:304), a pattern with implications for community and family persistence. Many but not all rancheros also expended little effort to alter Native American practices, beliefs, or lifestyles as long as workers performed their rancho jobs (see Hackel 1998:134). For instance, Vallejo claimed that to Native people he "made no mention of religion, for by principle I am consistently opposed to meddling in religious matters" (1875c:10–11).

Most ranchos with a sizeable Native American labor force were based in southern California (see Pauley 1997). Rancho Cañon de Santa Ana in southern California serves as a classic example (Bakken 1997). Here, Bernardo Yorba employed a large number of California Indian people during the 1830s and 1840s: twenty-six as domestic servants, more than one hundred as livestock workers, and fourteen other individuals in tasks ranging from wool combing and tanning to wine making and household entertainment (Green-wood, Foster, and Duffield 1988). The numbers of Indian workers grew during the rodeo and *matanza*, when cattle were branded and slaughtered, respectively. Similarly, some Native craftspeople were seasonal depending on the goods being manufactured on the rancho (Haas 1995:49). This distinction between permanent and temporary labor may prove to have had significant consequences for Native experiences of ranchos. Although most Native people who worked on ranchos before and after mission secularization received payment in goods, Yorba paid workers in silver dollars (Greenwood, Foster, and Duffield 1988:18).

Other ranchos ran similar operations. Isaac Williams's establishment at Rancho Santa Ana del Chino in the 1840s had seventy-five Native American people working as farm laborers and living "in huts near his home" (Black 1975:2). Similarly, at the Hugo Reid Adobe and others in the 1840s and 1850s, "Indian retainers—farmhands, vaqueros and house servants—undoubtedly dwelt nearby in brush- and grass-covered huts" (Wallace 1959:20, 36; see also Dakin 1939:54; Jackson 1997). American colonel Cave Couts, using his power as Indian agent in the 1850s, obtained Native residents in the San Luis Rey Valley to work as household servants and ranch hands in a rancholike situation (Moratto et al. 1994:3.15, 4.12). He paid them in money and *aguardiente* (Monroy 1990:185). At Rancho Los Cerritos in 1850, a census recorded twenty-two of the thirty-six individuals as California Indian, five of whom were female (Evans 1969:76). Many ranchos probably had forty to fifty Indians living nearby (Frierman 1982:157), and even the smallest of ranchos or the "poorest persons," at least as suggested by documents pertaining to the Monterey Bay area, tended to have one or more Native American servants who received food and some clothing for their work (Dana 1980:89).

The northern frontier of Alta California possessed its share of ranchos. Hundreds if not thousands of Native Americans worked Rancho Petaluma in the 1830s and 1840s as vaqueros (cowboys), field hands, weavers, tanners, cooks, and house servants. A contemporary of Rancho Petaluma after 1839 was New Helvetia, owned by the Swedish John (Johann) Sutter in the Sacramento region. Sutter's rancho employed hundreds of Native people for agricultural, military, and livestock purposes (Hurtado 1988:55–71; Phillips 1993:117–34). Generally, Sutter obtained workers through local alliances with village chiefs, raiding, and a hearty supply of trade goods. Work was seasonal, and Sutter paid workers in merchandise when they turned in punched disk "coins" that they had received as proof of a day's work. Sutter instituted stricter social control on the Native American residents than was the custom among other rancheros, keeping some laborers under lock and key at night to prevent their return to their villages (Hurtado 1988:58).

Quality of Life

Historical characterization of Native American life on ranchos has been inconsistent, which seems to reflect more the ethnic tensions in nineteenth-century California than simple inaccurate reporting. Early historians depicted indigenous people as "loyal" and "content" workers under kind and caring rancheros such as Reid (Dakin 1939:54–56, 118–19; see Jackson 1997:240–41, 250–51 for a contemporary example), Yorba (Stephenson 1963), and Vallejo (Engelhardt 1915:136). Some recent historians have also suggested that "Indians as a general rule were not at all loathe to spending a season or two in San Jose or Los Angeles, hoeing, weeding, plowing, planting, and harvesting. In exchange for such trifles as cloth or hardware and a consistent ration the laborers would gladly take over the more difficult tasks of the pobladores" (Mason 1993:179–80). Cook even believed that "the Indian adjusted himself [*sic*] with facility to the peonage system of labor" and "found it the easiest road to economic adaptation" (1976:305, 308). Similarly, he made a case that had the Native American workers "been unhappy, discontented, and rebellious, their labor would have been worthless, and the entire project would have disintegrated" (Cook 1976:305). But could not the same scenario be offered, quite mistakenly, for enslaved Africans on southern plantations?

These positive images of rancho labor are one-sided and not without serious interpretive and political implications. Several nineteenth-century Anglo visitors to California saw Native workers living a difficult existence. Although their words are frequently tainted by anti-Mexican sentiment, these observers exposed some of the darker sides of rancho life. Wilkes claimed that Native women and children "prisoners were apportioned as slaves to various families, with whom they still remain in servitude, and receive very harsh treatment" (1845:174). To some, Native Americans working at Vallejo's rancho were considered the "most miserable of the race" (Simpson 1847:177). Furthermore, life at Sutter's New Helvetia rancho in the 1840s had definite overtones of physical and sexual abuse and other forms of inhumane treatment (Hurtado 1988:62–65). Hastings, although particularly biased toward Mexico, stated in 1845 regarding California's aboriginal population: "It is usually understood, that slavery does not exist, in any form, in any portion of the Mexican dominions, yet the natives . . . are in a state of absolute vassalage, even more degrading, and more oppressive than that of our slaves in the south" (1932:132).

Ambivalence certainly infused the relationship between rancheros and their workforce, as recorded by George Gibbs during his 1851 visit to a rancho northwest of Petaluma. A ranchero named Féliz protested that "he should be utterly ruined were the Indians to be removed, as he could get no other labor, while at the same time he abused them as thieves who had killed his cattle and eaten his crop" (Gibbs 1853a:105). This sentiment captured the tensions that surrounded rancho owners, relying completely on the Indian population as the primary workforce but not accepting either the responsibility to fully compensate these workers or the potential resistance by individuals caught up in severely unequal economic and political relations.

Twentieth-century California Indian communities relate oral histories of the rough life endured by their ancestors on California's ranchos. It is not difficult to conceive of a hard life for those forced to labor as a prisoner of a military campaign or for those who had no village or land to which they could return. However, "remnants of the Indians persisted in staying with certain wealthy rancheros long after it became impossible for the latter to exert any physical pressure whatsoever" (Cook 1976:304–5), hinting that there was incentive for some Native individuals to remain on ranchos. Monroy (1990) has characterized this as dependency. As Hurtado's (1988) analysis revealed for New Helvetia and related colonial settings, the situation was complex and highly variable but probably never positive or comfortable for Native participants.

Native Americans and Labor Practices

Rather than relying solely on "dependency" to explain Native American participation in ranchos, it is imperative to understand how and why they came to ranchos as workers and what kinds of rancho labor organization and life they experienced. That is, we need a "peopled" version of the past. Some workers were ex–mission converts trained in the necessary trades for ranchos; others whom the Spanish called *gentiles* had never undergone missionization and provided unskilled labor. Likewise, some Indian people provided a permanent workforce for year-round activities, but most worked on a seasonal basis during peak rancho labor times such as crop harvesting or livestock slaughtering. Potential implications for social and cultural change along just these two planes are highly divergent. Some individuals joined voluntarily, while others were under physical and economic coercion (Salvatore 1991:445). Labor recruitment and participation were highly variable and often contested by the various parties involved, which is particularly clear given that many California Indians actively resisted and attacked rancho establishments (Phillips 1993:164). To examine this variability, I have classified Native American entry into ranchos into five types: legislation, indebtedness, capture by force, military alliance, and social incorporation. Only indebtedness might bring about the kind of dependency suggested by Monroy.

First, Native individuals were required by law in southern California's populous Los Angeles pueblo to be gainfully employed, at least during certain seasons. A law was enacted in 1836 that allowed *regidores,* or council members, to arrest intoxicated Native Americans and turn them over to public works projects, and another appeared in 1844 that required all Native Americans to be employed or to have documentation of dismissal from particular jobs (Phillips 1980:437–38). Infractions resulted in individuals having to "work off" their crimes, which insured their availability as laborers and provided a semblance of social control to Los Angeles residents amidst an influx of Indian workers. The auctioning to rancheros of imprisoned Native people for temporary labor projects and the system that led to repeat incarcerations have been well documented by Phillips (1980:444–46). This pattern continued following U.S. annexation of California in 1848. In 1850 "An Act for the Government and Protection of the Indians" further legislated California Indian people into subservient labor positions and filled rancheros' needs for workers "through criminalization of their quotidian activities" (Monroy 1990:186; see also Heizer and Almquist 1971:46–47). In other words, the number of crimes punishable by jailing increased not so much in proportion to their incidence but more in relation to a redefinition of social "problems" like intoxication and unemployment as criminal acts (Phillips 1980:438). This was true in both Mexican- and American-controlled Los Angeles.

Second, many Native American people, especially ex–mission residents, became indebted to rancheros as peon laborers. Ex–mission neophytes often placed their cattle and land, which they had received under the conditions of secularization, in the care of a ranchero. Monroy's (1990) analysis focuses on this situation, and it was probably the most common. (See chapter 3 for a description of similar arrangements by Vallejo.) Many Native people had no interest in private land alongside the old missions or in small herds of cattle, and some may have happily parted with these trappings of colonialism. More frequently, however, colonists assumed California Indians' incompetence with and lack of interest in cattle and land, and they had few qualms about trying to deceive them out of these resources. The transfer of care meant that Native individuals had to work for a ranchero in exchange for food provisions, alcohol, or material goods. Even nonmissionized groups became economically dependent on the frontier in northern California (Hurtado 1988:69–71) and in the growing urban climate of Los Angeles (Phillips 1980). The latter was due primarily to the interplay of increasing integration of Indian people into the pueblo's economic success (and, by extension, the surrounding ranchos) without corresponding social integration, expanding urbanism that prevented Indian people from returning to villages or familiar subsistence pursuits, and the consistent manipulation of their legal rights and compensation by government officials and non-Native residents.

Third, Native American people were kidnapped and physically coerced to join ranchos (Cook 1976:302, 457). Stated justification for this practice generally hinged on the punishment of reputed stock thieves or field burners or at least a scapegoat proxy (Cook 1976:5; Simpson 1847:195; cf. Wilkes 1845:174). As Cook noted, "The expanding economy of the private ranches demanded an increased supply of cheap labor, which was most easily obtained from the adjacent native tribes. Thus punishing stock thieves and capturing farm labor became almost the same in method" (1976:201). Similarly, he claimed that "long before the missions collapsed, both public and private parties were making some inroad on the more remote natives for this purpose [labor], and after secularization, when the christianizing motive had disappeared, practically all captives were utilized as day labor on the growing ranches" (Cook 1976:223).

Few rancheros may have participated in outright capture of Native people (Hackel 1998:134), but it seems to have been a colonial strategy on the northern frontier of Alta California (Almaguer 1994:48). Examples include Vallejo's Rancho Petaluma (see chapter 3) and Sutter's New Helvetia (Hurtado 1988:55–71). Covert Californio trade in Indian slaves has also been documented north of San Francisco Bay, presumably to secure servants or field hands at ranchos. Although Vallejo openly opposed this practice (Tays 1937:360–61), he was more than willing to use Indian people as workers if they had been captured in "authorized" military campaigns.

Fourth, political or military alliances between rancheros and local Native leaders often generated labor assistance. These alliances have been documented in northern California for Rancho Petaluma (Davis 1929:135–36) and New Helvetia (Hurtado 1988:48–49; Phillips 1993:121–24), and Jackson (1997: 258–59) recounts a case for Hugo Reid in southern California. Agreements forged between Native leaders and rancheros resulted in labor exchanges for military protection and support against neighboring or rival villages. Some Native allies were previously missionized groups; others were not. In fact, ex-neophytes who participated in the cattle-for-labor exchange described above may have participated in rancho labor willingly as part of a broader strategy of alliance.

Fifth, individuals may have incorporated rancho settlements into indigenous social rounds as a new material and political resource. That is, a rancho may have become a stopover during certain seasons for Native American people moving to take advantage of different gathering or hunting areas, trade opportunities, or social interactions. In cases such as New Helvetia, some individuals worked seasonally in exchange for trade goods; men often substituted rancho farming for hunting, while Native American women may have continued more traditional practices (Hurtado 1988:69). Although difficult to track in the historical record, this process reveals the active ways that some Native individuals could manipulate colonial communities to their own perceived benefit. Obviously, rancheros tried to entice individuals to join labor forces, but the choices to participate were, for some people at some times, entirely indigenous ones.

Given these facets of labor recruitment, Native American responses to or experiences of the rancho would have been highly variable. Experiences would have cleaved along lines of age, gender, social status, group affiliation, labor duty, and method of entry into the labor force. Some Native individuals participated by choice, some had their material resources seized through deception, and others were dragged to a rancho in the wake of a burned-out village and murdered family. Although a condition of dependency as argued by Monroy (1990) may have characterized some Native individuals on some ranchos, the notion does not exhaust the possibilities, nor does it make room for an understanding of indigenous choices and actions.

These aspects raise the critical issue of social agency in the interpretation of Native Americans and ranchos. The issue of indigenous people as active players rather than passive responders is a perspective central to historical anthropology (Comaroff and Comaroff 1991; Lightfoot, Martinez, and Schiff 1998; Sahlins 1985; Rubertone 2001; Silliman 2001a). Anthropologists and historians need to account for Native intentions and strategies in joining or leaving ranchos, and they need to recognize efforts of Native workers to mold their lives within rancho regimes. That is, Native American practices at ranchos must be seen as intentional acts and as "making do" in novel circumstances, even though the form and content of these practices may have been rigidly bounded. Native Americans were not simply victims of the colonial system; they were active players despite their lack of control over some aspects of their lives. Several ancillary questions spring from this reconceptualization. How did indigenous individuals perceive the colonial rancho? How did rancho labor control their daily lives, and how did they manipulate this labor to their own advantage? What comprised daily life for Native individuals on ranchos, and what impact did this have on identity and relationships?

With few exceptions (e.g., Hurtado 1988), scholars have not posed, much less answered, these questions. For example, Monroy consistently portrays Native American people in these secular laboring contexts as passive and "shepherdless" (1990:186; see 1998:190–91 for a more moderate position). The complexities of rancho recruitment, worker treatment, indigenous choices and agency, and the labor "agreement" call for a more nuanced interpretation of indigenous participation. Such nuances will not be available through a sole reliance on the written words of rancho owners and European visitors, because "privileging written sources over archaeology in constructing histories of Native Americans in culture contact situations is a highly problematic endeavor that binds Native peoples to someone else's history" (Rubertone 2000:434).

Archaeology and Rancho Life

Before introducing archaeology's role at this juncture, it is worth querying why the lives and experiences of Native American people laboring on ranchos have been neglected in many historical analyses and representations. Some but certainly not all scholars have simply lacked interest, but the real answer lies in a paucity of archival materials. With the exception of a few owners such as Yorba and Sutter, rancheros left insufficient surviving documents to illuminate specific aspects of California Indian life. In addition, many of the available archival resources tend to paint Native Americans at ranchos with broad brush strokes. California's Native people did not record their experiences in writing, and most colonial overseers and rancheros apparently found California Indian laborers unworthy of extensive description in their own letters and accounts. This does not mean that diligent archival research and creative syntheses cannot produce some information, but the details remain sketchy in archival sources such as ranchero records or reminiscences and visitor accounts. Native American voices are usually suppressed in or entirely absent from these records.

In this vacuum, archaeology may be the only way—outside of oral history—to adequately retrieve and analyze the Native component of California's rancho history. We must seek material evidence left by Native people themselves. Native Americans may have noticeably disappeared from much of the documentary record, but they have not done so from the archaeological one. A historian recently made an astute observation regarding Bernardo Yorba's adobe: "For the most part, Indian voices largely are silent, but the artifacts crafted by the natives are obvious and extant" (Bakken 1997:208). Others need to heed this realization. Even if documents abounded on California Indian lives on ranchos, archaeological data would still be necessary to explore the material and daily aspects of life left unrecorded in written texts and to counterbalance the biases of the written record. Archaeological information provides the foundation on which to anchor historical interpretations *and* the independence of data required to evaluate critically the archival sources. Stated simply, archaeological information grounds history, both figuratively and physically.

The archaeological record is not without limitations. Although material culture may speak more poignantly about Native American practices than many historical documents, it typically records particular kinds of information. For instance, archaeologists spend much time analyzing garbage and the residues of activity, and often they can peer into spaces created in the landscape and by architecture. These are critical elements in social life, but they can be remarkably different features from those noted in documents. Moreover, archaeologists are constantly faced with the daunting task of analyzing only a small portion of material culture, or that which has actually survived the ravages of weather and time. For the case of California's Native people, this means that historical archaeologists (and their colleagues working on precontact periods) rarely discover evidence of basketry. Baskets sat at the core of economic, social, and ritual life for many California Indians, and they have become material icons of this "culture area" to scholars and public alike. Yet archaeologists almost never find them. The same frequently holds for the multitude of wooden objects that comprised material life for people inhabiting the West Coast. For these reasons, archaeological research into rancho life for California's Native people requires focusing on those things that do survive: stone (or lithic) tools, local pottery, animal bones, plant remains, and a variety of mass-produced Western goods such as glass bottles, glass beads, imported ceramics, and metal. Because these are samples of a previously rich material existence, archaeologists must be creative yet cautious in interpreting them.

The remainder of this chapter offers a preliminary view of archaeology's current contribution to these research issues. It is preliminary because I draw on archaeological information previously published in cultural resource management reports and academic literature to outline the current state of knowledge regarding Native American presence on California ranchos. It is also preliminary because the available information is sparse, underdeveloped, and largely untapped. The paucity of data on individual ranchos precludes definitive statements at a broad level, so my discussion remains cursory. In addition to revealing the potential for examining California Indian material culture and lifeways on ranchos, the following discussion underscores clearly the need for more detailed archaeological studies focused specifically on recovering evidence of Native workers. The current information simply says too little too quietly. What is needed is an in-depth study of a single rancho, one that might unveil the material, spatial, and social parameters of Native American life to serve as a starting point for future work and broader synthesis. The Rancho Petaluma case study takes up that challenge.

Archaeological Research on California Ranchos

Archaeological research on California's ranchos in the last three decades has opened the proverbial door, allowing brief and dimly lit peeks into Native lives on ranchos. Numerous cultural resource management projects and some academic studies at rancho and adobe sites have added important details to rancho history and life, especially regarding ranchero households. Several archaeologists have taken additional but hesitant steps toward discussing indigenous workers after discovering material evidence for Native American activities. The process began as early as the late 1950s with excavations at the Hugo Reid Adobe by William and Edith Wallace (1958).

Native peoples have been retrieved from the shadows of rancho history in two primary ways: discovering specific items made or used by them that were discarded in general ranchero refuse and investigating specific archaeological contexts (e.g., trash areas, cooking features, houses) used by Native rancho workers. The former has been the more popular because interpretation can proceed from fortuitous discoveries, but the latter offers a clearer picture of Native American social and material practices, as will be seen in the Rancho Petaluma case. However, before either of these two avenues can "find" Native people on ranchos, scholars must be ready first to admit that they are there to be found. They must collectively "remember" Native participation and presence on these ranchos, regardless of the material signatures or lack thereof. This typically requires a conceptual reorientation—acknowledging Native American presence and social action in colonial spaces and making an effort to circumvent the vacancies in and biases of the written record to illuminate their experiences.

A variety of indigenous artifacts provides the most compelling evidence to date for California Indian workers on ranchos. These artifacts have been recovered from excavations in ranchero household contexts or mixed deposits on several southern California ranchos. Material remains include locally produced earthenware ceramics, stone tool and manufacturing debris, shell and glass beads, soapstone vessels, ground stones, and industrial material such as glass modified into projectile points and other indigenous forms (e.g., Frierman 1982:75–84; Greenwood, Foster, and Duffield 1988:129; Wallace and Wallace 1958:80). Some of these artifacts clearly represent Native Americans on the ranchos, but others may have resulted from the mixing of precontact and historic deposits at certain sites. However, the conclusion of "mixed deposits" is, I believe, premature for some excavated ranchos, but rather than detail all artifact types and the ambiguities of sorting out historic versus prehistoric artifacts, I discuss one artifact class in particular that can offer information on rancho life for California Indian people: the locally produced coarse earthenwares known as Brown Ware.

Brown Ware ceramics constitute the most abundant evidence of Native American presence at or near many nineteenth-century rancho sites in southern California (Frierman 1992:19). Historical Brown Ware pottery derived from a tradition of precontact ceramic manufacture in certain regions of southern California, part of a technology probably adopted from the American Southwest and Colorado River region around A.D. 1600 by the Gabrieleno, Juaneño, and Luiseño peoples of southern California (Frierman 1982:22, 1992:19). Native potters typically produced the ceramic by the paddle and anvil technique from local clays and with open firing (Frierman 1992:20). Contact-period changes in Brown Ware vessel technology included thickened walls and expanded types from primarily ollas (jars) to ollas, cooking bowls, and *cazuelas* (wide and shallow pots) (Frierman 1982:24). The Brown Ware manufacturing technique contrasts with the kiln-fired "mission wares" produced by Native artisans in the Spanish missions (Costello 1985).

Major rancho sites that contain this ceramic type are (1) Aros-Serrano Adobe, occupied from the early 1850s to the 1870s (Frierman 1987; Greenwood, Foster, and Duffield 1987); (2) Bandini-Cota Adobe, built by Juan Bandini in 1840 and occupied by the Cota family from 1850 to 1897 (Greenwood, Frierman, and Foster 1983); (3) Estudillo Adobe, occupied from 1842 to 1860 (Foster et al. 1996); (4) Rancho Los Cerritos, occupied primarily between 1844 and 1864 (Evans 1969); (5) Olivas Adobe (Greenwood 1989:461); (6) Ontiveros Adobe, inhabited during the 1815–35 period (Frierman 1982); (7) Sepulveda's Rancho San Joaquin, occupied from the 1820s to the 1860s (Chace 1969); (8) Yorba-Slaughter Adobe, occupied from 1849 until the late nineteenth century (Greenwood, Foster, and Duffield 1988); (9) Hugo Reid Adobe, occupied from 1841 onward (Wallace and Wallace 1958); and (10) Juan Antonio Yorba's Rancho Santiago de Santa Ana, occupied from 1810 to circa 1835 (Stephen Van Wormer, personal communication, 1999; map 2.1). The ware is also a primary link to the Native American presence at contemporary southern California pueblo sites (Frierman 1992), representing a continuity of local ceramic manufacture into the late nineteenth century in the Los Angeles area (Frierman 1987:81). The consistent recovery of these vessel fragments at rancho sites suggests that Native Americans in the southern California region continued their ceramic technologies well into if not beyond the rancho period and may have put a unique, indigenous spin on ranchero household material culture.

Although these ceramics denote Native production, the contexts of their use and deposition are ambiguous. At adobe sites, Brown Ware ceramics have been reported primarily in domestic and other debris from ranchero, not Native American, households (but see Foster et al. 1996:126–27). If Native workers (or spouses) actually introduced and used these ceramics in colonial households, then the ceramics are central elements in interpreting Native daily practices at ranchos. They may represent Native women using familiar pots for their cooking tasks. If, on the other hand, Brown Ware ceramics were only made and not really used by Native people in ranchero contexts, then they no longer necessarily represent indigenous choices and uses of material culture in colonial households. Instead, they represent the colonial use of the products of Native labor. Although such a scenario complicates the archaeological attempt to "find" Native American people at any given rancho, the presence of Native-manufactured items in ranchero contexts does indicate that Native labor took material form in the day-to-day lives of colonial households.

The second method of recovering Native American life at a rancho setting is through investigation of actual Native living or working areas. This requires looking outside of ranchero households and further opens the metaphorical door, dispersing more shadows left by the written record. Few archaeologists have investigated this potential, in large part due to the difficulty of locating and recognizing relevant archaeological contexts on ranchos. Native deposits often occur away from the adobe buildings studied as part of cultural resource management projects, and they may not present themselves in any straightforward manner as "Native."

Yet these problems are surmountable if three points are kept in mind. First, as presented in the next chapter for Rancho Petaluma, existing archives point to promising, although far from certain, areas for locating Native American residences and debris at certain ranchos. As I discovered in my field research at Rancho Petaluma, finding appropriate archaeological remains necessitated more than fortuitous discovery in a project with other objectives. It required multiple field techniques to explore favorable areas. Second, a combination of archival, archaeological, ethnographical, and oral historical data sets helps alleviate some problems that arise from presupposing what Native American material culture in a rancho context would have looked like. Renewed theoretical attention to the interplay between material culture and identity in these contexts is necessary, since we cannot assume that identity can be easily read from material remains (Upton 1996). A "Native American identity" in the nineteenth century was not a given and tied only to precontact practices and material items; it was actively recontextualized in the material and social array of colonial worlds. Third, the traditional distinction between historical and prehistoric archaeology outlined by Lightfoot (1995) exacerbates the problem of recognizing ranchos as potential contact period sites. As Greenwood suggests, many cultural resource management projects on ranchos confound the issue by predefining the "prehistoric" and "historical" deposits according to their expected constituents (i.e., European ceramics and metal versus chipped stone tools and shell ornaments) and assigning them to different research teams (1989:460). Frequently, this approach results in historic-period Native Americans falling through these arbitrary cracks because the potential for creative intermixing (at the social, not stratigraphic, level) is denied.

In addition to the Rancho Petaluma case, three other projects offer a glimpse into Native American living or working areas on secular ranchos.[3] The first is a site in the east San Francisco Bay area, reported by Luby (1995), that preliminary results indicate may have been a *ranchería*, or Native village, associated with Rancho Suñol in Alameda County. The second project is an investigation of an adobe house and associated debris at José Antonio Estudillo's Rancho San Jacinto Viejo in southern California. Based on evidence from two features, Foster et al. (1996) hypothesized that residents of the adobe site had been Native American sheepherders for the local ranchero from the 1860s to the 1880s. Evidence included sherds of Brown Ware, flaked lithic artifacts, ground stones, a high preponderance of sheep and goat remains, temporary residential structures, and few European goods (Foster et al. 1996:125–33). Located in the San Luis Rey Valley in San Diego County, a third project recovered the potential remains of Native adobe residences at a ranchería in Presley Hubbert's landholdings between 1890 and 1910 (Moratto et al. 1994:4.34). Evidence from Historical Feature 2 is particularly important because it includes the probable association of California Indian artifacts such as stone tools, ground stone fragments, *Olivella* beads, and Brown Ware ceramics with late-nineteenth-century Euro-American items such as earthenware ceramics, glass bottles and fragments, tile fragments, nails, and other metal items (Moratto et al. 1994:11.5–11.6).

These archaeological projects only scratch the surface regarding Native American participation on ranchos. Their insights are encouraging with respect to finding Native workers in historic contexts in California, but the data are ambiguous and sparse. Two of these three archaeological cases also include late-nineteenth- and early-twentieth-century material culture, well after the rancho period proper as defined for this book. Yet they demonstrate that Native American people on Mexican-Californian and Anglo American ranchos can be studied archaeologically and that their role as laborers might be a fruitful focus for future study. To truly expand that potential and to begin the journey of understanding Native American involvement in ranchos, much more archaeological attention must be devoted to finding, recovering, and analyzing sites or deposits that offer a richer foundation for this interpretive effort. The subsequent chapters are based on one such effort at Rancho Petaluma.

Summary

Because they were typically owned and operated by colonial settlers and worked by indigenous people, many of California's larger ranchos were multiethnic communities. Ranchos took a colonial backseat in the initial years of California's colonization by Spain and then Mexico, but the years following Mexican independence in 1821 and mission secularization in 1834 witnessed an exponential rise in the numbers and standing of ranchos. The growing significance was relevant to both colonial and Native American histories because ranchos became centers for sustained daily interaction between California's indigenous and new residents in the 1830s and 1840s. They became a major nexus of colonialism and culture contact in the postmission, pre-American era and exerted a profound impact on Native life too little examined by anthropologists and historians. "When we remember the blissful era of the *ranchos,* often romanticized, we must remember what it cost the Indians of California" (Mason 1993:177).

Ranchos operated basically as peonage systems in which Native people labored at various tasks for production and export in exchange for food, goods, and perhaps shelter. For some, colonial labor became the focal point of daily life; for others, it may have become one link in the complex chain binding Native Americans and colonists in the nineteenth century. Many California Indians joined rancho labor regimes out of indebtedness, choice, or affiliation with a leader allied to a local ranchero, but others found themselves on ranchos after capture or imprisonment. Some may have lived and worked on ranchos because they could see no other options. These factors, plus the mixture of diverse Native American groups and households, left ranchos entangled in a complex web of social relations. In its complexity, the context begs for analysis of Native American laborers as active social agents who were both constrained and empowered. Although the rancho form structured Native labor, it did not overdetermine Native American experiences of rancho life.

Faint outlines of Native American life on ranchos have appeared through documentary research, and archaeological data have begun to sharpen some of the borders and textures. The sharpening has hinged on the recovery of artifacts and contexts that suggest California Indian presence on particular ranchos. In spite of the ambiguity, these materials demonstrate not only that Native people can be pulled from the shadows of rancho history but also that these individuals were forging new identities that melded material aspects of traditional life with those of the novel colonial world. Stone tool and shell bead manufacture may have held sway, but individuals incorporated nonindigenous items of metal, glass, and ceramic into their daily repertoire. This may have continued well into the late 1800s and early 1900s. Yet these archaeological discoveries are only teasers, only tiny beams of light into the darkness behind the door now standing ajar.

The next step is to conduct archaeological research that does not preempt the material creativity of indigenous people negotiating periods of colonialism and contact, and the following chapters present a case where that research has been possible. The trick is not to second-guess what lies behind the opening door but to open it strategically, to move it without disturbing the objects behind it, to adjust one's eyes to the dim subjects behind it. In practical terms, archaeologists need to seek out Native American living areas on ranchos, to design areal excavations that tap into the spatial arrangement and diversity of daily practices, and, most importantly, to refuse to define archaeological sites simply by whether or not they contain stone tools or "historical" artifacts. The Rancho Petaluma case offers an example of what such a project might look like and what kinds of information are available to explore the details of Native American life on colonial ranchos. The foregoing discussion and succeeding chapters on Rancho Petaluma drive home the point that to understand the material culture of ranchos, even that contained within explicitly ranchero contexts, one must acknowledge the presence, activity, and experiences of California Indian people.

Chapter 3

Revisiting History

Native Americans at Rancho Petaluma

[Indian men] tilled our soil, pastured our cattle, sheared our sheep, cut our lumber, built our houses, paddled our boats, made tiles for our houses, ground our grain, killed our cattle, dressed their hides for the market, and made our unburnt bricks; while the Indian women made most excellent servants, took good care of our children, and made every one of our meals.

—Salvador Vallejo, 1874, in Myrtle M. McKittrick, "Salvador Vallejo"

To examine the participation of Native American people on California ranchos requires homing in on particular cases that have solid historical documentation and archaeological potential. Taken together, these lines of inquiry make for stronger interpretations of historical and anthropological issues. There are, undoubtedly, many such ranchos in California with untapped potential, but I examine here the Rancho Petaluma case. As the epigraph by Salvador Vallejo, a brother of Mariano Vallejo, sums up poignantly, the area north of San Francisco Bay epitomized nineteenth-century colonial use of Native labor. As outlined earlier, Rancho Petaluma is a unique case for the archaeological and historical anthropological study of colonialism for four reasons: the high number and diversity of California Indians laboring on-site, the large scale of economic productivity on the rancho, Vallejo's importance in the wider scope of politics and society as the regional Mexican-Californian identity known as Californio took hold in the late 1830s and 1840s, and the rancho's geopolitical position at the convergence of colonial frontiers and Native borders. This chapter focuses on the first two to highlight issues concerning Native labor, gender, and social relations on California ranchos.

Precontact Life in Northern California

To understand Rancho Petaluma requires situating it within a regional and political history, one that extends back well before the arrival of European colonists into the area. It only makes sense to place the Native American aspects into a more diachronic, long-term perspective. Precontact societies of the area immediately north of the San Francisco Bay were diverse (Fredrickson 1984; Moratto 1984), as were those recorded ethnographically (Heizer 1978). As I will discuss, it is also not possible to know with certainty which of these various late precontact and historic groups found their way onto Rancho Petaluma. For this reason, delving into specific precontact sites and linking them to particular cultural or biological descendants on Rancho Petaluma would not be prudent or useful. The best approach is to discuss the archaeology of late precontact times from the Pacific Coast to the Sacramento Valley in general terms, but terms that revolve around issues of diet, residential structures, technologies, and social life. These are the material culture commonalities shared by the region's various groups that can be considered in the rancho case. My goal is not to synthesize the regional precontact archaeological evidence or to outline it in its many changes over time but, rather, to provide a baseline summary for unfamiliar readers.

Although variable by group and location, northern California's people in late precontact times obtained their food from a lifestyle of gathering, hunting, and fishing. Diets included a variety of resources depending on season and geographic location. Popular plant resources included acorns, grass seeds, manzanita, and seaweed. Numerous other plants were consumed and used for ritual and medicinal purposes (Bocek 1984; Chesnut 1902). Most of these plants were processed by women in mortars and pestles or with handstones and milling slabs; most were also gathered by women, but men participated in the fall acorn harvest, according to ethnographic accounts. Community members would manage oak tracts with fire to improve acorn mast production, and many oak areas were probably "owned" by families.

From bays and coastlines, Native women, men, and children gathered shellfish such as abalone, chiton, clam, limpet, mussel, and oyster. Hunting and fishing were also important components of social life and subsistence. Individuals hunted large mammals such as deer and elk with bow and arrow or net, while they trapped or clubbed medium-size game such as rabbits. Individuals captured smaller mammals and many birds with traps, clubs, and stone-tipped projectiles, and they procured fish with hooks, traps, weirs, and netting. Groups with coastal access took and consumed marine mammals and coastal fishes. Men probably obtained the majority of faunal resources, perhaps with age-dependent strategies.

In addition to providing food, animal and plant resources provided raw material for other purposes. Bones were used to make awls, saws, beads, tubes, and whistles (Gifford 1940). They were also used to manufacture hooks and harpoons. Shellfish were particularly important as material for manufacturing body ornaments such as pendants and beads. Beginning in late precontact times, beads made of clamshell became a type of currency among Native groups in the area, and this practice continued well into the ethnographic period (Collier and Thalman 1996:195–96, 203). Abalone (*Haliotis*) and *Olivella* shell also were made into ornaments, pendants, and beads. One of the most famous organic technologies of northern California's indigenous populations was basketry. Both women and men made baskets, but the practices and types were typically gendered. Baskets served to cook, store, and transport a variety of materials, and they carried symbolic weight. Ceramic vessel technology was not known or used in the region.

Individuals accomplished many of their tasks with stone tools of various sorts, but wooden artifacts (e.g., arrows, bows, utensils) were of great importance, despite their absence from most archaeological contexts in northern California. Obsidian and chert comprised the majority of flaked stone, but basalt, igneous stones, and other microcrystalline silicates (geological relatives of chert) were also used. Native people obtained obsidian primarily from five well-known obsidian sources (Jackson 1986), and numerous chert outcrops dot the landscape. Individuals transformed these raw materials into unhafted bifaces to be used as cores or tools; projectile points for tipping arrows or spears; drills for wood, leather, and shell working; and expedient tools for tasks such as cutting or scraping. Magnesite was also an important raw material, used in large part for the production of beads.

Unflaked ground stone implements included a combination of mortars and pestles, milling stones and grinding slabs, charmstones, net sinkers, and hammerstones. Mortar-and-pestle technology, which involves grinding flour in a mortar depression with an elongated pestle, is typically associated with economies focused on acorn beginning around 2500 B.P. in the mountainous region immediately north of Petaluma and around 4000 B.P. in the San Francisco Bay area (Basgall 1987). Rock mortars can have deep depressions for holding the flour, or they can have shallow bowls that require the mounting of a bottomless basket to the hole to contain the processed meal ("hopper mortars"). Milling equipment frequently relates to hard seed processing in a technique involving the back-and-forth motion of a milling stone, also known as a mano, on the flat surface of a grinding slab, or metate. This technology is an older one in California than mortars and pestles. Shaped, often phallic charmstones are common finds in the graves excavated in northern California archaeology's early years, and large numbers were retrieved from the drained lakebed of Lake Tolay, just southeast of Petaluma (Elsasser 1955). They may have been used for rituals or for hunting waterfowl, but their meanings are currently elusive. Net sinkers, or rocks used to weight down fishing nets in water, often have notches in the sides for tying cordage. Finally, hammerstones are cobbles used in the production of chipped stone tools. They may display battering on one or more edges from repeated strikes to a core.

Housing varied by season, geographical location, and cultural group. In general, summer houses were conical thatched houses with poles tied at the top and grass woven around them to form walls. Individuals placed some houses directly on the ground; others were set within shallow excavated areas. Those who lived in the redwood belt frequently made houses from redwood bark, and those who lived in the valleys typically constructed their houses of grasses and reeds. Winter houses for some groups were more substantial, excavated into the earth and covered with wood and dirt. Sweat lodges were constructed to facilitate ritual cleansing, and these may or may not have been the same as dance houses, depending on the group in question.

Trade formed the core of social and economic life. Groups on the coast often traded marine products such as clamshell and dried fish to inland groups for obsidian and magnesite. Other common trade items included feathers, bows, and plants. Obsidian sources are relatively restricted in the southern North Coast Range, and resident groups often controlled their collection areas. The exchange of materials forged lasting ties between groups, but they did not insure the absence of conflict. Abduction and trespass seem to have been key sources of tension and fighting, if the ethnographic record is an accurate reflection of precontact life.

Rigid social inequality does not appear to have been a prominent feature of everyday life, although leaders and their families held some clout in community decisions and organization, as evidenced in historical and ethnographic accounts for many groups in northern California. A few groups may have even practiced craft specialization with regard to stone tool or shell bead production, but nowhere near the scale reported for the Channel Islands of southern California (e.g., Arnold and Munns 1994). Gendered divisions of labor were common in everyday practices of subsistence, material production, and use of space. Political power seems to have rested primarily at the village or tribelet level, meaning that it did not integrate peoples over great distances and did not provide large stratified settlement systems or regional elites. A variety of languages could be found in the area, and, although indicating a shared history, language does not seem to have been a critical feature of identity, alliance, or politics. Many individuals were multilingual, and proximity rather than language was the main factor influencing group interaction (Hughes 1992).

Albeit brief, this summary distills some of the critical political, social, economic, and material practices of California's indigenous people north of the San Francisco Bay area in the few centuries prior to and at contact. These practices have been reconstructed through wide-ranging archaeological research over the last century and careful extrapolations from historic and ethnographic sources, and I summarize them to give a generalized flavor for nonspecialists. Admittedly, the view is static and unrevealing of the changes in Native societies over time, but this is an unfortunate result of a need to condense information. I also focus on the latest precontact periods, since these are the cultural practices that collided with the colonial world in the late eighteenth and first half of the nineteenth centuries. The objective of the remainder of this book is to outline how these practices underwent change, sustained continuity, and marked Native struggles on the California rancho.

History of Colonialism and Settlement

The course of Native American history in northern California took an unprecedented turn from the thousands of years preceding it with the arrival of Spanish, Mexican, Russian, and American settlers in the late eighteenth and early nineteenth centuries. The advent of Vallejo and his Rancho Petaluma in 1834 marks only one point on a trajectory of political, demographic, military, and cultural impacts that had been experienced by the region's Native populations since the Spanish arrived in the San Francisco Bay six decades earlier. The historical setting of Rancho Petaluma and the greater region was well documented by historians in the nineteenth century (Bancroft 1885, 1886, 1888; Vallejo 1875a, 1875b, 1875c, 1875d) and twentieth century (Lothrop

Table 3.1
Timeline of some key events in northern California history.

1579	Sir Francis Drake visits harbor north of San Francisco for thirty-six days
1595	Sebastian Rodríguez Cermeño anchors north of San Francisco for more than a month
1769	Gaspár de Portolá expedition visits San Francisco Bay
1770	Pedro Fages visits southern part of San Francisco Bay
1772	Pedro Fages visits eastern part of San Francisco Bay
1774	Fernando Riviera visits San Francisco Bay
1775	Spanish naval vessel *San Carlos* explores San Francisco Bay
1776	Juan Bautista de Anza inspects San Francisco Bay area
	El Presidio de San Francisco founded
	Mission San Francisco de Asís founded
1777	Mission Santa Clara founded
	Pueblo of San José founded
1797	Mission San José founded
1800	Sem-Yeto (became Chief Solano) born to Suisun group of Southern Patwin
1806	Russian expedition under Nikolai Petrovich Rezanov visits San Francisco Bay
1808	Mariano Guadalupe (M. G.) Vallejo born in Monterey
	Gabriel Moraga explores Sacramento Valley
1810	Gabriel Moraga attacks Suisun village
	Sem-Yeto baptized at Mission San Francisco de Asís
1812	Russian Colony Ross founded on Sonoma Coast
1815	Francisca Benicia Carrillo born
1816	Camillo Ynitia born
1817	Mission San Rafael Arcángel founded
1821	Mexican independence
1823	Father José Altimira visits North Bay to seek new mission site
	Mission San Francisco Solano founded
	M. G. Vallejo joins military
1829	M. G. Vallejo leads military campaign against Estanislao in southern San Francisco Bay
1832	M. G. Vallejo and Francisca Benicia Carrillo marry
1833	M. G. Vallejo visits Colony Ross on secret mission
1834	Mission secularization begins
	M. G. Vallejo receives Rancho Petaluma in North Bay
	M. G. Vallejo launches first military campaign against Satiyomi
1835	M. G. Vallejo transfers military from San Francisco to Sonoma
	M. G. Vallejo converts Mission San Francisco Solano to pueblo of Sonoma
1836	M. G. Vallejo launches second military campaign against Satiyomi
	M. G. Vallejo grants honor guard to Chief Solano
1837	M. G. Vallejo launches military campaign against Yolotoi chief Zampay
	Chief Solano receives land grant in tribal territory of Suisun

1838	Smallpox epidemic ravages northern California
1839	New Helvetia founded by Johann (John) Sutter
	William Hartnell, inspector of the missions, investigates M. G. Vallejo
	William Heath Davis visits Sonoma for the first time after living in Yerba Buena since 1831
1841	M. G. Vallejo is denied permission to buy Colony Ross.
	Colony Ross sold to John Sutter
	Russians depart Sonoma coast
	Charles Wilkes visits Sonoma
1842	Edward Vischer, George Simpson, and Gustav Waseurtz af Sandels visit North Bay
1843	M. G. Vallejo launches third military campaign against Satiyomi
	Massacre of California Indians near Clear Lake by Salvador Vallejo causes local uproar
	M. G. Vallejo applies for and receives duplicate title to Rancho Petaluma from Governor Manuel Micheltorena
1844	Manuel Torres visits Sonoma
1846	William Boggs stays as guest in Petaluma Adobe
	Edwin Bryant visits North Bay
	Bear Flag Revolt in Sonoma, M. G. Vallejo jailed
1848	U.S. annexation of California in Treaty of Guadalupe Hidalgo
	Jaspar O'Farrell and James Hudspeth produce survey map of Rancho Petaluma
	James Ward visits North Bay
1850	California enters United States as official state
	M. G. Vallejo rents Petaluma Adobe to two French men (Deslander and Lebret)
	M. G. Vallejo helps to author "An Act for the Government and Protection of the Indians"
1851	Redick M'Kee and George Gibbs visit northern California
	The Vallejos move into a newly constructed Victorian-style home, Lachryma Mortis, in Sonoma
1852	M. G. Vallejo rents Petaluma Adobe to Leandro Luso
	M. G. Vallejo in U.S. land court to verify title to Rancho Petaluma
1856	Horace Bushnell inspects Petaluma Adobe as the potential site for what would become the University of California
	Camillo Ynitia dies
1857	M. G. Vallejo sells Petaluma Adobe and remaining Rancho Petaluma lands following confirmation by U.S. land court
1858	Chief Solano returns from travels outside of California and dies (?)
1867	The old Vallejo home, Casa Grande, in Sonoma burns
1890	M. G. Vallejo dies in Sonoma
1891	Francisca Benicia Vallejo de Carrillo dies in Sonoma
1910	Petaluma Adobe is deeded to the Native Sons of the Golden West
1950	Petaluma Adobe is transferred to the state of California

1926, 1932; Rosenus 1995; Smilie 1975; Tays 1937, 1938), and I provide only a synopsis here to frame my anthropological study (table 3.1).

Aside from a handful of landfalls by European explorers in the sixteenth and seventeenth centuries (Lightfoot and Simmons 1998), the official contact period in the greater San Francisco Bay region and northward began with the establishment of Mission San Francisco de Asís and the military post of El Presidio de San Francisco on the San Francisco peninsula in 1776 (Milliken 1995). Yet, more than simple culture contact, this event marked the beginning of Spanish colonization in the San Francisco Bay area and attempts at conversion and subjugation of northern California's Native populations. Other missions soon opened at Mission Santa Clara in 1777 and Mission San José in 1797 (see map 1.1). By the early 1800s, all three missions were actively proselytizing, recruiting, and decimating the indigenous populations that occupied the entire ring of the San Francisco Bay and adjoining waterways (Milliken 1995).

Due in part to poor health conditions at Mission San Francisco de Asís in the first two decades of the nineteenth century, local padres initiated a plan to establish a new mission north of the San Francisco peninsula that could serve as an *asistencia*, or adjunct hospital, to the main mission. This asistencia and later mission, Mission San Rafael Arcángel, was founded in 1817 on the eastern edge of the Marin peninsula. Mission San Rafael Arcángel served as a new base for missionization of indigenous populations that had remained out of immediate reach in the mountains and valleys north of San Francisco and San Pablo Bays, particularly after it achieved full, independent mission status in 1822. Areas just north of the San Francisco Bay and adjoining northern watercourses had already undergone missionization, with Native individuals relocated south under the efforts of Missions San Francisco de Asís and Santa Clara (Milliken 1978). As health conditions worsened at Mission San Francisco de Asís, several padres wanted to relocate the mission northeast of Mission San Rafael Arcángel in the Contra Costa del Norte frontier.

After much political posturing by missionaries and government officials, a new mission site was chosen in the Sonoma Valley in 1823, and Padre José Altimira founded Mission San Francisco Solano (Smilie 1975:16–18). This was the twenty-first and final Franciscan mission to be established in California; it was the only California mission established under Mexican governance. At the founding of the new mission, Native people at Mission San José, Mission Santa Clara, and Mission San Francisco de Asís who originally hailed from the North Bay were given the option to transfer to the new northern mission in the Sonoma Valley (Smilie 1975:18). Many chose to do so, a move the padres encouraged so as to secure a founding population because "by the time of the founding of the Mission San Francisco de Solano, the North Bay, south of a line drawn between Cotati, Glen Ellen, Yountville, and Vacaville, had been stripped of its people" (Milliken 1978:2.39). Father Altimira's visit to the North Bay in 1823 to look for the new mission site supports this abandonment with his repeated references to names of Native groups who *once* lived there (Cleaveland 1932:68–78; Smilie 1975:6–12).[1] Mission San Francisco Solano soon became a prosperous settlement by mission standards, but Mission San Francisco de Asís did not close.

Ten years later, in 1833, colonial eyes turned westward from the mission in Sonoma to the Santa Rosa Plain and Petaluma Valley as the Mexican government pushed for more secular settlements in the region. At this time, Lt. Mariano Guadalupe Vallejo made a historic journey to the Russian colony at Ross, established more than twenty years earlier, on a "secret mission" to discuss political matters and to scope out the armaments and composition of the Russian fort (Tays 1937:232–33). On the eve of mission secularization, colonists were dispatched to the Petaluma Valley, but they encountered some mission herders in the vicinity (Smilie 1975:45). The mission's focus had shifted to the Petaluma area only in 1833, when Padre José Gutiérrez at Mission San Francisco Solano sent neophytes to Petaluma Valley to take up residence in an attempt to thwart secular colonists arriving to settle "mission" lands (Bancroft 1885:255; Hoopes 1965:5–6; Tays 1937:235). The mission's effort to block secular settlement in Petaluma proved temporarily successful, but in June 1834 these "mission" lands entered Vallejo's hands (Tays 1937:235). Although the granting of Rancho Petaluma rode on the heels of mission secularization, ownership change arose at least partly out of a deal struck between Vallejo and the new resident padre, Father José Lorenzo Quijas, at San Francisco Solano (Hoopes 1965:16–17; Lothrop 1926:24, 85).

Vallejo and Rancho Petaluma

Vallejo was an important political figure in Alta California throughout the middle of the nineteenth century. Born in Monterey, California, in 1807, Vallejo joined the military at the age of sixteen. He made his first major appearance in the annals of history in 1829, when he led troops against Estanislao, a fugitive Native neophyte who had escaped from Mission San José in the South Bay (McNally 1976:53–63; Tays 1937:219–21). Vallejo maintained the military garrison at El Presidio de San Francisco from 1830 until 1834–35, when he transferred to the Sonoma Valley with orders to secularize Mission San Francisco Solano.

Vallejo's transfer to Mission San Francisco Solano was a turning point in North Bay history. Not only did Vallejo officially secularize the mission and turn it into the pueblo of Sonoma, but he also relocated his military headquarters there (Smilie 1975; Tays 1937:236–37). He did this at age twenty-seven. Mission secularization in October 1834 served to eradicate ecclesiastical control in the area and to disband most neophyte communities living around the mission quadrangle. Many of these Native American individuals left for any remaining homelands, received cattle and land as part of the secularization process, or performed various labor roles on surrounding ranchos or in the pueblo. The secularization process was slow because of the reluctance of Father Quijas at Mission San Francisco Solano to give up mission lands (Tays 1937:240–41). In 1835 Governor José Figueroa designated the Sonoma Valley the military and political headquarters for the northern frontier (Tays 1937:242–43). After Figueroa bestowed the title of Military Commander and Director of Colonization of the Northern Frontier upon him, Vallejo turned the secularized Mission San Francisco Solano into the pueblo of Sonoma (Tays 1937:242). At this time, Vallejo began to be called general, although his official military rank of colonel remained unchanged (Rosenus 1995:xv). From this position of power, Vallejo controlled an enormous colonial frontier and affected an equally large indigenous social landscape.

Military relocation in 1835 marked the beginning of ten years of significant armed conflict with Native groups outside the immediate reach of Mission San Francisco Solano. Vallejo, his brother Salvador, and his indigenous military ally Sem-Yeto (Chief Solano) from the Southern Patwin area near present-day Fairfield ran numerous campaigns against neighboring Native groups to the north to punish horse thieves, to alleviate fears of Native attack on the pueblo, and to secure laborers (Farris 1989a; Lothrop 1932; Vallejo 1875c). Some of these confrontations took place between newly forged enemies of Vallejo and Sem-Yeto; others developed out of traditional animosity between indigenous tribelet polities and individuals striving for positions of regional power.

A significant component of Vallejo's arrival in Sonoma County was his 1834 receipt of Rancho Petaluma. Upon his official request to Governor Figueroa for lands in Petaluma, Vallejo received the Rancho Petaluma grant as repayment for his services to the provincial government and as incentive for further colonization of northern California. The rancho provided material if not also symbolic compensation to Vallejo for his years of military service in Alta California. Even more explicitly so than the founding of Mission San Francisco Solano, the Petaluma land grant was designed to prevent Russian expansion inland from their settlements on the Sonoma coastline (Bancroft 1886:164; Lothrop 1926:47; Tays 1937:234). The military and political backing now existed in Mexican California to announce to Russian managers at Colony Ross that they were only tolerated guests.

Cultural Landscape

At its zenith, Rancho Petaluma stretched for approximately 270 square kilometers (66,600 acres) from Sonoma Creek (Arroyo Sonoma) in the east to the Petaluma River (Arroyo Petaluma) in the west and from the northern shore of San Pablo Bay to the north for over 30 kilometers inland (see map 1.1; Finley 1937:91). Rancho Petaluma was not the only rancho in the North Bay during the late 1830s and 1840s, but it was certainly the largest and most populated. Neighboring valleys were owned by Salvador Vallejo (Vallejo's brother), María Ygnacia López de Carrillo (Vallejo's mother-in-law), and George Yount. Under Mexican law, a land grantee had to immediately build a house and begin making "improvements" to the land (Sánchez 1986:216). In 1834 Vallejo complied as he began constructing a hacienda on a promontory in the Petaluma Valley alongside the western bank of Arroyo Lema, now Adobe Creek. This hacienda became known as the Petaluma Adobe, and this structure and its associated buildings and spaces comprised the residential and working core of the rancho. The state of California now preserves this core in the roughly 17-hectare (41-acre) Petaluma Adobe State Historic Park, situated northeast of the city of Petaluma (map 3.1).

Inside the Petaluma Adobe

The Petaluma Adobe was one of the largest of the Monterey style adobes in Alta California (Brack 1991:169–70). It sported the thick adobe brick walls, two-story design, and double verandas characteristic of the style. Vallejo designed the Petaluma Adobe with strong Hispanic elements: enclosed central courtyard, exterior stairways, and a single-file arrangement of rooms accessible primarily from an exterior porch (Brack 1991), although the building includes the American influence of a fireplace and plastered or paneled ceilings.

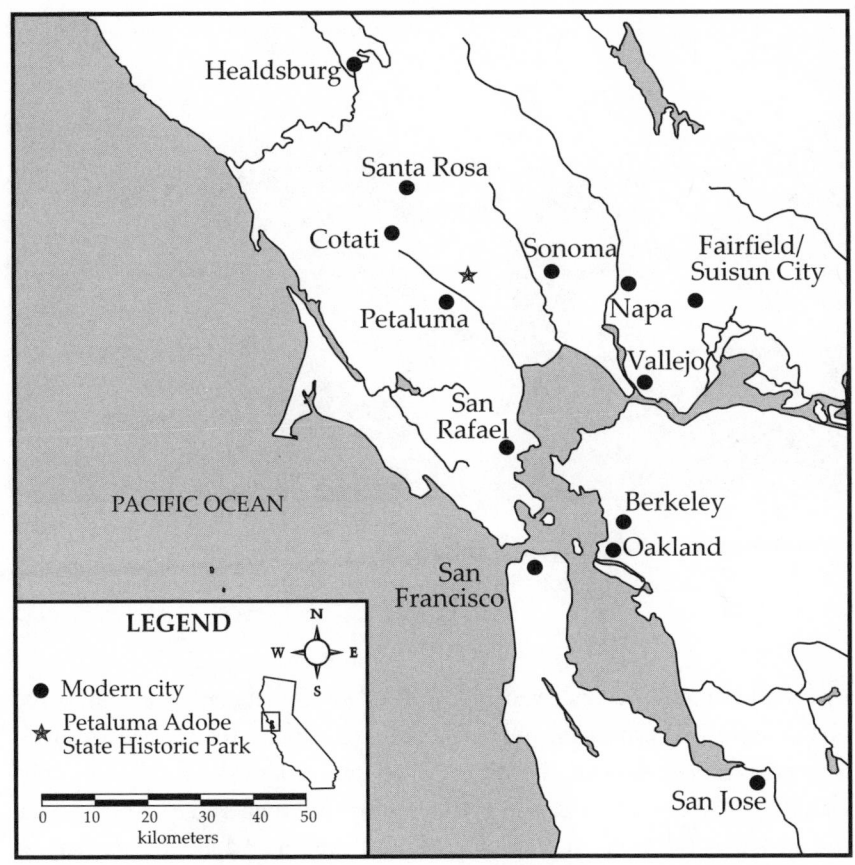

Map 3.1

Map showing location of Petaluma Adobe State Historic Park.

The Petaluma Adobe served multiple purposes, including residential quarters for Vallejo and his family on their seasonal or special occasion visits to Rancho Petaluma; housing for the labor overseer and artisans; work rooms for weaving, grinding, leather working, and other economic pursuits; and storage rooms for grain, hides, and other materials (Hoopes 1965).

The Petaluma Adobe measured approximately 60 meters along all four faces (figure 3.1). As it stands today, the structure forms a U shape facing eastward, but the deteriorated eastern half now recovered archaeologically would have completed the quadrangle (Gebhardt 1962; Treganza 1958). Archaeological research inside the extant western half suggests that the struc-

Figure 3.1
Photograph of extant Petaluma Adobe. Photo by the author.

ture was built on a preconceived architectural plan of large proportions, based on the sequence of room fill and construction (Silliman 1999:112–14). There is some question as to whether the now-missing half of the Petaluma Adobe was ever finished (see review in Hoopes 1965; Silliman 1999:17–19). Given the evidence, the construction date of the Petaluma Adobe proper may be traceable to 1836 (Hoopes 1965:18; see Vallejo 1875c:64) or to 1839 (United States District Court 1852:9). The former date is more likely.

The upper floor of the Petaluma Adobe consisted mainly of residential quarters and the Vallejo family dining room (Boggs 1913; Vallejo 1941:2). Although the dining area was upstairs, cooks prepared food in large ovens in the courtyard (Boggs 1913). Vallejo's family quarters, probably located in the second story of the south wing, were the most ornate rooms, with detailed woodwork on the ceilings (Hoopes 1965:68). Domestic quarters served Vallejo and his family when they resided in Petaluma, visitors and guests, and the resident majordomo, Miguel Alvarado, whose job was to oversee workers and manage the property (Vallejo 1941:2). Otherwise, Vallejo and his family lived approximately 15 kilometers away in Sonoma near the old Mission San Francisco Solano.

Lower rooms of the Petaluma Adobe contained work spaces and storage areas (Hoopes 1965:43; Vallejo 1941:1), but they had neither wooden nor tile floors (Silliman 1999; Treganza 1958:8; see also Boggs 1913). Manufacturing activities in these ground-floor rooms included tanning, weaving, woodworking, and blacksmithing. Workers at the Petaluma Adobe manufactured blankets, shoes for troops and vaqueros, men's and women's stockings, utilitarian carpets, field stools, saddles, bridles, and spurs (Vallejo 1875c:246, 1941:1). Letters from Alvarado make frequent mention of shoes and thread (1844b, 1845), and candles were important commodities (Hoopes 1965:46). Specific products and materials stored in these rooms included agricultural crops such as wheat, beans, barley, and strings of tomatoes and red peppers (Boggs 1913); probably lentils, garbanzos, oats, corn, and other crops, given their production at the rancho (Davis 1929:136; United States District Court 1852:10; Vallejo 1941:2); cattle and possibly deer hides (Boggs 1913); and tallow and lard (Vallejo 1941:2). Vallejo used these goods for activities at the adobe itself, for distribution to Native workers, and for trade with vessels at Yerba Buena (San Francisco) and nearby and with the Russian colony at Ross (Alvarado 1844b; Davis 1929:136). Large ranchos like Petaluma typically "had a room given over exclusively to the storing of field tools, another for the storage of fresh milk and cheese, and another in which was accumulated tallow and grease which, upon the arrival of ships that transported it to Peru or the United States, was placed in cowhide bags" (Vallejo 1875c:258). A similar configuration may have existed at the Petaluma Adobe, given that Vallejo himself penned this description.

Outside the Petaluma Adobe

During its heyday, Rancho Petaluma incorporated a number of outbuildings and work spaces to accommodate the multiple tasks associated with agriculture and the hide and tallow trade. Various natural and built features of the Petaluma landscape are depicted on a survey map produced in the late 1840s by Jaspar O'Farrell and James Hudspeth (O'Farrell 1848), and some have been investigated archaeologically (Clemmer 1961; Gebhardt 1962; Treganza 1958). Directly outside the main adobe structure on the northwest stood two stone foundations discovered through archaeological excavations and interpreted as corrals (Clemmer 1961). Alternately, these foundations may have represented initial construction of a "herders' house" and associated corral before the actual Petaluma Adobe (Hoopes 1965:17–18). Currently, no archaeological data can be mustered to support or even evaluate this claim.

The same nineteenth-century survey map by O'Farrell (1848) also depicts two rectangular adobe buildings across Adobe Creek to the east. Interestingly, these buildings existed on the survey map designed to accompany Vallejo's request for new title to his land under U.S. jurisdiction, but not a single individual referred to them in the depositions (United States District Court 1852). Similarly, I have located no reference to them in any archival document. One historian suggested that the buildings were a storehouse and granary (Hoopes 1965:31–32), but the archival evidence cited does not unequivocally situate Vallejo's known gristmill in that field. Although the granary possibility has not been discredited fully, others have suggested that the structure(s) may have been a housing complex for Native laborers (Bowman and Hendry 1940:312; Schuyler 1978:77). Vallejo hinted at a "house for the servants" (1875c:258), and ranchos generally had some laborers living nearby (Bancroft 1888:348; Cleland 1941:43; Monroy 1990:151).[2] Other California ranchos may have had additional Native workers living away from the rancho house near water holes and corrals for livestock (Cleland 1941:43; Híjar 1988:20).

Recent excavations in this field have revealed a wealth of nineteenth-century residential debris in the vicinity of the presumed building(s), but no actual building remains were discovered (Silliman 2000a). However, the buildings' residents or users certainly dumped many batches of food or material trash on the ground in this area. From stone tools to metal containers and from wheat and beef to acorns and fish, these material remains help clarify the rancho situation. As I discuss in subsequent chapters, the evidence clearly points to many Native American people living and working on Rancho Petaluma.

Labor at Rancho Petaluma

Native American people spent much of their days on ranchos as workers, and Rancho Petaluma was no exception. The labor force included former mission Indian neophytes working as artisans, specialized laborers, and subsupervisors; nonmissionized Native Americans, often called gentiles by the Spanish and Californio residents, working as menial laborers and assistants (Davis 1929:136); Mexican colonists serving as carpenters, painters, blacksmiths, and silversmiths (Hoopes 1965:19–20); and four Native Hawaiians (Canacas or Kanakas) laboring as wood carvers (Vallejo 1941:3). Native Americans comprised the bulk of workers, and their numbers were staggering, as they probably reached six hundred to a thousand during certain years.

Mexican artisans were few, and very little is known about the four Hawaiians. Vallejo's residence at the Petaluma Adobe was impermanent, since he or members of his family occupied the building only during particular construction episodes on the rancho, occasional crop harvests, or the entertaining of special visitors. The former two categories of residents were defining features of Vallejo's perceived control over the North Bay landscape, as "he always appeared to take pride in the title of 'labrador'" (Davis 1929:136), although a "plowman" he himself was not. In Vallejo's absence, daily operation of Rancho Petaluma rested in the hands of his majordomo, Miguel Alvarado, at least from 1839 to 1849 (Hoopes 1965:15).

Labor "Recruitment" Practices

California Indians entered the rancho system at Petaluma in four of the five ways outlined in the preceding chapter: indebtedness, capture by force, military and political alliance, and active social incorporation. They are critical elements of how and why Native people lived on Mexican-Californian ranchos, and the variety of "recruitment" practices makes Rancho Petaluma highly complex. These particular recruitment methods strongly characterized the frontier setting in northern California amidst Vallejo's heavy control of mission dismantlement, the numerous Native groups living outside the core of colonial settlement, and Vallejo's military strategy of divide and conquer among unmissionized Native American groups in the hinterland. Vallejo had even promised settlers in the region the use of Indian labor as a colonizing incentive (Cleaveland 1932:131), so he was certain about their availability.

The first and principal source of workers for Rancho Petaluma was indebtedness. Indebtedness related directly to mission secularization as many ex–mission neophytes from Mission San Francisco Solano and Mission San Rafael joined Rancho Petaluma after "investing" their cattle in Vallejo's care in exchange for their labor (Emparan 1968:201; Lothrop 1926:86–90; Tays 1937:241). Vallejo's son Platon noted that some ex-neophytes traded their cattle for material goods such as blankets, cooking utensils, and tools (Vallejo 1914:26), a strategy that may have dodged the labor requirements. As expressed by Vallejo, the logic behind the investment involved a California Indian inability and lack of interest in tending livestock or raising crops and his own willingness to take over the Natives' postsecularization "burden" and provide them with work to fulfill their material needs (Hoopes 1965:20).

From the indigenous side, however, the participation in such a labor contract may have stemmed from conflict with nonmissionized groups over livestock and land in the North Bay (Lothrop 1926:86) rather than through the presumed duping. A twist of epidemiological fate sealed Vallejo's claim to the neophyte cattle after a smallpox epidemic swept through the North Bay in 1838 and killed many of those ex-neophyte workers who had agreed to Vallejo's cattle-for-labor deal (Hoopes 1965:43–44; McKittrick 1944:142).

Native Americans entered Rancho Petaluma in a second, more violent way when they were physically forced into rancho labor in the Petaluma and Sonoma region after their capture in military raids (Brown 1878:14; Lothrop 1926:168). These military raids involved both Californio and allied Native participants as the aggressors. Based on his extensive research into Mexican and Spanish archives, Cook noted that for the secular ranchos "there are numerous records of Indians who were actually kidnaped [sic] and of fleeing Indians who were brought back by force and chastised for running away. In fact, the practice of sending out armed expeditions to catch fugitive laborers or procure new aborigines was universal" (1976:457).

In Petaluma Vallejo and his neighbors obtained prisoners from large-scale military campaigns against indigenous groups and from small-scale raids on Native villages. Large battles were fought between Native American groups who resisted the encroachment and political upheaval caused by Spanish and Mexican-Californian settlement and the Californios and Native allies who carried forth those agendas. Small raids generally involved Californio-led strikes against single villages to punish or prevent horse stealing or field burning (Lothrop 1932:181, 194; Tays 1937:360; see also Davis 1929:63).

Whether or not horse thieves were always present in ravaged villages is debatable. Gustav M. Waseurtz af Sandels, a Swedish visitor to Sonoma in 1843, illuminated the potentially shadowy purposes of these raids led by Vallejo or, more often, his brother Salvador:

> These barbarous incursions into the Indian territory are often made from mere wantonness, or result from the Indian being cheated out of their lands or the reward for their labor. As a consequence, they retaliate by stealing cattle; never, as far as I could learn, by committing murder. . . . The officers receive as *remuneration for heading these expeditions the prisoners that fall into their hands;* so, whenever a ranch requires laborers, you hear of some Indian outrage, followed by the taking of prisoners by the Californians. (Sandels 1880:551, emphasis in original)

It is unclear whether the particular raid that prompted Sandels's scathing comments was unique in its atrocities, but it may have been, given that the governor called for an investigation in response to public outrage (Bancroft 1886:363; Lothrop 1932:198). The pattern was not unusual, however. An Anglo visitor who displayed noticeable anti-Mexican sentiment in his accounts made a derisive claim against Vallejo regarding his treatment of Native people: "The commandant-general is frequently said to hunt them, and by his prowess in these expeditions he has gained some reputation" (Wilkes 1845:198). The practice of procuring people for labor tasks may have been common among the Californios in the 1840s, "but in this they were following a practice started by the missionaries" (Lothrop 1926:100).

The third reason that California Indians joined Rancho Petaluma involved the military and political alliance between Vallejo and California Indian leaders.[3] The primary ally in this relationship was Chief Solano, or Sem-Yeto, a leader of the Suisun (Suysune) group of the Southern Patwin living on the eastern flank of the North Bay who had been baptized in Mission San Francisco de Asís in 1810 at the age of ten (Milliken 1995:255). In fact, Solano may have turned over some of his own captives at the urging of his wife, Isadora Filomena, to Vallejo. She recalled in 1874 what she had told her husband: "Turn them loose with Vallejo, who will make them work the land" (Sanchez 1930:39). Although many Southern Patwin whom Solano was purported to lead probably joined the rancho as ex-neophytes, others may have offered themselves to Vallejo as part of a broader alliance.

William Heath Davis, an American who lived in the San Francisco area in the 1830s and 1840s, made the most direct reference to this alliance: "As a proof of General Vallejo's clearheadedness I will state that he always treated both Solano and Camilo with high consideration, because it was through these men that he conquered and controlled the numerous tribes of Indians without shedding blood. It was also by their assistance that he had command of all the laborers he needed for the vast improvements he introduced in Sonoma and Petaluma" (Davis 1929:135–36). Davis's mention of Camillo Ynitia, the Coast Miwok owner of Rancho Olompali located southwest of Rancho Petaluma, suggests that Solano was not the only Native leader involved in the labor-for-alliance exchanges (see Carlson and Parkman 1986 for details on Ynitia). Even though most Native groups had left the Petaluma region during the 1810s conversion efforts of Missions San José and San Francisco de Asís (Milliken 1978:2.39), the postsecularization ability of Ynitia to garner support and laborers hints that Coast Miwok individuals may have returned to the Petaluma vicinity or had not completely abandoned it. Secularization of Missions San Francisco Solano and San Rafael, much like that at other missions, would have also produced a flood of Native ex-neophytes. Many of them may have attached themselves to Rancho Petaluma.

The fourth and final reason for California Indian involvement in Rancho Petaluma was active incorporation of the rancho into indigenous social and political strategies. Unfortunately, there is little documentary evidence with which to develop this hypothesis. However, the large numbers of Native residents and workers on Rancho Petaluma and the presumed lack of available military force to keep them there suggest that some Native individuals may have chosen to incorporate the rancho into their seasonal and social rounds. More than likely, many of these individuals were seasonal workers from potentially distant, unmissionized villages. A visitor to the region in 1842 suggested that some Native groups camped near colonial settlements for work during certain seasons (Gudde 1940:7), and Davis noted that many of the "civilized Indians . . . were of peaceable disposition, were employed as vaqueros, and helped the rancheros at the planting season and at harvest time" (1929:34). I do not suggest that Native Americans flocked to Rancho Petaluma and its labor regime out of sheer enjoyment. Rather, it would not be surprising if the rancho had become a source of food resources, material items, and social relations to groups embroiled in the colonial world of the North Bay. Hurtado has carefully documented a similar situation at the Sutter rancho of New Helvetia in the Sacramento region (1988:55–71).

Population Estimates

Population numbers for Rancho Petaluma at any given time are unknown. When Vallejo and his family resided in Sonoma, the Petaluma Adobe itself probably housed no inhabitants other than Alvarado, one or two nonindigenous artisans, and guests of the Vallejo family. Although some guests stayed for months, the total number of visitors staying at the Petaluma Adobe appears to have been small. However, the Native population living and working at Rancho Petaluma was enormous, but most, if not all, resided outside the Petaluma Adobe structure itself.

Only one seemingly incomplete list of workers has surfaced, with 135 names demarcated by gender and occupation (Alvarado n.d.), but Vallejo and his contemporaries made helpful, albeit sporadic, references to other numbers in the Native American workforce.[4] Davis noted on his visit in 1838 that Vallejo "employed several hundred men to plow, sow and harrow the vast fields he had under cultivation. These laborers were trained in the art of plowing and sowing at the Missions with the Padres as instructors. The General also employed uncivilized Indians, known as 'gentiles,' as assistant plowmen and harvesters" (1929:135–36). Davis also stated that Vallejo "had to house and feed six hundred vaqueros and laborers" at Petaluma (1929:136). Vallejo claimed that he had two hundred men for plowing, and in an 1889 letter, he stated that he "made blankets enough to supply over 2000 Indians, also carpets, and a coarse material, used by them for their wearing apparel" (Vallejo 1941:2, 1).[5] Julio Carrillo, during his residence in the region during the 1830s, noted that Vallejo had 150 pairs of oxen for plowing the fields at Rancho Petaluma and that each pair was led by an Indian man (1877:131). In addition, Agustín Janssens reported that Rancho Petaluma had "a hundred Indian ploughmen all at work in one field, each at his plough" (Ellison and Price 1953:273). Another contemporary, Walter Colton, offered a higher number for Vallejo, suggesting that "a thousand Indians, whom he has won from savage life, cultivate his fields and garner his grains" (1854:1–2).

It would be imprudent to offer an exact or even average figure within this variation because the number of Native workers fluctuated seasonally and yearly. A primary factor in this dynamic state would have been the seasonality of labor for which Native Americans were employed or coerced. Planting and harvesting would have been important times for Native aggregation in agricultural fields. For instance, wheat and barley would have been planted during the winter and corn during the spring, and all would have been harvested throughout the dry summer (see Alvarado 1849; Brown 1956; Lugo 1950). At this time, the labor needs of the rancho would have been high. Similarly, the spring rodeo and summer matanza would have drawn in vaqueros for a few weeks of intensive branding, slaughtering, and processing. The rest of the year was replete with processing and manufacturing duties such as making candles and shoes, but it is unlikely that these required the large numbers of Native workers necessary to handle field crops and cattle. Household servants probably formed the core of permanent residents. In addition, I suspect that the numbers rarely reflected the children who would have lived on the rancho with their family members.

Just as strongly, indigenous schedules and preferences would have influenced the Native presence on Rancho Petaluma. Aboriginal schedules of gathering, hunting, and ceremonial life undoubtedly affected the numbers of resident laborers. Native people from unmissionized villages may have opted for rancho work in Petaluma only when it did not conflict with traditional seasonal subsistence rounds or ritual cycles. (See Phillips 1980:31 for a similar case in 1784 with Gabrieleno workers.) Allowing Indian leaders the opportunity to visit family away from the Sonoma pueblo was a common practice during Vallejo's control in 1835 (see Vallejo 1874a), and it probably prevailed at Rancho Petaluma. Francisca Benicia claimed that Indian servants at the Vallejo home in Sonoma were provided animals and guards to facilitate their visits to distant family members (Engelhardt 1915:136). The interest in visiting family, procuring foods, maintaining and forging trade relations, and attending to ceremonial life would have been key factors in the ways that Native people participated in the rancho. They would also have been points of negotiation and contest between those working and those supervising. Furthermore, Alvarado seemed to have been struggling with fugitivism: "I sent Simon with the other boys to round up the stock and Simon has not returned neither has the boy Allitre. Also on Sunday night Ventura and Anselmo left for I don't know where" (1848).[6] These individuals were likely to have been California Indians. Fleeing the rancho would have been a popular option for those forced into laboring roles, much as it had been for Native people caught up in the Spanish missions (Jackson and Castillo 1995), and turnover for field hands was probably quite high.

As in other regions in North America, the spread of diseases wreaked havoc on Native populations in the area and affected the rancho labor force. Rancho living areas probably did not become the strong disease vectors that preceding mission dormitories had been for Native people (Cook 1976; Jackson 1994; Jackson and Castillo 1995), but such a pattern may be partly an artifact of the reduced documentation on rancho life (see Simpson 1847:77). Nonetheless, regional epidemics posed serious problems, as evidenced by the virulent smallpox scourge that swept through northern California in 1838. Believed to have traveled from Russian Colony Ross through Vallejo's agent, Ignacio Miramontes, the smallpox epidemic killed thousands of California Indians (McKittrick 1944:140; Tays 1937:360). Vallejo's son Platon recalled that his father and Chief Solano had noted a drop in the Southern Patwin population from forty thousand to a mere two hundred people immediately following the outbreak (1914:30). Based on his conversation with Vallejo, Joseph Warren Revere claimed: "Twenty thousand of them were carried off in a single year by the ravages of smallpox, and the tribes of Sonoma have now been swept from the face of the earth" (1849:129). Hubert Howe Bancroft compiled a number of mortality tolls, including Vallejo's, that suggest upwards of seventy thousand deaths (1886:74).

Because of the devastating blow dealt by smallpox, the largest numbers of Native Americans working at Petaluma may have been in the years between 1834 and 1838. Alvarado hinted at a potential worker shortage in a letter to Vallejo written in late September 1844: "Sir in order to count the stock well it is necessary to have a large number of men" (1844a). The importance of disease in altering Native demography is illustrated by Carrillo: "If we had been able to save the lives of our Indians and more especially those of the Suysunes, we would cheerfully have done it, for they were our faithful servants and with their help we were enabled to till our immense fields and drive to pastures new our countless thousands of cattle and horses" (1877:130). The quotation accentuates both the rancheros' desperate reliance on Indian workers and their overall ambivalence regarding Native health and cultural survival. Only white settlers, Chief Solano, and a handful of Native individuals received smallpox vaccines during the late 1830s epidemic (McKittrick 1944:140). According to Vallejo's letters, he and other settlers encouraged vaccination, temperance, and "cleanliness" among Native people to halt the spread of the disease (Bancroft 1886:73). In Sonoma and Napa, for example, local officials applied lime whitewash to the sides of Native homes in an effort to curtail the disease's spread (McKittrick 1944:140), but many believed these efforts were hopeless as long as Native people continued their "stubborn reliance on sweat lodges" for curing (Carrillo 1877:129). Of course, these pseudomedical beliefs relate more to ethnocentric perceptions of undesirable Native practices leading to disease rather than to any understanding of epidemiology.

Cultural and Linguistic Origins

In much the same way that I reconstructed population size, so must I reconstruct the homeland and cultural identity of California Indian laborers at Rancho Petaluma. The task of identification is difficult and speculative because of the lack of adequate documentation. Very few California Indian names have been recovered from written sources (Silliman 2000a:table 4.1), but new data are slowly coming to light that may add some clarity (Alvarado n.d.). Because of the variable "recruiting" strategies of Vallejo and his contemporaries

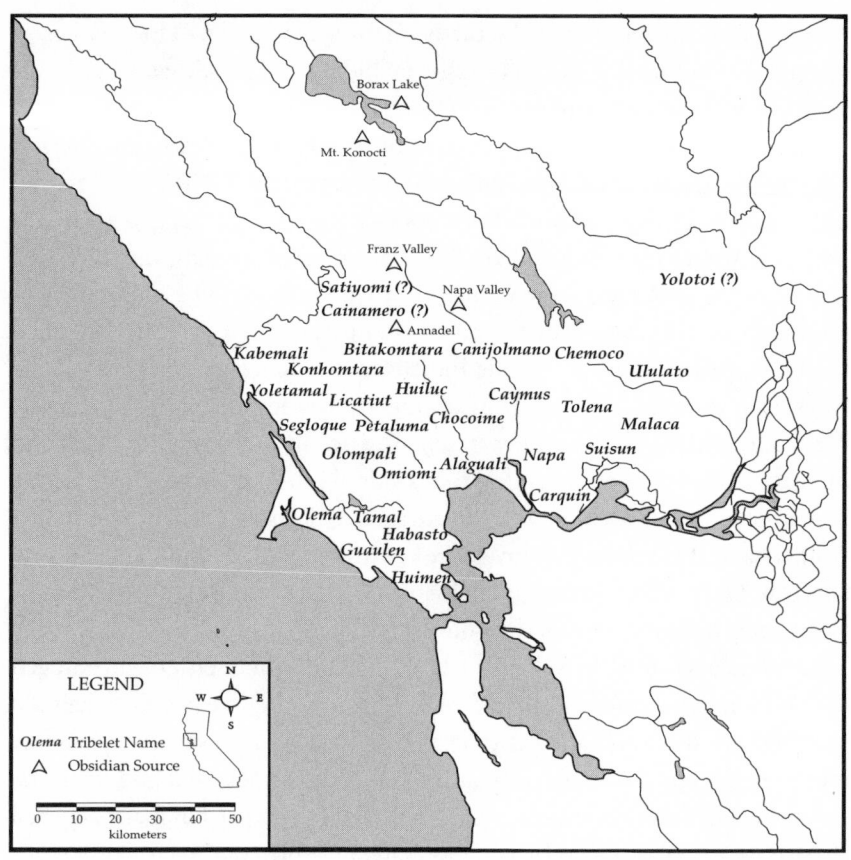

Map 3.2

Map of eighteenth- and nineteenth-century Native communities north of San Francisco. Names followed by a question mark are my additions to the results otherwise compiled, mapped, and published by Milliken (1995:map 4).

in the Petaluma region, Native people arrived at Rancho Petaluma from a number of different political and linguistic groups in northern California. A variety of mission records, historical accounts, and ethnographic data shed some light on the topic, especially through the innovative work of Milliken (1978, 1995), who has been able to reconstruct an ethnogeography, although tentative in some respects, during nineteenth-century missionization. To this I have added Native groups referred to by Vallejo during the postsecularization period (map 3.2). Drawing on these sources, I hypothesize four local but broad groups present at Rancho Petaluma: Southern Patwin, Coast Miwok, Southern Pomo, and Wappo.

Because Rancho Petaluma sat in traditional Coast Miwok territory and because Camillo Ynitia, a Coast Miwok (Olompali) leader, forged an alliance with Vallejo, the Coast Miwok linguistic group likely constituted a large percentage of rancho workers. When Native people who had been missionized in the second decade of the nineteenth century at Mission San Francisco de Asís and Mission San José arrived in the Sonoma Valley in 1823 to help found Mission San Francisco Solano, they were returning home. Many of these returning were Coast Miwok, probably from tribelets such as Alaguali, Chocoime, and Petaluma (Milliken 1995:234–61). The Alaguali had held the areas surrounding the mouths of Sonoma and Tolay Creeks, the Chocoime (Chucuien, or Sonomas) had occupied the area of the pueblo of Sonoma, and the Petaluma had once lived in the Petaluma River valley.

The Petaluma Indians had converts at Missions San Francisco (1814–17), San José (1815–18), San Rafael (1818–22), and San Francisco Solano (1824) (Milliken 1995:251). These baptisms may have virtually emptied the Petaluma area, because the only Native people whom Father Altimira noted on his way through the soon-to-be Rancho Petaluma in June 1823 while looking for a new mission site were eight to ten Petaluma Indians who were "wandering warriors hiding from the fury of the Indians of the *Ranchería* of the *Libantiloyomi*" (Smilie 1975:6).[7] The actual village of Petaluma seems to have been located northeast of the Petaluma River (Barrett 1908:310), making it the closest candidate (less than 3 kilometers from the Petaluma Adobe), if still inhabited, for association with Rancho Petaluma. Currently, no evidence has surfaced for this association or inhabitation, though.

The neophytes who returned to their Sonoma or Marin County homelands in 1823 were also many of the ones who turned over their cattle and lands to Vallejo in exchange for joining Rancho Petaluma. These individuals most likely gained supervisory positions at the rancho due to their familiarity with the landscape and their experience with agriculture and herding at missions. The Coast Miwok tribelets Licatiut, Yoletamal, and Segloque, which were located in central and western Sonoma County, entered Mission San Rafael Arcángel between 1817 and 1825 (Milliken 1995:247–61) and may have become involved with Vallejo's rancho through his secularization efforts. Oral histories of Maria Copa also indicate Coast Miwok involvement with Vallejo's operation. Maria Copa's grandfather was a Mexican captain of

Vallejo who married a "Solano" woman, presumably from Mission San Francisco Solano (Collier and Thalman 1996:26, 75). However, many of Maria Copa's maternal relatives had affiliated with Mission San Rafael Arcángel (Collier and Thalman 1996; Dietz 1976).

The Licatiut[8] appear repeatedly in Vallejo's accounts of the North Bay during the 1830s (1875a:10, 1875c:10–22), and they probably lived in the Cotati area and westward (see map 3.2; Merriam 1907:357; Milliken 1995:247). After extensive and well-documented resistance efforts by Chief Marín, the entire ninety-two-member Licatiut tribe seems to have moved to Mission San Rafael between 1820 and 1825 (Milliken 1995:247). They reportedly clung to the mission well into the 1830s to avoid conflict with unmissionized Native groups in the mountains to the north (Vallejo 1875c:18), suggesting that they may have been a critical labor source for Vallejo. Vallejo certainly portrayed them as numerous and relevant to political alliance building (e.g., 1875c:22). Vallejo also stated that Chief Marín was subservient to Chief Solano (1876:4), but there is the distinct possibility that Vallejo misconstrued the relationship or, at minimum, that it was a postcontact phenomenon.

Southern Patwin also likely represented a primary language group at Rancho Petaluma. In the eighteenth century, speakers of this broad language family resided primarily north of the Carquinez Strait in Solano and Yolo counties as well as in the lower Napa Valley (Johnson 1978). Mission registers from Mission San Francisco Solano indicate that numerous Native Americans were baptized from three different tribelets within this language group: Malaca, Ululato, and Chemoco (Milliken 1978:2.11–2.14, 1995:234–61). The Napa tribelet, presumably Patwin (see Merriam 1977:175), moved to the missions in San Francisco (1809–15) and San José (1814–18), and the Tolenas appeared only at Missions San Francisco and San José. Members of these latter two groups may not have had a solid presence in the North Bay after the 1830s. However, Napas, if equivalent to "Napahoes," comprised a substantial part of Sonoma's surrounding Native population and of Vallejo's military excursions, according to his own accounts (1875c:69, 103, 197, 242, 272).

Although individuals from the Suisun tribelet appeared only in the records of Mission San Francisco to the south (Milliken 1995:255), they were important players in North Bay politics in the 1830s and 1840s. In fact, George Gibbs noted in the early 1850s that "in Petaloma [sic] Valley, the original inhabitants are reduced to almost nothing, and they have been replaced by the Indians of Suisun, from the bay of that name, above Benicia" (1853b:421).

The further likelihood of their presence at Rancho Petaluma stems from the political power held by Sem-Yeto (Chief Solano) and his ability to garner laborers for Vallejo's operations. As noted earlier, Chief Solano was a Suisun, one of the southernmost tribelets speaking a language within Southern Patwin. Presumably, many Southern Patwin ex-neophytes under his leadership participated in the cattle-for-labor exchange at Rancho Petaluma. In addition, Vallejo's battles with Zampay, a Yolotoi Patwin leader who was supposedly trying to win the allegiance of Napahoes (Vallejo 1875c:103, 199), undoubtedly allowed him to secure Patwin prisoners who may have found themselves subsequently working at Petaluma.

Native people from the Southern Pomo linguistic group also may have been present at Rancho Petaluma. Three lines of evidence are pertinent. First, individuals from several Southern Pomo groups—Kabemali, Konhomtara, and Bitakomtara—were baptized at Mission San Rafael from 1820 to 1831 (Milliken 1995:234–61). Vallejo's efforts to secularize that mission while controlling Mission San Francisco Solano may have placed several Southern Pomo ex-neophytes under his supervision in Petaluma. Second, a group known as the Cainamero, who occupied the Santa Rosa plain south of Healdsburg,[9] tended to ally with Vallejo's forces in battles against other indigenous groups, but their seemingly inconsistent alliance (Vallejo 1875c:236) may have resulted in occasional imprisonment and forced labor on ranchos. One Sonoma Valley resident also remarked on large numbers of Cainamero women in Sonoma's town plaza during the Mexican period (Carriger 1874:8). Third, the chief California Indian antagonist to Vallejo's occupation of the North Bay was a man named Succara who led the Satiyomi. Although their exact location and linguistic affiliation are unknown, the Satiyomi appear to have been a Southern Pomo group near Healdsburg (Barrett 1908:218–19; Kroeber 1925:233; Lothrop 1932:173, 181; Merriam 1977:74–75). The numerous military campaigns launched against the Satiyomi by Vallejo and his allies would have resulted in prisoners being captured during some of these raids and used as laborers on local ranchos.

Members of the Wappo language group probably worked at Rancho Petaluma as well. Registers at Mission San Francisco Solano record individual baptisms from the tribelets of Canijolmano, Caymus, and Huiluc; many individuals from these groups transferred to Mission San Francisco Solano from Mission San Francisco (Milliken 1995:234–61). They may have been previous neophytes who were willing or forced to join Rancho Petaluma after mission secularization.

Although these four broad language groups very likely comprised the majority of California Indians at Rancho Petaluma, relying too strongly on these linguistic categories as cultural markers would obscure the subtleties of social and cultural variation among individual tribelets. In general, language groups in northern California did not cleave along ethnic or cultural lines (see Hughes 1992; Milliken 1978:2.29). Evidence also points to Native people from the Clear Lake region—probably speakers of Southeastern Pomo, Eastern Pomo, Wappo, or Lake Miwok—working on ranchos nearby if not at Rancho Petaluma itself. Examples of Clear Lake peoples include Davis's observations of Vallejo's mother-in-law's rancho to the northwest (1929:34), Ward's journal entries in the late 1840s (1878b), and oral histories collected from the Southeastern Pomo (McLendon and Lowy 1978:319).

Furthermore, identity politics in the Sonoma and Petaluma Valleys during and especially after the mission period may have been volatile and unprecedented. In fact, the new amalgamation of members of multiple Native groups around Mission San Francisco Solano was termed Sonomellos, or "Sonoma Indians" (Barrett 1908:312). As mentioned earlier, Gibbs noted the virtual replacement of Coast Miwok speakers in the Petaluma Valley by Southern Patwin (1853b; see also Kroeber 1925:353), a pattern also suggested by Milliken's research into group and linguistic relationships (1978:2.6). If true, these observations confirm the prominence of Southern Patwin speakers at Rancho Petaluma. Prior missionization and the ambiguity of Native American group geography and composition in the North Bay during the historic period further complicate any ethnogeographic scenario. Tribelet locations and intermarriage have been adeptly reconstructed by Milliken (1995) during and just prior to the mission period in the North Bay, but it is unclear how these tribelets or villages withstood the onslaught of postsecularization labor requirements and military confrontations. For this very reason, my earlier summary of cultural practices in the North Bay region was based on a more general characterization of common features.

Structure of Native Labor on Vallejo's Rancho Petaluma

Evidence for the condition of California Indian life and work duties on Rancho Petaluma is frequently as ambiguous and scarce as that found for laborer demography and composition. Despite the lack of detail, some archival sources touch on issues of labor organization, quality of life on the rancho, and compensation and provisioning.

Organization

Life and labor at Rancho Petaluma were organized around activities of production. Prominent activities included tending and slaughtering cattle, herding and shearing sheep, planting and harvesting agricultural crops, and manufacturing goods. The economic mainstay of the operation was cattle ranching, and these animals ran loose and wild on California ranchos. Head counts for Rancho Petaluma grew from three to four thousand in 1834, according to Vallejo's brother Salvador, to around ten thousand in the late 1830s (Davis 1929:31; United States District Court 1852:12, 14). Davis projected an inconsistently larger figure when he claimed that Vallejo branded roughly ten thousand calves, or one fifth of the herd, every spring, propelling the total to fifty thousand (1929:138). The succeeding decade saw Petaluma cattle herds perhaps totaling fifteen thousand in 1841, just over two thousand in 1844, fifty thousand in 1845, twenty thousand in 1846, and only three thousand in 1850, according to Hoopes's documentary research (1965:44). These numbers are drawn from a variety of correspondences and letters, and I present them as illustrative rather than exact amounts. The discrepancies are noteworthy, though. During his visit to the Petaluma Adobe in 1846, Boggs (1913) reported only four thousand cattle, or 20 percent of the total projected by Hoopes. In addition, the radically diminished herd size reconstructed for 1844 seems discrepant with yearly trends, but the majordomo himself provided this total to Vallejo, saying that "all the stock was let out to the vaqueros on shares because it can no longer be done otherwise" due to a shortage of laborers (Alvarado 1844a). Oddly, Alvarado penned this letter in September, which should have been almost six months after the regular rodeo counts in early spring. The only herd size changes that appear to correspond to known historical events are the sharp upswing in the late 1830s, when Vallejo acquired cattle from ex-neophytes after the smallpox epidemic, and the sharp downturn after the late 1840s, when Vallejo lost control of many rancho resources during American annexation of the region.

At Petaluma, as at other Mexican ranchos, vaqueros rounded up cattle in the rodeo during the spring months of February, March, and April (Alvarado 1848; Davis 1929:138; Richman 1965:349). Vaqueros then branded and counted livestock in preparation for slaughtering in late summer. "Don Guadalupe [Vallejo], as he was generally called by his countrymen and the merchants, castrated, earmarked and branded about the first of March each year some ten thousand calves, or one-fifth of his great herds" (Davis

1929:138). The matanza began in July or August and involved butchers slaughtering thousands of cattle to secure highly prized hides and tallow (Hoopes 1965:44; Revere 1849:99). After a butcher dispatched an animal, workers dragged the carcass off for hide removal. Sanchez's general description of California practices probably fits Rancho Petaluma: "Skinners, *peleadores*, took off hides, and butchers, *tasajeros*, cut meat into strips [while] Indian women gathered tallow and lard in bags made of skin" (1929:47–48). The lucrative hides made it to the Petaluma River for shipment downstream in oxcarts, by mules, or stacked on the heads of Native workers (Hoopes 1965:44).

At Rancho Petaluma, Vallejo had approximately eight thousand steers over three years old, or 80 percent of the annual herd increase, slaughtered during a yearly matanza (Davis 1929:138). An average steer would produce 100 pounds of tallow, or *sebo*, and 50 pounds of lard, or *manteca* (Sánchez 1993:224; see Davis 1929:138). The huge number of cattle killed and processed would have produced immense quantities of beef. Portions of this meat undoubtedly served to fill the plates, bowls, and baskets of those living on the rancho. However, since the primary reason for the matanza was to obtain hides and tallow, the ultimate destination of the meat probably proved more a burden for the rancho manager than it did a boon for human nutrition. Much of it was discarded or left for carrion feeders.

Sheep were an important livestock commodity for Rancho Petaluma. Estimates varied by year and report, numbering between three and six thousand sheep in the late 1830s (Bancroft 1885:720; Lothrop 1926:86; United States District Court 1852:14). Cloth goods were woven from their wool (McKittrick 1944:174), especially serapes with black-and-white stripes (Fitch 1874:47). Vallejo even had special sheep imported from England after 1842 for their higher-quality wool (McKittrick 1944:174). Sheep may have served as a food resource for the Vallejo family and the worker populace, but visitors to the region claimed that mutton was not common, even at Vallejo's own dinner table (Simpson 1847:175).

Like livestock, agriculture served as a seasonal timepiece for rancho activity. Oxen dragged plows made of wooden poles with iron bars, churning only the upper 5–8 centimeters of soil (Davis 1929:136; Simpson 1847:176; see Lugo 1950:228 for a similar description). Generally, rancheros like Vallejo planted wheat and barley in December or January (Lugo 1950:228; Alvarado 1849) and corn during March (Brown 1956:8). Field hands then harvested barley in May or June and wheat in July and August (Lugo 1950:228). These months surely brought increased numbers of Native American workers to

Rancho Petaluma. In the early years, laborers processed all grain by hand, but a water-powered flour mill was built in Petaluma in 1838 (Fitch 1874:43; Vallejo 1874b).

Like agriculture and livestock, manufacturing and processing were principal activities on the rancho. Workers processed raw materials and manufactured finished products such as blankets, shoes, and candles year-round, but resource availability and task focus depended on the season. For example, in the fall Native workers concentrated on making tallow candles from the summer's fresh supply of cattle fat (Hoopes 1965:46). Native workers who filled these manufacturing positions probably lived and worked at Rancho Petaluma on a relatively permanent basis, and these artisans were joined by household servants who cleaned Petaluma Adobe and prepared food. Due to their training in "domestic" tasks and their trustworthiness in the eyes of Vallejo, these individuals are likely to have been ex-residents of the mission.

Vallejo's Rancho Petaluma strongly resembled the Franciscan mission in both labor scheduling and organization. Native workers at California ranchos arrived for work around sunrise (Híjar 1988:20; Monroy 1990:151). At this time, Vallejo would have called the "chief taskmasters" into the courtyard of the adobe for roll call (Vallejo 1941:2). Following breakfast in the form of *atole* (a soup of ground grains),[10] Indian workers went to their various tasks to labor until the midday meal between 11:00 A.M. and 12:00 P.M., which was followed by a siesta until around 2:00 P.M. and continuation of work until early evening if not dusk (Hoopes 1965:36).

The division of labor was based on both gender and prior work experience in the mission system. Women generally performed tasks related to cooking, cleaning, grain processing, weaving, basket making, and hide working, whereas men usually plowed agricultural fields, herded and butchered livestock, and cared for horses. Based on the pattern established with mission work assignments, both men and women constructed adobe buildings and corrals, worked the crop fields, processed hides, and rendered tallow. Few documents speak to the role of children in rancho labor, but it is likely that they performed jobs reminiscent of mission duties such as guarding fields and adobe bricks being dried or assisting in household or production tasks (see Geiger and Meighan 1976).

Prior experience in mission communities was a significant factor in labor organization. Ex-neophytes who had been trained in mission crafts were frequently given positions as vaqueros, house servants, and primary plowers and harvesters (Cleland 1941:42; Davis 1929:136; Sanchez 1929:197).

Unchristianized Indians worked in the field as heavy manual laborers or assistant plowmen (Davis 1929:136; Sanchez 1929:197). Much like the "trusted" household servants, Indian artisans who worked in the crafts of candle production, smithing, and leatherwork had probably once lived at a mission. Complementing the skill-based divisions, task specialization may have been common practice, at least as represented in Vallejo's household in Sonoma. As reported by Manuel Torres in 1841, Francisca Benicia stated:

> Each one of my children, boys and girls, has a servant who has no other duty than to care for him or her. I have two for my own personal service. Four or five grind the corn for the tortillas; for here we entertain so many guests that three could not furnish enough meal to feed them all. All six or seven are set apart for service in the kitchen. Five or six are continually occupied in washing the clothes of the children and of the rest employed in the house; and finally, nearly a dozen are charged to attend to the sewing and spinning; for you must know that, as a rule, Indian women are not much inclined to learn many things. (Engelhardt 1915:136)

Whether this task specialization was imposed by the Vallejos and others to rift any cohesion between Native workers or whether it developed out of Native individuals staking claim to a worker identity is unclear. I return to this issue in the penultimate chapter.

In addition, given that at least some Native workers were prisoners of war, a system of hierarchical supervision must have been in place. The rancho probably mimicked the mission system by establishing a series of watchdogs and subsupervisors to enforce labor demands and to prevent flight. Following the tradition of mission Indian alcaldes, or judicial and administrative officers, and their reputation for harsh treatment and vigilance over other Indian workers, the rancho may have utilized a similar system for tasks—tending livestock or harvesting crops—outside the majordomo's immediate watch (see Sanchez 1929:197). Only one document thus far discovered alludes to this structure: an undated list of workers compiled by Alvarado (n.d.) that specifically names four individuals—Nasario, Pio, Bisente Pablo, and Aulirio—as alcaldes. The social implication is that Native people would have occupied positions of authority over fellow village members or even potential political rivals. Many of these appointed leaders were probably previous mission residents at San Francisco Solano or San Rafael Arcángel, although some may have been Californios. In many ways, this system mirrored the divide-and-conquer military strategy that Vallejo employed to combat Native groups in northern California but on a smaller scale (1875c:73). That is, Vallejo maintained order by pitting Native people against one another in his system of labor supervision.

Native individuals probably had little flexibility in work commitments due to economic indebtedness, the urgency of seasonal work, or their frequent status as prisoners. This meant that indigenous resistance to work, especially fugitivism, would not have been tolerated (see Cook 1976:457). A Coast Miwok woman, Maria Copa, recalled a story that "Vallejo was mean to his men and abused them; he had those who ran away followed" (Collier and Thalman 1996:75). Although the standard practice at Rancho Petaluma was to retrieve fugitives, it was not always consistent. As mentioned above, several named individuals working at Rancho Petaluma disappeared in 1848, and the majordomo was unsure of their whereabouts (Alvarado 1848). Presumably, these were Native workers, but Alvarado did not recommend a search for them, and the records do not suggest that Vallejo ordered one.

Coercion and violence structured Native entry into Rancho Petaluma, but more Native workers lived and labored there than could be restrained by physical force. Cook believed that "in order to obtain and hold the necessary labor supply, they treated their peons well, kept them supplied with food and clothing, and paid them what cash they could. As a result their Indians were reasonably contented and labored faithfully" (1976:304–5). Those close to Vallejo spoke favorably of his relations with California Indians. Davis claimed that "General Vallejo would never tolerate injustice or brutality toward the natives" (1929:137–38). Similarly, Francisca Benicia claimed that local Indians held a deep respect for her husband: "'They were happy in building our new home in Sonoma, the Casa Grande and to work at the Petaluma Rancho'" (Emparan 1968:201). Davis relayed an interesting story about Vallejo's mother-in-law, who managed a rancho near modern-day Santa Rosa and had a few hundred unmissionized Native people working and living near the family adobe.

> I asked the good Señora once if she was not afraid for the safety of her family, with so many unchristianized Indians among her household. She said that she had perfect confidence in her raw help because she treated them so well, giving them abundant food, beef, *frijol* and corn. She also learned their dialect and managed them with a uniform system in their labor and otherwise. It was the treatment and government of the early fathers she had adopted, and these Indians would do anything for her and perform it most cheerfully. (1967:25)[11]

The observations convey not only the relative stability of rancho labor and social relations but also the expectations of subservience and dependency shared by rancheros with regard to local Native people. The system bears remarkable similarity, explicitly in Vallejo's mother-in-law's case, to that of the preceding Franciscan missions.

Although these rancheros' views of "their" Native workers may have held some truth, their perspectives euphemized the realities of hierarchy and forced labor. In fact, the positive views of Native laborers espoused by Californio residents such as the Vallejo household frequently went hand in hand with the paternalism that discursively justified the rancheros' use of Indian people as a laboring class. Plantation owners in the American South envisioned similar relations with enslaved Africans. As Almaguer stated, "Indians were viewed as stepchildren of the ranchero class, as dependents bound by a series of mutual duties and responsibilities as well as binding *compadrazgo* (godparent) relationships" (1994:49). Many rancheros and their families constructed quasi-familial ties with some Native workers, presumably as an outgrowth of daily interaction with favored servants. However, it is unlikely that rancheros shared these sentiments with all field hands or vaqueros, many of whom they never even knew. More importantly, it is dubious that Native workers would have reciprocated and accepted this subordinate relationship as wholeheartedly as the rancheros liked to believe.

These various perspectives convey that there is not one correct side of the debate. All Native workers were not willing servants, but all were not under lock and key. Instead, these stories demonstrate the multiplicity of views and experiences that existed within the rancho context. Some Native people may have lived at Rancho Petaluma comfortably, voluntarily, and relatively content with their situation, but others probably resented Vallejo and all that he stood for and were constantly on the watch for ways to escape the rancho's hold. Adding to this complexity, this period may have represented "a time of little choice," if, as Milliken (1995) suggests for the preceding mission period in the San Francisco Bay, other means of survival had become increasingly limited in the cementing colonial world.

Compensation and Provisioning

Issues of labor compensation and provisioning are important for understanding colonial-Native interactions at Rancho Petaluma. On the northern frontier, colonial currency would have had little value for Native Americans, who had no company store from which to buy and who may have had no desire for Mexican-Californian money, except perhaps as material items to be modified for body ornamentation. In fact, few rancheros anywhere in Alta California paid Indian workers in money instead of material goods (Bauer 1953:7; Mason 1986:12; Sánchez 1986:25). In a system of indebted peonage, Native individuals received goods and provisions in exchange for their labor.

In Petaluma, part of the verbal deal between Vallejo and those Native Americans choosing to pasture their cattle with him involved provisioning laborers for their work. Like other ranchos in Alta California, Native workers received clothing and food for their labor, but food was certainly the main commodity, given the economic orientation of the rancho. At Rancho Petaluma, Carrillo commented that a male worker "for his trouble only obtained a scanty amount of clothing and the food he required for the support of his family" (1877:131). Vallejo's son Napoleón recalled his father's provisioning practices, although he referred primarily to the workers and soldiers residing in Sonoma:

> Every week a certain number of beeves would be killed and divided among the Indians and soldiers' families. The amount each household received being governed by the number of its members. During the week, the squaws were required to pound up in mortars a certain quality of *pinole* (corn-flour), and [place?] it into a great bin in the storehouse, whence it was distributed per capita. The same with lard, which when prepared, was kept in bladders. Shoes and blankets in plenty, were made and dealt out as required. (N. Vallejo 1890:4)[12]

Beef was also likely distributed as dried strips, if the situation at all paralleled that of the missions (Farnham 1947:147). Revere remarked in the late 1840s while visiting ranchos in the nearby Napa Valley that Native American workers were "always paid in merchandise" (1849:100), and there is no reason to suspect Vallejo's operation was much different. In his synthesis of documents on Rancho Petaluma, Hoopes concluded that "there was simple food, primitive shelter and a scant supply of crude homemade clothing as labor payment" (1965:35; see also Smilie 1975:84). Such a conclusion agrees in data, although not in tone, with Cook's claim that rancheros treated Native workers well, provided ample food and clothing, and paid them cash whenever possible (1976:304–5, 458).

Although Vallejo provisioned his workers, the constancy of these goods may be questioned. Alvarado wrote to Vallejo in February 1848: "Sir, Pietro the Indian says that you have given them nothing and that for that reason they are not happy here. They do not say that to me, but from others who do not belong here I learn that people from here say it, and at other ranchos they are paid something, and for that reason they want to go to work at other ranchos" (1848). The quotation is a tantalizing glimpse into Native choice in the rancho context, revealing that some individuals at certain times could leave on their own accord. The letter suggests also that Native Americans had some opportunities to manipulate rancheros to improve their own compensation or laboring conditions. Timing may have been critical, though. Alvarado penned the letter during the year of U.S. annexation of California, when Vallejo and his estates were in turmoil. This context may have been the first time that Native workers had such leverage on Rancho Petaluma. However, the quality or quantity of provisions on Vallejo's rancho may have been a problem long before 1848. Seven years earlier, Sir George Simpson of the Hudson's Bay Company observed that Native Americans who worked for Vallejo ate "the worst bullock's worst joints" (1847:77). In 1851 Vallejo's mother-in-law's rancho near Santa Rosa had Native workers who apparently received only "a bare support beyond what they can steal, and then only in the summer" (Gibbs 1853a:100).

Residential Life

Simpson's observation about the quality of provisioned food prompts a consideration of Native American residential and material life at Rancho Petaluma. Since virtually no accounts exist for the Petaluma case, I draw heavily on observations made in other colonial contexts in the North Bay between 1830 and 1855. Simpson painted perhaps the most complete picture of Native life associated directly with Vallejo's labor force. His statement is worth repeating in full:

> During the day, we visited a village of General Vallego's [sic] Indians, about three hundred in number, who were the most miserable of the race that I ever saw, excepting always the slaves of the savages of the northwest coast. Though many of them are well formed and well grown, yet every face bears the impress of poverty and wretchedness; and they are, moreover, a prey to several malignant diseases, among which an hereditary syphilis ranks as the predominant scourge alike of old and young. They are badly clothed, badly lodged and badly fed. As to clothing, they are pretty nearly

in a state of nature; as to lodging, their hovels are made of boughs wattled with bulrushes in the form of beehives, with a hole in the top for a chimney and with two holes at the bottom towards the northwest and the southeast, so as to enable the poor creatures, by closing them in turns, to exclude both the prevailing winds; and as to food, they eat the worst bullock's worst joints, with bread of acorns and chestnuts, which are most laboriously and carefully prepared by pounding and rinsing and grinding. (Simpson 1847:77)

Simpson probably visited a camp closer to the pueblo of Sonoma than to Petaluma, but living conditions for Native people had to have been similar at the two localities under Vallejo's supervision. Despite Simpson's perceptions of the Natives as "badly clothed, badly lodged and badly fed," which reflected perhaps as much his preconceptions of appropriate attire and housing as the actual condition of Vallejo's workers, his observation recorded several key features of rancho provisioning and a continuity of traditional economic and subsistence pursuits. Namely, California Indians were given or at least allowed beef portions considered suboptimal by Western standards, *and* they continued to practice indigenous methods of house construction and acorn preparation.

In 1842 Edward Vischer encountered a Native encampment located between Sonoma and San Rafael, probably near Petaluma. Again, the visitor's observations are worth repeating.

We passed a camp of migratory heathen Indians. They were used to camping during certain seasons near frontier settlements to earn, by means of communal labor, a better living than is possible for them in the wilderness. . . . The *rancheria* consisted of about fifteen or twenty cone-shaped huts of straw. There was only one opening through which one could crawl. Unless they were on duty with their white neighbors or on a fishing or hunting trip, old and young, male and female, lay inside around a fire. Knowledge of Spanish was of no use with these people; we had to resort to signs and gestures if we wanted a drink of water from their basket-work pitcher. Similar vessels were used for cooking utensils. They do not place them over a fire, for fear that the close basket-work may start to burn. Instead, they place heated rocks in them to make the contents boil. (Gudde 1940:7–8)

Despite Vischer's ethnocentric assumptions, this statement indicates that entire villages may have moved seasonally to engage in rancho labor tasks and that these groups may have settled temporarily in territories not formerly their own. The lack of spoken Spanish suggests little previous association with mission communities (or an unwillingness to comply with "expected" modes of colonial discourse). Coupled with Simpson's statements, Vischer's observations confirm the continued use of conical thatch houses in the nineteenth-century North Bay. These were undoubtedly the residential mainstays on ranchos, although one visitor reported Indian servants sleeping on the floor of an adobe home in Marin County (Ward 1878a). However, most, if not virtually all, Native American people at Rancho Petaluma would have lived outside the adobe, and they would have done so in their own housing or in adobe dormitories.

Conclusion

Vallejo retained the Petaluma Adobe, the large building erected as the rancho's hub, and about half of the surrounding rancho lands until 1857, when he sold the property for $25,000. He had sold the other half earlier, in the 1850s. The expansive "colonial" Rancho Petaluma was greatly reduced by 1848, when the United States annexed California in the Treaty of Guadalupe Hidalgo, after an earlier diminution in operation when American rebels of the 1846 Bear Flag Revolt jailed Vallejo in Sacramento. At this time, Vallejo claimed that he "lost more than a thousand live horned cattle, six hundred tame horses, and many other things of value which were taken from my house here and at Petaluma. My wheat crops are entirely lost for the cattle eat them up in the fields" (Larkin 1953:237). One of the last solid archival references to a Native presence on Rancho Petaluma dates to February 1848 in a letter from the rancho's majordomo to Vallejo (Alvarado 1848). An archive in the intervening period between the Bear Flag Revolt of 1846 and Alvarado's reference in 1848 gives a sense both of the final days of the rancho and of the continued presence of Native workers. While traveling through the Petaluma Valley in 1847, James Ward stated that the Petaluma Adobe "was never finished, and is now partly in ruins. The scene now before us was very gloomy with scarcely anything to disturb its monotony, and not a soul in sight but the General's Indians" (1878a).

A few of these Native workers may have stayed on until approximately 1854, but their numbers would have been significantly reduced. Vallejo rented the Petaluma Adobe property to Leandro Luso between 1852 and 1854 under

Figure 3.2
Mariano Vallejo standing with an elderly Pomo woman, 1878. Photo courtesy
of the Sonoma County Library, Santa Rosa, California.

an ultimately unsatisfied agreement that Luso would supervise the few re-maining Indian workers in the final construction of the building (Vallejo 1874c). An 1853 letter to Vallejo regarding his Petaluma property also men-tions "your Indians" (Vallejo 1874d). However, there must have been very few workers available, for Vallejo had rented the property to two French colo-nists named Deslander and Lebret in the preceding period of 1850–52, and these occupants complained about the lack of available vaqueros to capture the wild cattle for food (Hoopes 1965:27).[13] These agreements referred al-most exclusively to the Petaluma Adobe itself and immediate fields, since Vallejo had sold almost 30,000 acres of Rancho Petaluma before 1857 (Hoopes 1965:12). The historical details of Vallejo and the Petaluma Adobe after this date are beyond the scope of this work, except that relations forged between Vallejo and Native Americans during the Mexican period extended well be-yond the end of Rancho Petaluma. Not only were the Vallejo family, particu-larly the children, in close contact with Indian people in the 1850s and 1860s (Emparan 1968:380–82; Vallejo n.d.b; Vallejo 1914), but Vallejo himself main-tained at least some connections (figure 3.2).

Although a short period of time in the grand scheme of colonialism in the American West, the Rancho Petaluma episode was not an insignificant or uneventful one. For approximately fourteen years, in spite of variation in production and participants, Rancho Petaluma maintained a strong but some-times archivally unnoticed presence in the North Bay. That is, this center of colonial and Native activity seems not to have come under the same level of description and scrutiny by its contemporaries as did the nearby Spanish missions, Russian fort, and growing urban centers. Yet the rancho did not go unnoticed by those individuals engulfed within it. This is perhaps most true for the many Native Americans caught up in the hard labor and toil of the enterprise whose voices have become only faint whispers in the historical record. Beginning in 1834, Vallejo developed Rancho Petaluma into a large manufacturing, processing, and residential center west of the dismantled Mission San Francisco Solano. Rancho Petaluma also became a colonial cen-ter for interactions between numerous types of people: nonmissionized in-digenous groups, ex–mission neophytes, and nonindigenous overseers and artisans. Although unique in its large size and position on the northern fron-tier of Mexican California, Rancho Petaluma was not entirely unique with respect to its dealings with Native people. Ranchos across California, par-ticularly the larger ones, survived by the labor of California Indian people, and we have only begun to understand the nature of this interaction. The

Rancho Petaluma case is poised to refine that understanding due to the wealth of archaeological potential and the vast numbers of indigenous laborers it employed.

In this chapter, I detailed archival evidence for Rancho Petaluma and focused attention on the experience of Native lives on this rancho. In addition to tracking the multiple cultural origins and large numbers of Native Americans working on Rancho Petaluma, I highlighted the variable treatment of workers, the provisioning of food and supplies, the quality of the workers' diet, and the daily activities of labor and residential life. I gleaned all of these from historical observations and ethnographic notes. However, what I did not do was analyze fully the material and spatial aspects of labor on Rancho Petaluma. I could not attempt this because the historical documents are largely silent on these aspects, perhaps because Vallejo did not reside consistently at the Petaluma Adobe or because many of the relevant documents burned in a fire at his Sonoma home in 1867 (Hoopes 1965:16). I have garnered some insights from archival sources, but these written materials cannot suffice for a detailed examination of labor and colonialism. As it stands, historical documents provide only the interpretive parameters for studying labor at Rancho Petaluma; they supply only a few edge pieces to the puzzle. To accomplish a more detailed anthropological analysis requires archaeological data, the subject of the next chapter.

Chapter 4

Lost Laborers in Northern California

Search and Recovery

It remains to be demonstrated whether any single trait or assemblage of cultural materials of the later [postmission, rancho] years can be identified archaeologically as Indian. Because the Native Americans adopted farming, domestic animals, and metal tools and other products of commerce with such rapidity, there are few remains of aboriginal lifeways or crafts to be excavated.

—Roberta Greenwood, "The California Ranchero: Fact and Fancy"

Information gleaned from historical accounts provides a cursory glimpse into the nature of life for California Indian people on Rancho Petaluma in northern California. These accounts underscore the significance of rancho labor for Native people, the daily and seasonal schedules in which Native workers maneuvered, and the system of provisioning that linked rancho owner with rancho worker. The archives suggest the possible mix of Mexican-Californian adobe buildings and California Indian conical thatch houses in the rancho landscape, both of which were part of the daily movements of Native individuals. Moreover, the documents suggest the expected role of material culture in the negotiations between Vallejo and Native workers. These items served as tools in the home and in the workplace, as objects for trade and provision, and as elements in the construction and expression of social identity and gender in the colonial world.

Despite these tantalizing clues and partial glances, historical records fail to provide a true entry into the material and social issues that California Indian people faced inside the colonial rancho regime. The documents give very little voice to the Native side of the colonial discourse, to the particulars of daily life that involved Native workers, and to the specific spaces that they may have carved out as their own in the landscape that Vallejo attempted to control. To circumvent the limitations of the written record and to open up the historical and cultural world occupied by Native American people in nineteenth-century northern California requires a turn to archaeology. Archaeological research must take center stage as the primary source for understanding indigenous experiences of rancho colonialism but not the archaeology of fortuitous discovery of Native artifacts or the archaeology of strictly ranchero households. The limitations of these were revealed in the previous two chapters, and the problems of "recognizing" Native Americans in rancho archaeological sites was discussed. Rather, what is needed is a full-scale explicit attempt to focus on the Native American aspects of ranchos. Thankfully, Greenwood's fears expressed at the opening of this chapter have not come to fruition, even when California Indian people adopted European material culture. In fact, the assumption is theoretically flawed, because the biggest danger is presuming that Indians are any less "Indian" when they materialize their identities with European goods. Understanding the link between material culture and identity requires more contextual studies and fewer preconceptions.

To illustrate, I turn once again to Rancho Petaluma. To begin the archaeological journey into rancho labor and daily life, this chapter elaborates on the field methods and general results of archaeological research undertaken in the last six years to examine the spaces and materials of Native workers on Vallejo's rancho. Specific interpretations of material culture and food remains are detailed in subsequent chapters.

The Search

The center of my archaeological attention was land preserved inside the Petaluma Adobe State Historic Park in Sonoma County. Restricting the project to these current political boundaries met the needs of state park interpretive efforts and cultural resource evaluation, but it also made good research sense. What better place to begin (but never stop) looking for evidence of Native life on a 27,000-hectare rancho than at its very core, the Petaluma Adobe headquarters and immediate environs. The search initially focused outside of the main complex formed by the Petaluma Adobe, where some archaeological work had already taken place and had not revealed clear evidence of Native American activities (Clemmer 1961; Gebhardt 1962; Treganza 1958). My limited excavations inside the Petaluma Adobe further verified that it was not a prime location for studying Native workers, since the results revealed more about the building's construction than its use (Silliman 1999). Although the Petaluma Adobe was constructed by the hands of California Indians and perhaps bears the most visible mark of their laboring presence on the landscape, the building itself does not evidence the everyday lives and activities of those workers.

The search for archaeological evidence of Native Americans on Rancho Petaluma required a two-tiered program in the lands surrounding the Adobe proper. The first step involved ground reconnaissance through pedestrian survey, shovel-test survey, and geophysical (remote sensing) techniques and aerial reconnaissance using vertical and oblique aerial photographs taken between the 1950s and 1980s (Silliman 2000a:106–15). These methods all served to trace changes in the landscape over time and to delimit areas that were to become top priority for the second step of archaeological research. Each of these survey methods narrowed the scope of research in the state park to one area of high potential for a successful excavation. This area was marked by artifacts such as stone tool debris and bottle glass fragments visible on the surface and significant geophysical "hits" from both gradiometer (magnetometer) and electromagnetic conductivity surveys (Silliman 2000a:111–13; Silliman, Farnsworth, and Lightfoot 2000). Upon its recording with the state, this archaeological site, located less than 150 meters east of the Petaluma Adobe, was given the official designation of CA–Son–2294/H.

The second step of the process involved the backbone of archaeology: subsurface excavation. Excavation took place in the area delimited by the previous research efforts, the field just south of the current parking lot that contained Son–2294/H (figure 4.1). Excavation proceeded through a combination of surface testing units, test units, trench excavation, and block excavation. The excavation types and locations all had the goals of evaluating the geophysical "anomalies" detected by remote sensing techniques and finding artifacts and cultural features such as trash deposits, cooking pits, and architecture that would tell the story of Native life on the rancho. Because this second phase of the research provided the most tangible information for addressing Native life and labor on Rancho Petaluma, I restrict the remainder of my discussion to it.

Excavation focused on two areas that had been distinguished by surface artifacts and remote sensing images of the subsurface (see figure 4.1). The first locus, flanking the eastern bank of Adobe Creek, was named Area A. A nineteenth-century midden deposit, it contains a dense accumulation of habitation

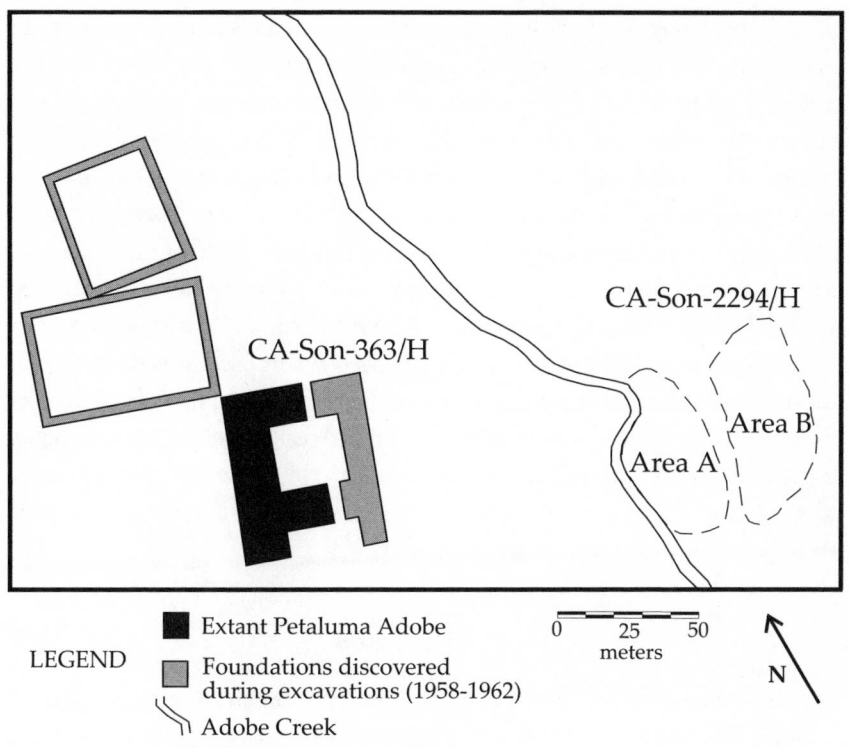

Figure 4.1
Archaeological site map.

refuse, with its rough boundaries set by Adobe Creek on the west and a lack of strong geophysical signatures on the east. Research began here with a surface collection strategy in which we turned over and examined the upper few centimeters of soil in a semirandom sample of thirty-six 1-by-1-meter units. Following the discovery of dense and varied artifacts in these surface testing units, a series of subsurface excavation units were placed in the most artifact-rich portions of this area in 1997 and 1998, and they joined to form the Midden Trench (Silliman 2000a). Additional excavation along the bank of Adobe Creek at the western perimeter of Area A took place in 2000 in the Stream Trench (Silliman 2002).[1]

The second area was pinpointed by geophysical surveying, and it underwent excavation based solely on expectations drawn from the geophysical data. The locus, labeled Area B, sat several meters east of the Area A midden on a slight topographic rise, revealed almost no surface indication of the archaeological richness beneath the ground, and displayed a wide variety of remote sensing targets. During "ground truthing" of these geophysical signatures, excavation revealed them to be both buried streambed deposits of cobble, gravel, and sand snaking their way across the field and cultural features comprised of burned bone, baked earth, fire-cracked rock, and many artifacts (Silliman 2000a:115–20). Initially, the buried stream deposits appeared in the geophysical survey images and very early test excavation as potential adobe building foundations (given their linear nature and narrow width), and this accounts for why we exposed several sections during excavation. The cultural features appeared in the remote sensing survey as more discrete, pronounced signatures. Excavation in Area B involved three trenches of contiguous 1-by-1-meter units and a larger "block" excavation of eleven 1-by-1-meter units in an areal excavation format. These areas were labeled Trenches 1, 2, and 3, and Block, respectively.[2]

The Recovery

The combined Midden Trench, Stream Trench, Trench 1, Trench 2, Trench 3, and Block excavations covered a total area of 79.75 square meters and removed 34.45 cubic meters of sediment (table 4.1). More details concerning unit designations and measurements, stratigraphic descriptions, plan maps, and provenience information are reported elsewhere (Silliman 2000a:115–90, 2002). Although numerous artifacts appeared in every unit opened, the Midden Trench, Block, and Trench 1 provided the keys to unlocking the cultural secrets buried in the field. Before elaborating on those discoveries, I outline the excavation methods and areas as a way of contextualizing the discoveries.

The geomorphology and stratigraphy of the site dictated a certain excavation and recording methodology. Relevant site characteristics included (1) few cases of stratified deposits, meaning that the alluvial matrix encasing the archaeological record had little vertical differentiation; (2) relatively shallow historical deposits that rested on or just above old fluvial surfaces; (3) heavily bioturbated deposits, especially in the midden, that were the result of many decades of gopher burrowing and possible agricultural activity; (4) discrete cultural features in only some excavation areas; (5) a lack of discernible precontact deposits except below the large fluvial deposits; and (6) clay-rich soils that slowed excavation and impaired traditional dry screening of dirt

Table 4.1

Total area and volume excavated.[a]

	Midden Trench	Stream Trench	Block	Trench 1	Trench 2	Trench 3	Total
Area	6.0 m²	33.75 m²	17.0 m²	11.0 m²	6.0 m²	6.0 m²	79.75 m²
Volume	3.2 m³	11.77 m³	6.85 m³	5.5 m³	3.35 m³	3.8 m³	34.45 m³

[a] See Silliman (2000a, 2002) for details.

to recover artifacts. These characteristics became clear as excavation progressed, but the field methods had been designed to accommodate such potential conditions. Excavation and recording involved mixed stratigraphic and arbitrary (10-centimeter levels) excavation techniques, depending on whether cultural layers could be distinguished, and a wet-screening method using 1/8-inch mesh for retrieving artifacts not collected in situ at excavation units. To complement the data from these recovery techniques, I collected soil samples from various units and features for processing through a flotation system, which served as a double check on recovery and a controlled method for the retrieval of plant remains.

Area A

Surface testing units allowed the initial collection and quantification of the midden by sampling 3.6 percent of a 1,000-square-meter gridded area using 1-by-1-meter surface units. The finer details of the stratified, systematic, unaligned sampling strategy used to examine this area are provided elsewhere (Silliman 2000a:114–15). Artifacts recovered from the inspection of the upper 2–3 centimeters of soil in the surface units included obsidian, chert, and other stone tools and associated manufacturing debris; animal bones; shellfish remains; nails and other metal artifacts; ceramic sherds; glass bottle fragments; glass beads; baked-clay roof tiles; ground stone; burned wood fragments; and thermally affected rock (table 4.2). These same artifact classes were subsequently recovered during subsurface excavation in the Midden Trench, which was placed in the highest surface density of artifacts

Table 4.2
Artifact and ecofact counts for Area A.

Category	Surface Testing Units	Midden Trench	Stream Trench	Total
Baked earth pieces	0	38	7	45
Beads, glass	50	560	176	786
Beads, other	0	7	0	7
Buttons	0	22	2	24
Ceramic	49	248	57	354
Charred wood	42	8,606	1,416	10,064
Fauna, unidentifiable	3,038	42,370	2,141	47,549
Fauna, identifiable	—[a]	2,561	110	2,671
Fauna, worked	0	6	1	7
Floral remains[b]	0	411	33	444
Glass	469	2,448	461	3,378
Glass, worked[c]	0	106	0[d]	106
Ground stone	5	6	0	11
Lithic artifacts	108	546	228	882
Lithics, obsidian[e]	66	290	145	501
Metal	140	829	116	1,085
Other[f]	0	38	27	65
Pipes	0	5	1	6
Schist	0	4	2	6
Shellfish	213	572	42	827
Tile	4	9	6	19
Wood	0	35	143	178
Total	4,184	59,321	4,969	68,474

[a] Faunal remains were not divided into identifiable/unidentifiable during this phase of research.

[b] None of these floral specimens retrieved from wet screening were analyzed. Only those remains secured from controlled flotation were identified.

[c] Worked glass is listed here as a subset of glass; the row is not counted separately in the totals.

[d] Some glass artifacts showed evidence of potential working, but they were not quantified (Silliman 2002:38–39).

[e] Obsidian is listed as a subset of lithic artifacts for illustration purposes; the row is not counted separately in the totals.

[f] "Other" includes a variety of rocks, potentially baked clay, plastic, rubber, and miscellaneous objects.

in 1997 and 1998, and in the Stream Trench, which was positioned along the precarious and eroding eastern bank of Adobe Creek in 2000. All surface artifacts are tabulated here but not integrated into any discussion unless otherwise noted.

Midden Trench. Using the artifact data available for the sample of surface units, I selected an area with the highest density of artifacts for subsurface excavation (figure 4.2). As part of full-scale excavation, the midden underwent a series of three 1-by-1-meter test units, two of which were later connected by three additional 1-by-1-meter units to form a trench. Total areal coverage equaled 6 square meters, and excavated volume totaled 3.2 cubic meters. The subsurface revealed the same artifacts recovered in the near-surface studies but added examples of shell beads; kaolin pipe fragments; buttons; and metal artifacts such as ammunition, thimbles, buckles, files, and tableware (table 4.2). The high fragmentation of artifacts and disarticulated faunal elements suggest that the midden received materials from nearby locations rather than from specific activities in that area, meaning that the midden is truly a secondary deposit, or one that had materials dumped into it from their original use or place of deposition. Despite the lack of stratified deposits, vertical density of archaeological materials indicated that the nineteenth-century ground surface was approximately 30–40 centimeters below the present ground surface and that the vertical dispersal of materials was primarily the work of burrowing animals or agricultural activities (Silliman 2000a:fig. 5.16).

The only discrete cultural feature discovered in the Midden Trench was Feature A, a pit filled with animal bones, charcoal, and metal in the southwestern corner of the southernmost unit (figure 4.2). Very little of it (0.03 square meter) could be seen in the excavated unit, and its depth prevented our opening another unit to expose the rest of it. The best evidence of a pit shape was the depth of its contents and a definable feature edge, or interface. The diffuse upper limit of Feature A in the 30–40-centimeter level reinforced the conclusion that this zone represented the nineteenth-century ground surface. The pit shape, large size of the artifacts, and charred wood suggest that Feature A was a place where individuals dumped burned materials in the otherwise undifferentiated midden. There was no evidence that any burning occurred in situ in this feature or anywhere else in the midden. In fact, the midden contained only 2.5 percent of the 1,548 variably sized pieces of baked earth recovered during wet screening from the entire site.

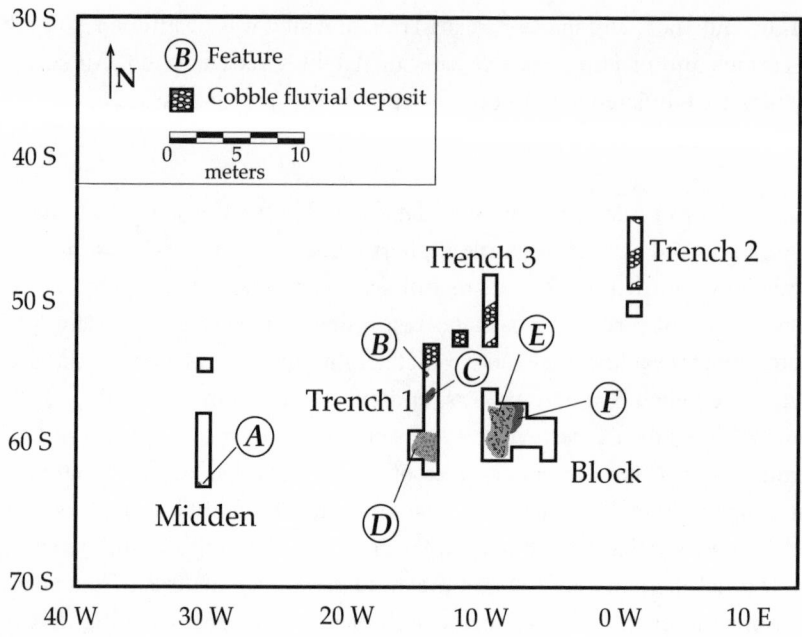

Figure 4.2
Excavated areas with features, minus Stream Trench. See text for details.

Stream Trench. In the fall of 2000 additional excavation took place alongside the eastern bank of Adobe Creek at the western edge of Area A. These fifteen units, 1.5 by 1.5 meters in size, were designed to evaluate erosion of the site edge by Adobe Creek, determine the western boundary of the dense midden area, and seek new artifacts or features previously unknown for the site (Silliman 2002). The larger units were developed to meet the management needs of the state park to stabilize the stream bank, and they were excavated in a three-step contour pattern (Silliman 2002:19–24). Areal coverage reached 33.75 square meters in the defined units, and the excavated volume totaled 11.77 cubic meters (Silliman 2002:25). The Stream Trench units contributed additional quantities of artifacts and ecofacts to the collection produced from the Midden Trench, but nothing stood out as significantly different (table 4.2).

The Stream Trench did, however, reveal two linear cobble features (figure 4.3), but no interpretation is yet possible. Their roughly parallel position and similar construction and the lack of gravel and sand surrounding the

Figure 4.3
Cobble features in Stream Trench. Photo by the author.

cobbles suggest that they are cultural in origin and that they may be related to one another (Silliman 2002:30–31). Additional probing into the nearby unexcavated areas demarcated the extent of the features inside and outside the Stream Trench and suggested that the southernmost of the two cobble features (top of figure 4.3) has been truncated at its western edge by stream erosion. The features may have been a foundation for a field wall, but they seem too small to have been a footing for any substantial architecture.

Area B

Trench 1. Trench 1 was the first trench opened in South Adobe Field in the summer of 1997. As stated above, the purposes for doing so included exposing two geophysical anomalies (at the northern and southern ends of Trench 1) and searching for artifacts and features in the intervening space. This succeeded on all counts, even though the northern geophysical anomaly proved to be a natural stream deposit. Trench 1 stretched over nine units as a linear

Table 4.3
Artifact and ecofact counts for Area B.

Category	Trench 1	Trench 2	Trench 3	Block	Total
Baked earth places	459	68	318	665	1,510
Beads, glass	97	123	37	269	526
Beads, other	0	1	0	0	1
Ceramic	3	8	4	10	25
Charred wood	6,384	606	2,295	28,977	38,262
Fauna, unidentifiable	9,314	1,382	943	17,943	29,582
Fauna, identifiable	945	361	28	3,875	5,209
Fauna, worked	3	0	0	17	20
Floral remains[a]	4	2	8	75	89
Glass	139	53	85	170	447
Glass, worked[b]	2	2	15	4	23
Ground stone	7	3	3	10	23
Lithic artifacts	361	237	383	1,386	2,367
Lithics, obsidian[c]	132	110	150	552	944
Metal	21	95	4	49	169
Other[d]	219	14	8	39	280
Schist	0	0	3	124	127
Shellfish	187	30	14	349	580
Tile	6	1	0	2	9
Wood	19	36	40	86	181
Total	18,168	3,020	4,173	54,046	79,407

[a] None of these floral specimens retrieved from wet screening were analyzed. Only those remains secured from controlled flotation were identified.

[b] Worked glass is listed here as a subset of glass; the row is not counted separately in the totals.

[c] Obsidian is listed as a subset of lithics for illustration purposes; the row is not counted separately in the totals.

[d] "Other" includes rocks, fused ash, potential petrified wood, red ochre, plastic, and aluminum foil.

1-meter-wide trench, with two additional 1-by-1-meter units westward from the southern end to accommodate the investigation of Feature D, described below. Ultimately, the excavated trench was 11 square meters in area and 5.5 cubic meters in volume.

The two pit features (Features B and C, below) uncovered here could be excavated separately along clear interfaces with the surrounding matrix; in other areas, most matrix removal was via arbitrary levels. Artifacts and organic remains were numerous and diverse (table 4.3). Like the midden artifacts, the materials seem to be predominantly residential in nature, but the archaeological deposits in Trench 1 were more bounded than those in the midden. In addition, the artifacts and ecofacts seemed to be less churned beneath the surface, since there was no evidence that plows had ever scarred the rocks or ripped through the features.

Feature B was a small pit near the northern end of Trench 1 (figure 4.2). The pit was approximately 0.7 meter in diameter (north-south) and 0.3 meter in maximum depth; its full westward extent is unknown. The pit was dark and rich with charcoal, and orange-colored baked earth ringed the feature on the northern edge. Feature B contained not only burned wood and fire-cracked rock but also ground stone, roof tile fragments, burned bone, stone tool debris, and a stone net sinker. The feature had visible internal layers of ash, dense charcoal, and baked earth, indicating that the pit had at least some of its constituents burned in place. No stones ringed or comprised the feature's deposits, suggesting that controlled heat for cooking or processing was not desired.

Feature C was a large, shallow pit farther south in Trench 1. The visible pit measured approximately 1.2 meters long and 0.7 meter wide in an elliptical shape. Feature C was composed of loose silty loam replete with heavily burned bone, some unburned bone, charcoal, and ash. Orange-colored baked earth ringed the pit in some locations, especially along the eastern perimeter. The baked-clay interface sloped downward toward the base and formed a hard-packed undulating interface; this burned interface indicated that at least some of the burning of materials happened in situ. One of the most intriguing aspects of Feature C was its association with large, articulated, unburned faunal remains. Most of these bones rested directly above the feature and at an elevation commensurate with other large, unburned faunal remains in a nearby unit to the north. The pit feature thus predated the deposition of these animal remains. Much like Feature B, this pit feature contained refuse burned in place or elsewhere. The presence of the baked-earth interface and the occurrence of 80 percent of the trench's 459 baked–clay chunks in the two excavation units associated with this feature indicate that most of the burning actually occurred in place. The pit may have been used as a hearth for cooking, which would account for the baked soil, but the calcined and charred bones could also have been discarded into it afterward. However, the hypothesis of an earlier hearth is weakened by the lack of associated thermally affected rock, unless the rocks had been cleared out and dumped elsewhere. On the other hand, the feature may have first been an earth oven like that described for the Coast Miwok (*hupa,* Collier and Thalman 1996:149) and Pomo (Barrett 1952:61), a cooking feature made by digging a hole, lining it with rocks, heating the rock-lined pit, adding the food, and covering it for in-ground roasting.

Feature D was a large concentration of fire-cracked rock, cobbles, faunal remains, and charcoal in the southern four units of Trench 1 (figure 4.2). The feature corresponded precisely to a semicircular magnetic anomaly detected during the 1996 gradiometer surveys (see Silliman 2000a:fig. 5.5), a result of the large concentration of igneous rocks with variable thermal histories. The feature consisted primarily of fire-cracked rock and cobbles stacked to form a roughly circular shallow basin, stretching across 3.5 square meters. Rocks in the central area of Feature D were sizeable, with some angular scars from possible thermal fracturing, while fire-cracked rocks on the southern perimeter were smaller, thinner, and stacked on top of one another. On top of the rocks were large, unburned faunal remains concentrated in a small depression. Charcoal and baked clay rested below the rocks, at least on the northern and southern borders of the eastern end of the exposed feature. I interpret this deposit as a large cooking feature with stream cobbles placed in a shallow basin of burning wood, undoubtedly to control and intensify the heat for cooking. The significant amount of expansion-fractured rock slivers in the charcoal-rich basin suggests high heat, but the unfractured rock above these may indicate a reduction in heat or a rock "cap" to extinguish it. It is possible that the feature was once an underground earth oven, but it seems to be too shallow, expansive, and covered with numerous unheated rocks for such a purpose. The unburned bones on its surface may or may not indicate its first use.

Trench 2. Trench 2 was also excavated in the summer of 1997 with a purpose similar to that of Trench 1. I designed the trench to search for an additional segment of a large, linear magnetic anomaly and to expose associated archaeological remains. Trench 2 covered six units, totaling an area of 6 square meters and an excavated volume of 3.35 cubic meters. Excavation proceeded solely with arbitrary 10-centimeter levels because of the difficulty of detecting stratigraphic changes. We observed no cultural features. As in the Trench 1 and Midden Trench excavations, the historical surface seemed to be approximately 30–50 centimeters below the present ground surface, given the concentration of artifacts and faunal remains at that level. However, no buried ground surfaces or living floor were visible in excavation or profile. Although the geophysical anomaly in the northern end of Trench 2 proved to be a natural deposit, there were numerous artifacts (table 4.3). Most artifacts occurred as small, dispersed items, but a distinct cluster appeared in the middle of the trench. The cluster primarily contained animal bones but also glass, metal, ceramic, and lithic artifacts in close proximity.

Trench 3. I opened Trench 3 in the summer of 1998 with the goals of exposing fully, from one side to the other, the anomalous cobble feature that had been explored in Trenches 1 and 2 and to search for deposits away from the concentrated amounts in the Block and Trench 1. This trench included five units in a contiguous series and a single unit 1 meter away, equaling 6 square meters of ground covered and 3.8 cubic meters of dirt removed. Artifact density was low and material diversity restricted compared to the other excavation areas (table 4.3). Like Trench 2, neither features nor significant artifact concentrations were discovered. Trench 3 did confirm the geomorphological nature of this rock deposit and its lack of immediate cultural significance.

Block. The 1998 excavation of the Block had two objectives: to broaden the understanding of spatial use and site structure and to expose several distinct and presumably cultural magnetic anomalies. Like Trench 3, the Block also bridged the physical gap between Trenches 1 and 2. The Block locus covered seventeen 1-by-1-meter units in an open-area style of excavation for a total of 17 square meters and 6.85 cubic meters. The only cultural stratification was the delineation of Features E and F from the surrounding matrix and the position of Feature E's eastern border over Feature F's western perimeter (see below). The only other stratification was between historical artifacts and features and the underlying geomorphological surfaces.

The Block produced significant amounts of nineteenth-century material culture, especially faunal remains (table 4.3), and two discrete cultural features:

Feature E and Feature F. These two features may be responsible for the sub-dued magnetic anomalies in the center and western portions of the area (see Silliman 2000a:fig. 5.5). The Block is characterized by refuse concentrated in two moderately bounded feature areas, and these refuse deposits rival the Midden Trench units in density and diversity and demonstrate remarkable integrity despite the previous plowing and burrowing in the field. No rocks had unmistakable plow scars, and the integrity of fish bones, articulated cattle elements, and brittle shellfish in Feature E reaffirmed their position in their original resting place. Gophers had still made their way through most of the deposits, but they seem to have spared sections of the dense rock-strewn areas of Features E and F, perhaps due to the impenetrability. Many artifact types are shared with the midden in Area A such as lithics of various raw materials, glass beads, glass bottle shards, ground stones, ceramic sherds, nails, other metal objects, thermally affected stone, and large quantities of animal and plant remains. However, unlike the midden findings, the artifacts and faunal remains were larger and less impacted by postdepositional dis-turbances.

Feature E, an extensive and rich refuse deposit from the rancho period, was one of the most important discoveries of the project. The core of the feature matched the high magnetic anomaly target in the western half of the block. The refuse deposit did not reveal a pit or basin, but it did contain an abundance of materials. Deposits held not only large quantities of unburned faunal remains of both domestic and wild species but also many types of artifacts, including stone tools, glass, metal, and glass beads. Charred wood and seeds occupied this deposit as well, and all were associated with numer-ous thermally affected rocks and unbroken cobbles. Although no old ground surfaces were discerned, the feature seemed to have rested on rather than in the nineteenth-century ground surface. Its amorphous shape, diversity of contents, and mostly unburned faunal remains point toward this feature be-ing a secondary deposit of household and perhaps some processing refuse. The burning indicated by the charcoal must have occurred elsewhere, since most artifacts and ecofacts were not burned. A reasonable scenario is that individuals discarded the debris on the ground in one or more dumping episodes. Drawing a parallel to the evidence suggested by Lightfoot et al. (1997:405) for Native activity at the nearby Fort Ross settlement such as the lack of many burned faunal remains, the presence of wood charcoal, and (in this case) baked earth, I tentatively suggest that these may represent, in part, materials cleaned out of an earth oven.

Feature F, a shallow basin filled with charcoal, fire-cracked rock spalls, and few artifacts, occurred just east of the northern terminus of Feature E. The western edge of Feature F's heavily burned matrix also sat beneath the eastern border of Feature E's unburned faunal remains and large rock concentrations, indicating that Feature F predated Feature E or at least the expansion of bone scatter at the eastern edge of Feature E. Invariably, we detected the charcoal-rich contents of Feature F as we removed large rocks, one of which proved to be an overturned shallow stone mortar, from the eastern edge of Feature E. Along the eastern feature lip was a dark orange border, a result of baking of the soil that framed the pit, and rock spalls were primarily small slivers oriented horizontally in the feature. Interestingly, this basin rested directly on a cobble and pebble fluvial surface, suggesting that someone had excavated it slightly into the rock bed. The total area of the visible Feature F was approximately 1.25 square meters, and the feature contained only 3–5 centimeters depth of charcoal, fire-cracked rock, and sediment, the latter of which occupied very little feature space. Unlike Feature E, which lies above it on the western edge, Feature F reflects a particular use other than refuse discard. The shallow basin shape and numerous expansion-fractured rock slivers are reminiscent of those found in the bottom of Feature D but without the density of overlying rock. The feature undoubtedly served as a cooking or processing area, but its large size weighs against its identification as simply a hearth or perhaps even an earth oven. Artifacts and ecofacts are relatively limited compared to its neighbor, Feature E.

Considerations of Context

To make the excavated data useful for interpretation of rancho life for Native American people, I discuss two aspects: precontact use of the Adobe Creek floodplain and the relatively synchronic nature of excavated site deposits. The relationship between these two aspects forms the crux of my interpretations.

To understand the material remains from the nineteenth-century use of the Adobe Creek floodplain, the precontact archaeological record of this site must be acknowledged. Not only does the prehistoric record relate directly to some of the rancho workers' ancestors who had once occupied this area, but the precontact deposits also should be analytically separated from those of the colonial period. Because of gopher- and plow-mixed soils and shallow cultural deposits overlying geomorphological surfaces, it was difficult to stratigraphically delineate a precontact component. I detected some pre-contact lithic materials in the obsidian collection through obsidian hydra-tion analysis (Silliman 2005), but we encountered no discrete or even poten-tial prehistoric layers during excavation.[3] Similarly, we located no precontact features and no items of what might be precontact Native American material culture outside of solid historical contexts. Precontact components, if only diffuse lithic scatters, certainly exist in South Adobe Field, but their spatial distribution, depth, and age are sketchy.

For this reason, I have combined all artifacts together per site locus for discussion purposes and have disregarded for the most part any vertical rela-tionships. Three factors led me to this simplification. First, the obsidian hy-dration data do not show a correlation between older dates (i.e., larger hy-dration rims) and greater depths (Silliman 2000a:221). Simply stated, this means that the precontact obsidian is just as likely at the surface as at 40 centimeters below it. If obsidian follows this pattern, the other lithic arti-facts probably do so as well. With the exception of a higher proportion of formal tools than debitage and of bifaces than projectile points in the obsid-ian collection that was directly dated by hydration, the precontact obsidian artifacts differ little from the nineteenth-century ones (Silliman 2005). Sec-ond, some of the precontact obsidian occurs in genuine historical contexts. This characteristic, coupled with the obsidian hydration pattern just noted, points to the likelihood of lithic recycling (Silliman 2005). That is, older obsidian may have been picked up and used or reflaked during the nine-teenth century. Third, the clustering of materials at approximately 20–40 centimeters below the current ground surface indicates that this zone must reflect the nineteenth-century ground surface. The fact that items cluster rather than occur exclusively there indicates vertical smearing. Therefore, the near impossibility of distinguishing mixed components combined with the likelihood that the excavation deposits reflect short duration nineteenth-century activity support considering the deposits as a whole.

Treating the site deposits as roughly equivalent in time does not mean that I apply the protocol blindly. For instance, I considered feature contents separately (or at least additionally) per locus, since these entities were bounded. In addition, I respect the superposition that existed between items or features with depositional integrity. Since artifacts are more likely to have moved relatively short distances horizontally compared to the number of vertical "levels" through which they might have migrated, I have paid more attention to spatial differences between loci rather than to levels within them.

Conclusion

I began the project with a search for evidence of residential structures, either traditional indigenous thatched houses, more substantial semisubterranean dwellings, or adobe dormitories, but I located not a shred of structural evidence aside from metal nails and small fragments of clay roof tile. The absence of structures was conspicuous given the nineteenth-century map depicting two adobe buildings in the excavated area, the foundation previously reported in the southwestern corner of the field (Gebhardt 1962), the mounded topography, and the large anomalies located during geophysical surveys. Although the first two facts indicated that building remnants should exist somewhere beneath the surface of the broad field encompassing the Son–2294/H site, my excavations and geophysical surveys did not reveal them. In fact, my excavations demonstrated that the field topography and geophysical anomalies were primarily the result of noncultural, geomorphological events.

In spite of the lack of structures, an unexpected wealth of residential and domestic debris emerged. The abundance and diversity of this material not only provided the opportunity to document and interpret the material culture and diet of Native people at the rancho but also hinted at the proximity of their residences. This amount of refuse would not be far from locations of its use or production, and, given its domestic nature, some of these locations would have been residential spaces. Again, the question of "why no structures?" looms. A reasonable answer seems to be that the absence was a combined result of (1) the difficulty of recovering archaeological traces of ephemeral, seasonal thatch houses used by some Native residents during the late spring through fall; (2) the bioturbated nature of areas that may have contained the residential structures, rendering them even more difficult to detect; and (3) sheer chance. I propose the latter simply because there may have been at least one and likely two substantial adobe buildings in the field, and, through the vagaries of chance, we may have "just missed" them. Similarly, we may have fortuitously tapped into the refuse rather than the home.

The cultural remains detected through surface collection and full excavation provide data for interpreting Native American residential and working life on Rancho Petaluma. These data include an extensive and dense sheet midden near Adobe Creek, six distinct cultural features, and numerous nineteenth-century artifacts scattered in and around these features in every excavation unit opened in the field. The midden served as the dumping area for large amounts of domestic refuse. Materials were quite fragmented, and site residents may have redeposited them there. I could discern only slight spatial differentiation, and artifact diversity was extraordinarily high. Like the midden, the area exposed by trench and block excavations sported refuse rather than floor deposits, but the remains were more bounded and less fragmented. In all locations, I detected little cultural stratification, a factor that accentuates the relatively synchronous nature of the historical deposits. Although bioturbation can be faulted for some of the vertical homogeneity outside of features, the data attested that at least some of the deposits were laid down over a very brief period of time. Given the short duration of Rancho Petaluma, this period may have been less than twenty years.

The features indicate a variety of activities and purposes. Three pits (Features A, B, and C) seem to have been for burned refuse, although they may have first served as hearths; one feature of cobbles and bones in a charcoal basin hinted at cooking or other processing activities (Feature D); one feature full of heavily fire-cracked rocks and burned wood suggested cooking activity due to the stones' use in controlling heat (Feature F); and one feature marked the piling of faunal and other debris on the historical ground surface (Feature E). Perhaps the latter signifies a time of partial site abandonment when less care was taken to remove or contain garbage.

Recovered objects include common artifacts of nineteenth-century industry such as mass-produced ceramics, bottle glass, nails and metal objects, buttons, and clay pipe fragments alongside artifacts strongly associated with Native lifeways such as stone tools made from obsidian and chert, ground stones, worked glass, glass and shell beads, incised bone, and a rock net sinker. High quantities of animal bone, charred plant remains, and shellfish capped the list. No human bones were discovered during excavation. The artifact types and their associations are strongly linked to Native individuals living and working on the rancho in the 1800s, although some individual artifacts pre- and postdate the rancho period. Several hundred California Indian people worked and lived at the rancho, and the material remnants of such a large population would be sizeable. In contrast, very few non-Native individuals lived or worked on Rancho Petaluma, and those who did tended to do so in and around the Petaluma Adobe proper. Therefore, the bulk of materials away from the Petaluma Adobe itself is likely to be Native produced and used. The small population of non-Native people who spent their time at the adobe dumped trash on the western bank of Adobe Creek and the downslope of the knoll beneath the Petaluma Adobe, as indicated by the trash pits and scatter found near the adobe (Clemmer 1961; Gebhardt 1962; Treganza 1958) and along the western bank of the creek (Gebhardt 1962). It is rather unlikely that adobe residents would have hauled their garbage down the hill and across Adobe Creek, especially in the winter, when the stream would have been treacherous to cross without a bridge.

All available evidence indicates that the refuse deposits and sheet midden recovered through excavation were deposited primarily by Native people who lived and worked on Rancho Petaluma. These items and deposits undoubtedly held key roles in Native social, domestic, and working relations on the rancho. Although residences were not discovered, the material residue of residential life was. The material remains reveal not only the constraints and parameters of colonial imposition but also the opportunities, choices, and struggles of those engaged with it. The data convey a picture of traditional Native practices and materials intertwining with novel European-manufactured goods in the forging of identities and social life under the mantle of colonial labor.

Chapter 5

Things of Everyday Life

Material Culture on Rancho Petaluma

> Ranchos such as that of Manuel Nieto used scores of Indians who were paid
> in grain or with such bits of hardware as knives, strings of beads, clothing, and
> whatever else struck an individual Indian's fancy.
>
> —William Mason, "Alta California's Colonial and Early Mexican Era
> Population, 1769–1846"

Archaeology is about material culture. Items of material culture, or artifacts,
are what archaeologists find while excavating and what they devote much
time to classifying, identifying, and measuring. More importantly, these things
filled the lives and practices of people in the past. They may have been tools
of productivity, facilitators of everyday tasks, products of and for survival,
physical forms of communication, meaningful referents for day-to-day life,
symbols of personhood and gender, and elements of domination and resistance. The same item could have been some or all of these, depending on the
perspective of the one who made it, used it, discarded it, found it during
excavation, wrote about it in an article, or viewed it in a museum display.
Artifact meaning is not immutable and is not constant even for the same
individual. This complexity of multiple meanings infuses colonial contexts
due in large part to the struggles between colonizers and colonized for control and use of the material world. Some of the most important issues for
deciphering material culture in colonial contexts revolve around sorting out
who made, used, and modified material items and how material culture participated in social, political, gendered, and physical worlds of the past.

This framework is crucial for understanding rancho contexts in California. Native Americans on these establishments often adopted new material

items, used finished colonial goods as raw material for other artifacts, held tightly to indigenous technologies, or melded introduced and traditional objects into complex new material practices. Often, determining what group of people actually used certain items is not a straightforward process. We cannot even always assume that only Native people used stone tools or that only colonial settlers in California used European or Asian ceramics. For instance, there are cases of Spanish and Mexican settlers in the American West using stone tools or flaking glass bottles into workable edges (e.g., Marshall 1982; Moore 1992) and numerous cases of Native Americans introducing Western ceramics, bottles, and metal objects into their sixteenth- to nineteenth-century households across North America. This does not mean that we have to discard our analytical key that assigns items such as stone tools and worked bone mainly to Native Americans, but it does mean that simply classifying artifacts into broad cultural categories is not sufficient to sort out the complexities (Loren 2001a). To fine-tune interpretations of Native American lives in these colonial settings, archaeologists must seek deposits that contain material items used (although not necessarily made) by Native people and must rethink how they interpret the materials of everyday life to answer questions of social and political consequence.

The Rancho Petaluma site serves as a solid starting point for this endeavor. Archaeological deposits point overwhelmingly toward Native American use and discard of material objects on this nineteenth-century rancho. The evidence includes the documented presence of hundreds of Native workers on this rancho, the site location slightly away from the Petaluma Adobe residential and working center, and the types and contents of cultural features found during excavation. These spatial and documentary contexts permit me to interpret the mixture of stone tools with metal flatware, ground stones with broken bottles, glass beads with metal buckles, bones of local fish and fowl with those of cattle and sheep, and acorns and grass seeds with domesticated wheat and barley as predominantly Native American and not as a result of postdepositional mixing. The constellation of material items and their associations rather than any one class of item underwrites this interpretation.

Rancho Petaluma holds a wide variety of artifacts that chase away some of the historical shadows surrounding Native participation on California's ranchos. The goal is to provide more nuance, more material grounding, to the scenario implied in Mason's "bits of hardware" and "whatever else struck an individual Indian's fancy." To describe and discuss them all in great depth for Petaluma would be unwieldy, so I choose to focus attention on several material categories. I opted to classify the artifacts by raw material and techno-logical attributes not because this method of classification is carefully attuned to artifact function and meaning but because it is standard and replicable. I can then turn these empirical categories to broader cultural questions that require the reintegration of different material items based on their place in social life for Native workers. The material categories are ground stone tools such as mortars and pestles, chipped stone tools and associated debris, metal ob-jects, glass bottles, nonindigenous ceramics, bone and shell artifacts, and glass beads.[1] With the exception of artifacts made from stone, bone, or shell, all items were products of nineteenth-century mass production and indus-try. They were not made on the rancho itself, nor were they likely to have been made in other colonial settlements of the region. The only exception might be some metal tools, since blacksmithing was documented for Rancho Petaluma and would be expected for Mexican-Californian, Spanish, British, or American artisans in nearby towns. Yet all of these items comprised the daily practices of site residents, who combined, used, displayed, and dis-carded them in meaningful and purposeful ways.

Stone Tools: Old Practices in New Contexts

An important discovery of the Rancho Petaluma excavations was the pres-ence of significant stone tool use in the nineteenth century. Evidence in-cluded chipped stone tools and debris, or debitage, associated with their pro-duction and ground stone fragments from items such as mortars and pestles. At the most basic level, the presence of these lithic artifacts signals the ef-forts of Native American people to maintain practices that had been a central part of their cultural heritage and personal experience well before contact with Western colonists. The production and use of these stone tools in a colonial world may have indicated a material necessity in the face of unavail-able metal or other tools, a maintenance of material comfort and familiarity, a political and social statement about identity and gender, or perhaps all three. They were certainly more than just a favorite pastime to be enjoyed during a worker's free time.

The ground and modified stone artifacts hint at these issues. Such items recovered during excavation include pestles, mortars, manos, one or perhaps two hammerstones, and a net sinker. Pestles and pestle fragments dominate the collection at eight specimens (seven are shown in figure 5.1). Mortars and mortar fragments number only four. The largest is a complete hopper

Figure 5.1
Pestle fragments. Photo by the author.

mortar with a shallow work surface found overturned in the center of the
Block. Other specimens include one mortar bowl fragment from the Block
comprised of two conjoining fragments (figure 5.2a) and two mortar bowl
fragments from Trench 1 (figure 5.2c–d). Of the two mano fragments recovered, only the specimen from the Midden Trench is unambiguously identified
as such. Trench 1 produced the only good example of a hammerstone, although Trench 2 contained a possible specimen. The low frequency is particularly striking in light of the quantities of chipped stone, discussed below,

Figure 5.2
Mortar fragments: *a*, conjoining mortar fragments with distinct lip and polish; *b*, mortar fragment; *c*, mortar fragment, two views; *d*, mortar fragment with some basin smoothing, two views. Photo by the author.

since these would have been used to produce the flaked tools. The only net sinker came from Trench 1, lodged in Feature B (figure 5.3).

These artifacts illuminate two aspects of Native life. First, the ground stones indicate that Native individuals continued to use mortar-and-pestle technology in their cooking practices. Likely plant products undergoing the grinding process were acorn, wheat, and barley, based on the evidence presented in the following chapter. The flour could have been used in the preparation of atole, the popular gruel in missions and ranchos, or baked goods such as acorn bread. The mano attests to some milling stone use for corn or

0 cm   6 cm

Figure 5.3
Rock net sinker. Photo by the author.

seeds, but currently nothing more can be speculated. The ethnographic and historical records in northern California suggest that Native women were the primary users of these tools; therefore, these tools may be a direct line into considerations of gendered activity. If nothing else, they reveal Native women grappling with the colonial rancho world by continuing some precontact food-processing technologies despite the alteration to the dietary products themselves. Second, the net sinker demonstrates the use of nets for capturing fish, as these items served to weight woven nets. Coupled with the many fish bones found at the site, this artifact is indicative of food-getting strategies on the rancho. Whether Native fishers netted fish out of the adjacent Adobe Creek or headed to the larger rivers in the nearby area, it is clear that these wild foods were sought.

Complementing the grinding tools are flaked stone tools and chipping debris. Two key characteristics of the chipped stone tools and debitage further highlight issues of life on the rancho: raw material and tool production and use. The raw material used to make the stone tools pertains directly to questions about access to and preference for rock resources, trade relationships

Table 5.1

Frequency of chipped stone lithic artifcats by raw material.

Raw Material	Midden Trench		Stream Trench		Trench 1		Trench 2		Trench 3		Block		Total	
	N	%	N	%	N	%	N	%	N	%	N	%	N	%
Obsidian	359	55.5	145	63.6	132	38.0	110	46.6	150	39.3	552	39.8	1,448	44.7
Chert, other silicates	193	29.8	58	25.4	172	48.0	89	37.7	161	42.1	572	41.3	1,245	38.5
Igneous/felsite	27	4.2	9	3.9	35	9.8	24	10.2	34	8.9	146	10.5	275	8.5
Quartz	20	3.1	7	3.1	18	5.0	11	4.7	30	7.9	86	6.2	172	5.3
Petrified wood	44	6.8	7	3.1	1	0.3	1	0.4	4	1.0	21	1.5	78	2.4
Basalt	0	0.0	2	0.9	0	0.0	0	0.0	0	0.0	2	0.1	4	0.1
Sedimentary	0	0.0	0	0.0	0	0.0	1	0.4	0	0.0	2	0.1	3	0.1
Schist	4	0.6	0	0.0	0	0.0	0	0.0	3	0.8	5	0.4	12	0.4
Total	647	100	228	100	358	100	236	100	382	100	1,386	100	3,237	100

between site residents and nonresidents, and the mobility of workers on and off the rancho (Silliman 2003b). The nature of stone tool production highlights whether or not objects were made on-site or traded in from elsewhere and how they might have been used on the rancho. For purposes of discussion, I group the flaked stone analysis by raw material and then consider the process of tool production and use per raw material category. My analysis draws on the methodology proposed by Andrefsky (1998).

The lithic assemblage is composed of the following raw materials: obsidian, cherts and related microcrystalline silicates, felsite and related igneous rocks, quartz, petrified wood, basalt, and sedimentary rock (table 5.1). The list reflects the order of abundance in the assemblage. Obsidian and microcrystalline silicates together occupy 83.2 percent of the total 3,237 lithic artifacts. Obsidian (44.7 percent) outnumbers microcrystalline (38.5 percent) artifacts only slightly across the site. Of the total assemblage, felsite/igneous and quartz each holds less than 9 percent, petrified wood slightly over 2 percent, schist only 0.4 percent, and basalt and sedimentary stones barely 0.1 percent. Because of their low numbers and ambiguous functions, I do not discuss further the latter four categories.

Obsidian

Obsidian artifacts number 1,448 at the site (table 5.2). Although predominantly debitage with some flake tools, the collection includes ten cores (0.7 percent), nine unmodified nodules (0.6 percent), and sixty-seven formal tools (4.6 percent), including bifaces and projectile points. The highest density of obsidian occurred in the Midden Trench, with 112.2 artifacts per cubic meter; the Block followed at 80.6 artifacts per cubic meter. Obsidian materials indicate the full spectrum of lithic production, from flaking cores to finishing tools. The forty-seven formal bifaces and parts thereof are predominantly fragmented and in the middle stages of production, perhaps having broken during manufacture rather than use (figure 5.4). These may have served as formal cores for later modification, or they may have been designed or used as knives or scraping tools. At least one bifacial drill was present, defined by its long, narrow shape rather than any microscopic examination of use-wear. Numbering twenty, projectile points are less abundant than unhafted bifaces, but they are slightly more complete. Those complete enough for stylistic identification were corner-notched points, used in tipping arrows in the latest phases of California Indian cultural history (figure 5.5). Projectile points

Figure 5.4

Obsidian formal bifaces and biface fragments: *a*, biface fragment with potential broken drill tip, Napa Valley source; *b*, drill fragment, Napa Valley source; *c*, thinned, almost complete biface, Napa Valley source; *d*, biface tip and midsection fragment, Annadel source; *e*, biface tip and lateral fragment, Napa Valley source; *f*, biface tip fragment, Annadel source; *g*, biface tip fragment, Napa Valley source; *h*, biface tip (?) fragment, Annadel source; *i*, biface tip fragment, Annadel source; *j*, biface midsection fragment, Napa Valley source; *k*, biface midsection fragment, Annadel source; *l*, biface midsection fragment, Napa Valley source; *m*, biface edge fragment, Napa Valley source. See text for discussion of obsidian sources.

Photo by the author.

0 cm   10 cm

Figure 5.5

Obsidian projectile points and point fragments: *a*, complete, may have tip
resharpened considerably; *b*, thin corner-notched point fragment, Annadel
source; *c*, corner-notched point fragment, Napa Valley source; *d*, corner-
notched point fragment, Annadel source; *e*, corner-notched point, almost
complete, Annadel source; *f*, corner-notched point fragment, Napa Valley
source; *g*, thin corner-notched point, almost complete, minimal flaking on
opposite side, Napa Valley source; *h*, coarse, perhaps resharpened, point,
Annadel source; *i*, point fragment, Franz Valley source; *j*, corner-notched
point fragment, some cortex, Napa Valley source; *k*, point tip fragment,
Annadel source; *l*, point fragment, resharpened side has removed tang, Napa
Valley source; *m*, corner-notched point base fragment, Napa Valley source; *n*,
corner-notched point fragment, Borax Lake source; *o*, point base fragment,
Annadel source; *p*, point midsection and partial tip, Napa Valley source. See
text for discussion of obsidian sources. Photo by the author.

Table 5.2

Frequency of obsidian lithic artifact types.

Area	Nodule		Core		Formal Tools		Angular Shatter		Flake		Proximal Flake		Flake Shatter		Total	
	N	%	N	%	N	%	N	%	N	%	N	%	N	%	N	%
Midden Trench	0	0.0	6	1.7	8	2.2	72	20.1	111	30.9	18	5.0	144	40.1	359	100
Stream Trench	4	2.8	1	0.7	3	2.1	43	29.7	42	29.0	0	0.0	52	35.9	145	100
Trench 1	1	2.8	0	0.0	13	9.8	30	22.7	46	34.8	0	0.0	42	31.8	132	100
Trench 2	0	0.0	0	0.0	6	5.5	17	15.5	50	45.5	1	0.9	36	32.7	110	100
Trench 3	2	1.3	0	0.0	9	6.0	12	8.0	70	46.7	3	2.0	54	36.0	150	100
Block	2	0.4	3	0.5	28	5.1	85	15.4	266	48.2	12	2.2	156	28.3	552	100
Total	9	0.6	10	0.7	67	4.6	259	17.9	585	40.5	34	2.4	484	33.5	1,448	100

Table 5.3

Frequency of chert and other silicate lithic artifact types.

Area	Nodule		Core		Formal Tools		Angular Shatter		Flake		Proximal Flake		Flake Shatter		Total	
	N	%	N	%	N	%	N	%	N	%	N	%	N	%	N	%
Midden Trench	0	0.0	4	2.1	0	0.0	90	46.6	36	18.7	2	1.0	61	31.6	193	100
Stream Trench	9	15.5	2	3.4	0	0.0	24	41.4	11	19.0	0	0.0	12	20.7	58	100
Trench 1	3	1.7	3	1.7	0	0.0	85	49.4	40	23.3	2	1.2	39	22.7	172	100
Trench 2	2	2.2	2	2.2	0	0.0	49	55.1	15	16.9	0	0.0	21	23.6	89	100
Trench 3	0	0.0	3	1.9	0	0.0	83	51.6	40	24.8	1	0.6	34	20.5	161	100
Block	0	0.0	13	2.3	1	0.2	291	50.9	158	27.6	2	0.3	107	18.7	572	100
Total	14	1.1	27	2.2	1	0.1	622	50.0	300	24.1	7	0.6	274	22.0	1,245	100

peak in density first in the Block and then in the Midden Trench, and they do not occur at all in Trench 3.

The cores are both multidirectional and unidirectional in the ways that knappers removed flakes, and many of them are small and exhausted beyond further usefulness. Just fewer than 10 percent of the recovered debitage had been modified into flake tools, meaning that these pieces showed evidence of additional trimming, sharpening, or usage. Trench 1 contains the largest percentage of flake tools at 18.6 percent, and Trench 3 contains the smallest at 6.4 percent. The debitage proper contains mostly flakes (40.5 percent) and flake shatter (33.5 percent), but angular shatter (17.9 percent) occurs in noticeable proportions.[2] Debitage reveals its peak density in the Midden Trench, followed closely by the Block. The relationship between debitage size, amount of dorsal cortex, dorsal scars from prior flaking, and platform preparation in the debitage further clarifies the spatial aspects of production on-site (Silliman 2003b), and I summarize the main points below.

Cherts and Other Microcrystalline Silicates

Chert and other microcrystalline silicate artifacts number 1,245 across all site loci (table 5.3), and they have their highest artifact density in the Block, with 78.8 artifacts per cubic meter, and their next highest in the Midden Trench, with 54.7 artifacts per cubic meter. The assemblage differs notably from obsidian in its lack of formal tools, more angular shatter in the debitage, and more abundant cores. Only 3.4 percent of the entire subassemblage is anything other than debitage, including twenty-seven cores (2.2 percent) and fourteen nodules (1.1 percent). Only one artifact (0.1 percent) qualifies as a formal biface tool, and it was retrieved from the Block. It is in the very early stages of manufacturing, with short flakes and no thinning. Interestingly, no gunflints were identified in the collection.

The cores are consistently larger than those made of obsidian. The Block produced not only the highest percentage of total cores (48.1 percent) but also the highest density (1.8 cores per cubic meter). All other areas had densities of less than 0.9 core per cubic meter. Reduction trajectories are exclusively multidirectional, and four cores show evidence of thermal alteration with either potlids (small round flakes ejected when water in the rock expands during heating) or differential luster. Like obsidian, chert and other silicate debitage is classified as angular shatter, complete flake, proximal flake, and flake shatter. Summary percentages for the site as a whole reveal the

1,245 artifacts to be 50 percent angular shatter, 24.1 percent complete flakes, 0.6 percent proximal flakes, and 22 percent flake shatter (see table 5.3). Like the obsidian, the various physical and spatial attributes of the debitage clarify the methods of production, signaling that individuals did not devote serious efforts to producing formal chert tools (Silliman 2003b). Unlike the obsidian, the microcrystalline silicate assemblage displays a significant percentage (13.1 percent, or sixty-three) of artifacts with thermal alteration. Whether or not thermal alteration on cherts is from controlled heating, accidental exposure to heat, or purposeful refuse burning is currently unclear. However, the lack of thermal alteration on obsidian suggests that cherts were singled out for intentional heat treatment.

Felsite and Other Igneous Rocks

This category comprises the most variable and intractable raw material at the site. Identification hinges solely on macroscopic inspection; important attributes are the presence of phenocrysts of various sizes, a coarser grain than generally seen in the sedimentary microcrystalline silicates, or a combination of both attributes. Many of the igneous rocks appear to be felsite, which is a general term for aphanitic igneous rocks that are light colored and composed primarily of quartz and feldspar and that may or may not contain phenocrysts (Bates and Jackson 1984:181). No petrographic thin sectioning was conducted to refine this classification, and for this reason it probably collapses a fair amount of petrological diversity.

A total of 275 artifacts (8.5 percent of all lithic artifacts) are assigned to this raw material (table 5.1). These reveal an overall site density of 11.4 items per cubic meter, but this mean belies significant spatial variation. A variety of lithic debitage types exists in the felsite/igneous materials, but no formal tools were recovered. The average percentage of angular shatter for the entire material subassemblage is 45.5 percent, leaving complete flakes with 28.7 percent, flake shatter with 22.2 percent, cores with only 2.9 percent, and proximal flakes with barely 0.7 percent. Compared to obsidian and chert, the pieces of debitage tend to be relatively large.

Quartz

Unlike felsite/igneous, quartz is a relatively straightforward raw material to recognize, but its ambiguity rests in the identification of its cultural or natural origins at the site. Any of the quartz recovered during screening is presumably too large to be a background constituent of alluvial soils at the site. Therefore, the transport of at least the larger pieces to the site can be assumed to be by human agency. Quartz occurs as 172 pieces across the entire site, rendering it only 5.3 percent of the lithic assemblage, with a density of only 6.8 items per cubic meter. The quartz pieces are all small, with more than 78 percent under 10 millimeters in size; two items in the 10–15-millimeter size class are definite crystals.

Synthesis and Summary

It is clear that individuals at Rancho Petaluma made noticeable use of stone tool technology and that they put different raw materials to very different uses. These patterns are visible in both tool and debitage characteristics. The obsidian and chert artifacts offer the most salient comparisons because of their large sample sizes (Silliman 2003b). The other raw material categories offer only limited insight, such as the felsite/igneous materials showing manufacturing patterns like chert, petrified wood revealing no apparent modification, and quartz being unclear as to its use.

Lithic reduction and use patterns for the obsidian and chert raw materials differ significantly. Initial stages of reduction are present in both, as evidenced by cores, nodules, and flakes having 100 percent dorsal cortex. The raw material patterns diverge beyond this. Evidence points to individuals focusing on obsidian for the full range of production from cores to formal tools while using chert and other microcrystalline silicates primarily for early stage reduction of cores. At the terminal end of the sequence, the presence of numerous broken obsidian bifaces and projectile points confirms the production of formal tools. Only one chert biface was found, and it is thick and minimally flaked. Some obsidian bifaces might have been manufactured elsewhere, but the small size of the debitage, the number of flake scars on the dorsal surface of complete flakes, and the platform preparation suggest that, in contrast to cherts, obsidian reduction was devoted in large part to later stages of reduction and biface production (Silliman 2003b).

Obsidian was worked on-site from core to finished tool, and chert and other microcrystalline silicates were the focus of early and middle stage reduction of cores. The latter pattern holds for the felsite/igneous materials as well. Given the pattern of lithic production, the infrequency of hammerstones and the complete absence of antler are unexpected. However, these tools of lithic production, particularly antlers, are often retained for several years without breakage, and the short duration of the rancho site may weigh against their abundant recovery. Almost all recovered bifacial tools were made from obsidian, but flakes of both obsidian and microcrystalline silicates were retouched and utilized for particular, perhaps on-the-spot uses. As determined by obsidian hydration analysis, obsidian tools included several predominantly nineteenth-century corner-notched projectile points, a mixture of precontact and nineteenth-century bifaces and associated fragments, and a likely precontact drill fragment.

Although not certain, individuals likely obtained the cherts and other silicates from nearby streambeds and outcrops in the surrounding landscape. For example, the Franciscan Complex, which contains the main chert sources of the area, outcrops just west of the Petaluma River. The prevalence of felsite/igneous material suggests fairly local sources, perhaps the thermal spring areas of Sonoma County or even nodules in the nearby Adobe Creek watercourse. However, the obsidian came from a variety of more distant locations, from sources within 20–30 kilometers (Annadel, Napa Valley, Franz Valley, Oakmont) to sources more than 50 kilometers away (Borax Lake, Mount Konocti) (see map 1.1).[3] Even streambeds with secondary deposits of obsidian from these six sources are similarly long distances from the Rancho Petaluma site.

The variety of obsidian sources used during the 1800s contrasts sharply with the more restricted sources of the precontact period recorded at this site and elsewhere in the park (Amaroli and Origer 1984; Silliman 1999, 2005). This contrast may indicate the possible diverse origins of Native workers, the maintenance of trading and exchange relations between those working on ranchos and those residing near obsidian sources, the likelihood that individuals had opportunities to procure raw material while away from the rancho, or some combination of these factors. Any of these options unequivocally testifies to the sustained interest by Native American workers on Rancho Petaluma in seeking out obsidian, regardless of the varying distance to the common sources or the trading networks needed to acquire it. The role obsidian played in formal tool manufacture was a virtually exclusive one compared to other raw materials—no other rock must have sufficed for projectile points or formed bifaces (Silliman 2003b). Obsidian was a significant resource, and individuals expended noticeable effort to get it.

Metal in Other Affairs

The study of stone tools in colonial and contact period sites always seems to take place in relation to the presence and use of metal tools. For some this relationship hinges on a faulty assumption: Native American individuals quickly dropped their traditional stone technologies when offered the chance to acquire "superior" metal implements. This is not the logic behind my juxtaposition of metal and stone tools, as I find it problematic and dangerous (see Silliman 2001a, 2003b). Instead, I seek to understand the decisions and politics behind Native American choices to continue making stone tools, to adopt metal objects, or to combine the two "options" in a single household or community, depending on the task at hand. Others have offered similar perspectives on this process in historical Native American archaeological contexts (Bamforth 1993; Cassell 2003; Hudson 1993; Nassaney and Volmar 2003). Were metal artifacts available, and could they supplant stone tools as the artifacts of choice? As the Petaluma case illustrates, California Indians faced limitations and opportunities with introduced Western technologies, and the outcome of their decisions makes a remarkable story.

Metal artifacts were certainly numerous at the site, and they represent a substantial component of Native American daily practices at Rancho Petaluma. Many of these metal artifacts were located in the dense residential debris of the midden. Here I want to highlight some categories of the recovered metal artifacts. A variety of unique, hard-to-categorize scrap pieces and miscellaneous metal objects found during excavation will not be discussed here (Silliman 2000a:346–48, 2002:39–41). Buttons are included in this analysis, since more than half of them are metal and since they logically fit into the discussion of clothing and adornment.

Clothing and Adornment

Clothing and adornment artifacts are represented by a variety of items, including buckles, hooks, a decorated silver band, and a ring. The buckles include three large belt or strap buckles made of iron and one small strap buckle reminiscent of garter buckles used to hold knee-length stockings (Silliman 2000a:fig. 8.18). The large size and iron composition suggest that the former two buckles may have not been worn on the human body.[4] Excavations also produced two indeterminate clothing hooks, a thin silver band with decorated borders, and a thin-gauge, presumably silver ring (Silliman 2000a:fig. 8.18).

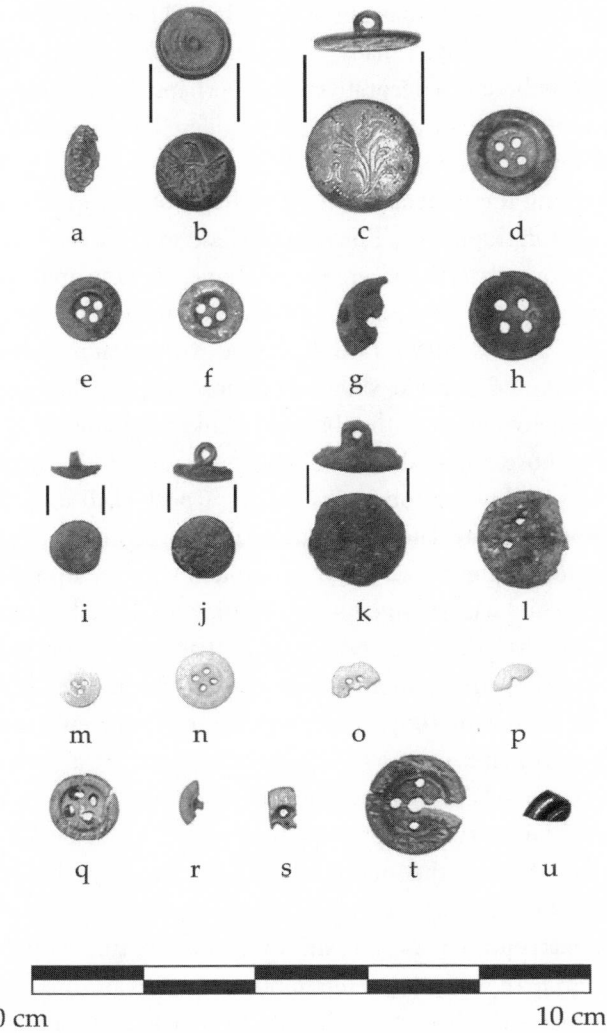

Figure 5.6

Metal, bone, and ceramic buttons: *a*, brass button fragment with leaf designs;
b, brass United States Army artillery button with eagle on face, two views; *c*,
brass "Wadhams Coe & Co. Extra Rich" gilt button, two views; *d–e*, metal
button; *f*, copper/brass button; *g*, fragment of metal button; *h*, metal
button; *i–k*, metal shank button, two views; *l*, heavy metal (lead?) coat
button; *m*, milk glass button; *n*, ceramic button with scalloped edge; *o–p*,
ceramic button fragment; *q*, bone button; *r*, bone button fragment; *s*, bone
button fragment; *t*, five-hole bone button; *u*, unidentified black button.
Photo by the author.

The former may be part of a hairpin or brooch, and the latter has the classic shape of a thin finger ring. Finally, a punched bronze/copper disk is included tentatively here as a decorative item, perhaps as a spangle. All clothing and adornment items came from the Midden Trench; one buckle was found in the Stream Trench.

Complementing these metal items related to clothing were twenty-four buttons and button fragments. Thirteen of these were metal, but the other eleven included one glass, three ceramic, six bone, and one unidentified material. The metal buttons include both shank and hole-sewn varieties. One is a fragment of a brass button face decorated with presumed leaf designs (figure 5.6a). Another example, shown in figure 5.6b, is a three-piece brass United States Army button with a broken shank, decorated on the surface with an eagle whose recessed chest shield holds an "A" for artillery (see Wyckoff 1984:44). The button probably has a post-1850 date (Luscomb 1967:11), although it may date to the late 1840s (Wyckoff 1984:45).

A third button is a gilt coat button complete with an alpha shank and floral decoration and backstamped with "Wadhams Coe & Co. Extra Rich" (figure 5.6c). The lettering and style indicate that it was manufactured between 1835 and 1837 in Torrington, Connecticut, during the "golden age" of buttons (see Luscomb 1967:78–79, 89). Four buttons are undecorated varieties of differing sizes (figure 5.6i–k, one not pictured), and the other six metal buttons are four-hole sew-through buttons. Three are brass with sunken eyelets (figure 5.6d–f), two are possibly iron with folded-down lips on the back (figure 5.6g–h), and one seems to be a heavy metal, perhaps lead, coat button (figure 5.6l).

The single glass button is a white, shiny milk glass button with three holes set in a tight circle (figure 5.6m). Three other buttons are small china buttons probably made in a Prosser mold, and two are complete enough to show that they are four-hole varieties. One is larger, with raised designs around the surface edge, giving it what some have termed a piecrust border (figure 5.6n), and the other two are fragments (figure 5.6o–p). The bone buttons show more design variety, including one four-hole button with a raised lip (figure 5.6q), four fragments with indeterminate holes but raised lips (figure 5.6r–s, two not shown), and one larger specimen with five holes that includes a center perforation for a cutting tool (figure 5.6t). The only other button is fragmented and made of a black, nonporous material (figure 5.6u). With the exception of the larger five-hole bone specimen, all of these buttons are in the size range for shirts, dresses, vests, and pants.

Containers and Vessels

Metal containers and vessels are represented by 11 pail and bucket pieces, 18 kettle fragments, 140 fragments of cans or similar items, and 5 barrel straps. The pails and buckets were found in the Midden Trench, Trench 1, and Trench 2, and they are recognizable by their large size, tall folded lip, and reinforced rims. We also recovered seventeen iron and one bronze/copper kettle fragments. The bronze/copper artifact includes part of a kettle rim and a lug for suspending the container by a wire handle. Found in Feature B in Trench 1, it was the only kettle fragment discovered outside the midden. The iron kettle fragments are strikingly different, being thick walled (2.5–3.6 millimeters) and unreinforced, and they occur exclusively in the Midden Trench. Such iron kettles may have rested on legs or rocks or may have been suspended. Barrels are represented by five fragments of metal barrel hoops; all but one of these were found in the midden. The metal can pieces occurred only in the midden and pose somewhat of an enigma, since they could postdate the final days of Rancho Petaluma. For this reason, I suspend detailed interpretation of them (Silliman 2000a:342–43).

Sewing

The artifacts related to sewing include scissors, thimbles, a pin, and a fastener. The pin is a common straight pin with ball end (figure 5.7a), and the fastener strongly resembles a needle but with a flattened end and no eye (figure 5.7b). Two thimbles were also recovered, both of which are probably copper, even though one is heavily oxidized like a ferrous metal (figure 5.7c–d). The final sewing items are a scissor blade fragment (figure 5.7e) and a pair of scissors that lacks handles (figure 5.7f). Like the adornment and clothing items, all sewing-related artifacts came from the midden.

Flatware

Artifacts of the flatware (or silverware) category are few, numbering only seven. Objects include a silver (or similar metal) knife tip and knife blade, likely from different items. Also present are various handles in decorated and plain styles, only one of which retains the look of silver. All others are heavily corroded but with hints of visible silver metal. The sixth item is crudely shaped and designed and can be only tentatively assigned to the

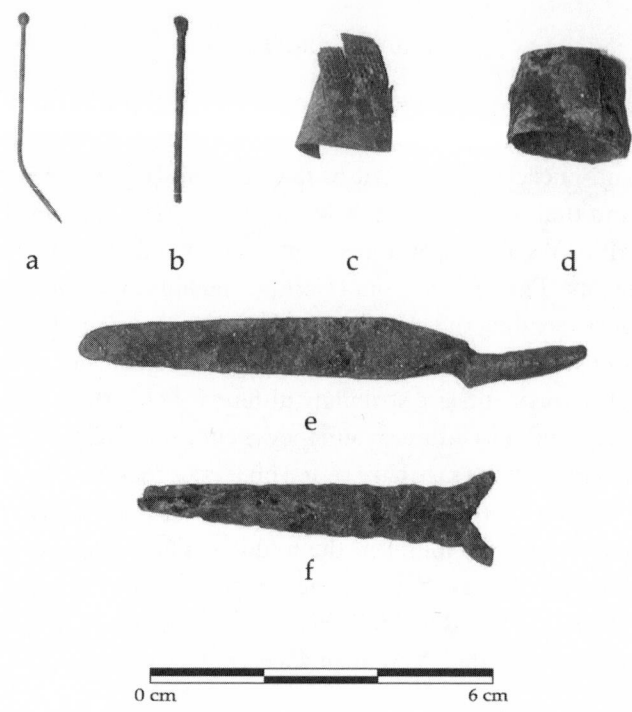

Figure 5.7
Metal sewing artifacts: *a*, pin; *b*, fastener; *c–d*, thimble; *e*, scissor blade and part of hinge; *f*, pair of scissors with missing handle. Photo by the author.

flatware category. We retrieved all of these metal flatware artifacts from the Midden Trench. We also located a white-metal spoon fragment on the midden surface.

Firearms

Gun-related artifacts were somewhat common across the site, represented primarily by ammunition. Excavations revealed forty-six lead shot and twelve lead ball pieces. Based on size, the lead shot is best termed "bird shot." The lead balls represent either pistol or rifle (although not musket) projectiles, and they appear to have been mold cast. All lead balls and 93 percent of the lead shot are from the midden. In addition, five percussion caps and three bullets were discovered (figure 5.8, one not pictured). All but one percussion

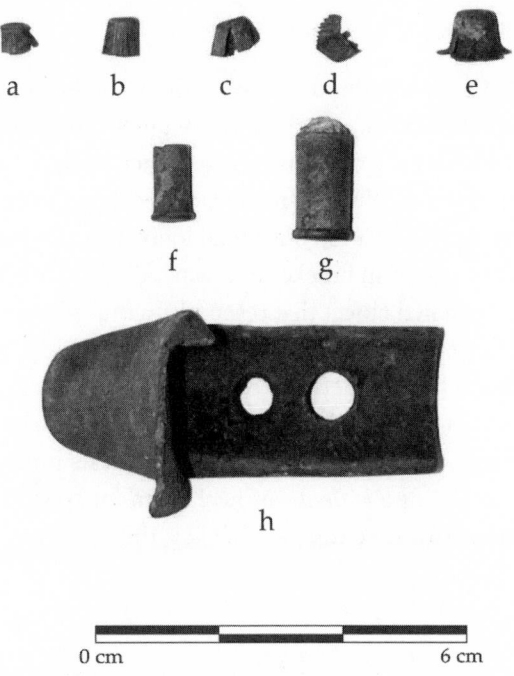

Figure 5.8
Firearm artifacts: *a*, percussion cap, pistol; *b–d*, percussion cap, rifle; *e*,
percussion cap, musket; *f*, .22-caliber short case, fired; *g*, .38-caliber Smith &
Wesson, unfired; *h*, rifle buttplate. Photo by the author.

cap have been fired, and all were found in the Midden Trench. Cap-lock
guns that would have used these particular items include pistol (figure 5.8a),
rifle (figure 5.8b–c) and musket, military rifles, and breechloaders (figure
5.8d). The two bullets are an expended .22-caliber short case and an unfired
.32-caliber Smith & Wesson shell (figure 5.8e–f). In contrast to the other
ammunition, these two casings occur in the Block. These latter items probably date to sometime in the late nineteenth or early twentieth century and
are intrusive to the historic deposits of interest here. Moreover, one shotgun
shell cap and one pellet were found in the Stream Trench, and these may
well be much more recent additions to the site. Complementing the ammunition is the only gun artifact recovered: a cast brass rifle buttplate found in
the Midden Trench (figure 5.8g).

Tools and Hardware

We retrieved metal tools and hardware of various sorts during excavation. The most easily identifiable ones include two segments of files or rasps. One is broken and very worn; the other is largely intact, with the filing surface still visible. Other objects include a snips blade too large for sewing; a brass clock or similar winding key; a ferrous metal looped handle possibly from a candleholder; a large iron wall bracket for suspending a lamp or similar object; and a curved, flattened object that resembles a thumb-depressed button latch. The final artifact in this category resembles part of a key used for doors, padlocks, or trunks. The hammerlike end is broken but hints at a previous looped end, and it has a hollow but thick-walled shank. Finally, one small chain segment was recovered, and its small size suggests it may have been a *cabestrillo,* or rein chain, or a *pialeras,* or heel chain for spurs (see Simmons and Turley 1980:101–10). Like the possible key, this identification is highly speculative.

Nails

Nails were frequent finds at the site. The 490 nails include cut nails, wire nails, and tacks made of iron, steel, bronze/copper, and aluminum (table 5.4). The Midden Trench contained 75.1 percent (368) of the 490 nails at a density of 115 nails per cubic meter; the Stream Trench produced another 14.3 percent but at a density of only 5.9 nails per cubic meter. The Block produced 6.1 percent (30) with a density of 3.8 nails per cubic meter, and Trench 2 produced 4.1 percent (20) with a density of 6 nails per cubic meter. Cut nails occupy more than 95 percent of nails in all loci but the Midden Trench. The Midden Trench also has the only tacks, thirteen in all. Nails complete enough for measurement were predominantly of the final carpentry and multipurpose sizes, consisting of 2d (1 inch, or 25.4 millimeters) to 16d (3.5 inches, or 88.9 millimeters) pennyweights, respectively.

Summary and Synthesis

The metal artifacts help to sharpen the understanding of Native life on Rancho Petaluma. A variety of activities are recorded in the metal artifacts: cooking and eating (kettles, silverware), sewing (thimbles, pins, scissors), heavier tool use (files, snips blade), clothing and adornment (buttons, hooks,

Table 5.4
Nail types and frequencies.

Area	Cut	Wire	Indeterminate	Tack	Total
Midden Trench	290	62	1	15	368
Stream Trench	70	0	0	0	70
Block	29	1	0	0	30
Trench 1	2	0	0	0	2
Trench 2	18	1	1	0	20
Trench 3	0	0	0	0	0
Total	339	64	2	15	490

buckles, ring), hunting or armed conflict (lead shot, lead balls, percussion caps, bullet cases, rifle buttplate), and construction (nails).

Nails are numerous at the site, and they offer some insight into construction activity. Although we recovered no evidence of wooden structures, the nails suggest that they may have existed on or near the site. A simple correlation of nail density and probable building location is not warranted, however, since the high density of nails in the midden correlates with high densities of other materials and reflects the refuse nature of this locus; that is, building debris with nails, or simply nails, may have been discarded here. Similarly, the lower density of nails in the Block may reflect their use for postconstruction purposes, given the fact that many of them were bent and hence presumably extracted specimens.

The metal artifacts also reveal aspects of Native cooking and eating practices. The iron and brass kettles likely indicate a shift in some aspects of cooking and vessel technology. The kettles, although now very fragmented, may have served as direct-heat cooking vessels that complemented stone boiling in baskets. The latter practice has been inferred from the historical evidence and the numerous thermally altered stones with contraction fractures discovered during excavation. At the same time, the kettles may have served other purposes such as rendering tallow in an outdoor processing facility, much as they did at the Petaluma Adobe proper. The open-mouthed buckets or pails may have coexisted with baskets for transporting or storing food and other items at the site.

The sewing and heavy tool use categories are those that dovetail closely with labor tasks on the rancho, but they may relate to residential activities outside of the daily labor regime. In other words, Native women were often assigned tasks involving sewing leather and cloth goods (Engelhardt 1915:136), and these items may mark those physical tasks. For instance, a surviving letter from Alvarado (1844b), the majordomo of Rancho Petaluma, to Vallejo requested thread for sewing. At the same time, these items indicate the material infiltration of rancho work tasks into domestic practices. There is no evidence that Native women performed "piecework" at home—that is, completed a quota—rather than time-based work duties. This suggests that women introduced sewing items into the home for domestic tasks (perhaps the maintenance of tailored clothing) that are evidenced in the adornment artifacts. The buttons represent coats and shirts, the hooks point to shirts or other thin garments, and the buckles indicate stockings or belts. Visitors and non–Native residents of California commonly noticed Native individuals in cast-off clothing, if, in fact, Native people wore any European garments at all (e.g., Bryant 1985:265–66). In addition, rancheros often "paid" Native workers in clothing (Bauer 1953:7; Carrillo 1877:131; Cleland 1941:43; Hastings 1932:132). The variety of metal clothing hooks, metal buckles, and buttons of metal, bone, glass, and ceramic may indicate the hodgepodge nature of clothing available to workers on the rancho, just as it may suggest the variety of provisioning protocols used by Vallejo and his rancho staff.

The files or rasps probably indicate metal- or woodworking, and these tasks were most often assigned to Native men. Again, because men were probably not bringing their jobs home, these items represent the translation of labor duties into household uses that perhaps extended their functionality. Yet it is of particular significance that no metal tools associated with livestock herding or butchery, agriculture, hide processing, or tallow rendering were recovered, despite the fact that Native men and some women spent many of their working hours devoted to these tasks. It would be premature to associate the small chain segment with vaquero boots or bridles. When compared to the presence of metal artifacts related to women's assigned duties, the lack of items from men's assigned tasks is striking. The appearance of "domestic" rancho artifacts in the "domestic" space of Native life away from rancho work is perhaps unremarkable in and of itself, since domestic tools may have been useful in both places, but I explore the additional interpretive implications in a later chapter.

Some initially surprising metal objects are those related to firearms. Although discontented armed workers would not have been a welcome sight for the handful in control of Rancho Petaluma, it appears that Native residents may have had access to firearms. A likely explanation is that these firearms were devoted to hunting, complementing rather than replacing stone tools. These guns may have been used for fowling, given the high quantities of bird shot and waterfowl bird remains. Additionally, it would not be unreasonable to expect that Vallejo and Alvarado armed some of their trusted workers such as alcaldes in the event that the Petaluma Adobe required defense from either insiders or outsiders. The number of battles between Vallejo's troops and outlying Native American communities certainly made the northern frontier of Mexican California a volatile place.

More perplexing is that the arms-related artifacts seem to evidence guns that typically postdate American annexation in 1848, or they would have been rare commodities before then. The combination of percussion caps and no unequivocal gunflints points to an exclusive use of cap-lock rifles, pistols, and perhaps muskets. Although cap-lock guns existed in the 1840s, their availability in California was rare and their price high (Glenn Burch, personal communication, 2000). Cap-lock arms were most popular between 1850 and the 1870s (e.g., Dietz 1976:147–48). Prior to U.S. annexation in 1848, Vallejo may have owned one or two cap-lock guns for personal use, but he would have neither outfitted troops with these arms nor given them to Native laborers. This makes it unlikely that these arms reflect the brief stationing of his soldiers at the rancho in 1835, noted by Vallejo (1875c:227). Therefore, the gun parts indicate the very real possibility that some artifacts postdate the period of interest. They may indicate some limited non-Native use of the site after the denouement of Rancho Petaluma, or they may suggest Native people living at the site into the mid-1850s, perhaps using guns to dispatch waterfowl when not working for the new residents of the Petaluma Adobe. The .22 and .38 cases most certainly indicate later use, but they could have easily made their way into the site after being discarded on the surface.

Broken Glass

Glass artifacts, both complete and fragmentary, provide a central element in historical archaeological studies. Like their ceramic counterparts, glass artifacts are often classified by archaeologists with respect to their production techniques and presumed contents, since these attributes are thought to best capture important features for archaeological interpretation. Manufacturing processes often give clues to dates for glass-bearing deposits. Body shape, embossed labels, and the form of the finish (lip, rim, and bore) often indicate the likely contents such as alcohol, medicinal products, condiments, or preserves. This content- and manufacturing-based analysis holds great potential, but glass may take on a slightly different meaning in colonial and contact period sites. Many archaeological projects have recovered Native American tools manufactured from chipped bottle glass across the United States, and California offers several notable examples (Allen 1998; Hoover and Costello 1985; Layton 1990; Silliman 1997). As such, the import of glass as raw material has to be considered vis-à-vis the availability and use of rock for producing stone tools. For this reason, it is appropriate for glass artifacts to follow the discussion of metal artifacts, since they offered, when juxtaposed with rock, yet another tool option available to site residents.

Methods and Results

For the sake of simplicity, I summarize some key points of the glass collection here. I draw bottle nomenclature, dating, and manufacturing descriptions from Jones (1971, 1986), Jones and Sullivan (1989), Lorrain (1968), Newman (1970), and White (1978). I have presented all analytical details elsewhere (Silliman 2000a:334–40).

I found no complete or even mostly complete glass bottles. A variety of bottle finishes and bases were present, and these offer opportunities for specific identifications. A total of 3,357 glass pieces was recovered from the five main excavation areas, and 86.7 percent of these came from the Midden Trench and the Stream Trench at a density of 765.3 and 39.2 shards per cubic meter, respectively. Trench 1 contains the second highest density, with 139 shards, but this translates to only 66.5 shards per cubic meter, or over eleven times less density than in the Midden Trench.

Color categories were kept to a minimum: dark green, medium green, light green, brown/amber, blue, aqua, and colorless. Dark green is the standard "black glass" of the nineteenth century. Green glass comprises 83.8 percent (2,813) of this total, split between dark (33.5 percent, or 942), medium (32.8 percent, or 922), and light (34.1 percent, or 959). Other colors are considerably less numerous, with colorless or clear at 9.9 percent, aqua at 4.8 percent, brown/amber at 1.0 percent, and blue at 0.4 percent. Four (0.1 percent) shards have a patina too thick to determine color. The dark and medium green typically indicate wine and other alcohol bottles, and the light

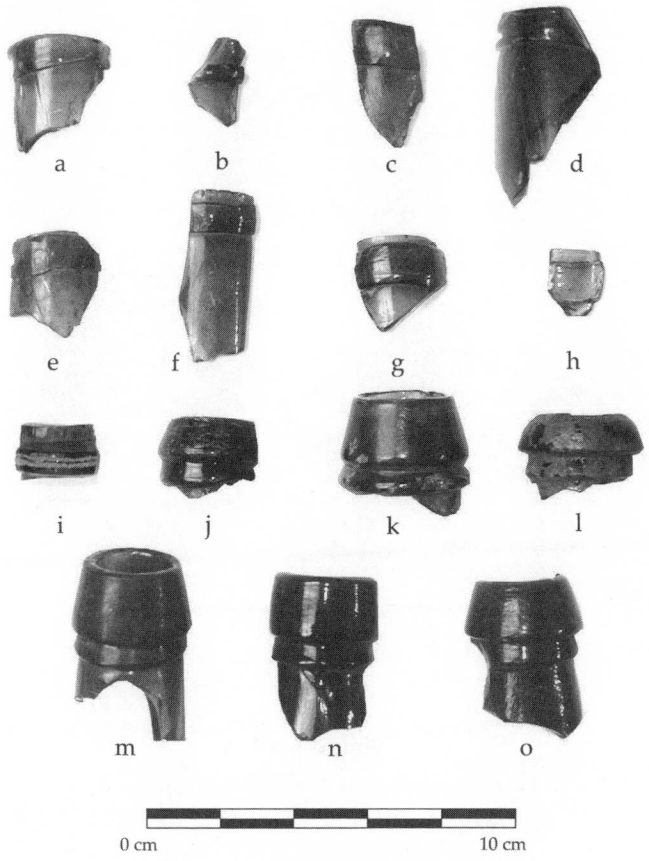

Figure 5.9

Green glass bottle finish and finish fragments: *a–h*, applied, untooled string rim; *i*, flat lip, even string rim; *j–k*, down-tooled lip with down-tooled string; *l*, round lip with down-tooled string; *m–o*, down-tooled lip with down-tooled string rim. Photo by the author.

green and brown/amber are primarily alcohol bottles as well. The black glass fragments belong in large part to the nineteenth-century "wine" and sometimes beer bottles common at historical archaeological sites in North America (e.g., Jones 1986). The colorless or clear glass indicates a variety of items, including medicine and condiment bottles, preserve jars, tumblers, and lamp globes. The aqua shards suggest bottles for medicinal purposes or preserves, whereas the cobalt blue indicates late-nineteenth-century medicine.

Figure 5.10
Embossed bottle glass: *a*, Saint Julien shoulder seal; *b*, "R" or "B" on body
shard; *c*, "E" on shoulder shard; *d*, "Y" below "N" (?) on body shard.
Photo by the author.

Most shards are indeterminate body fragments, but numerous base, heel,
and finish fragments exist in the collection. Dark green glass contains thirty
base/heel pieces and twelve finishes, medium green has six base/heel and
two finish fragments, and light green has eight base/heel and eleven finish
shards. A minimum of fourteen bottles are represented across these green
colors, including both finishes (figure 5.9l–n) and bases in styles common to
the mid-1800s. In addition to these common forms, two other bottle types
are present: a potential Rickett's three-piece mold and a snap case. The former
is identified by a single base fragment with distinct mold lines, abrupt heel,
and base embossed with "TS." toward the midline of the bottle. The snap-
case method is indicated on at least one base fragment that displays no distinct pontil marks and two base mold lines.

The excavated medium and light green base and heel fragments provide minimal assistance in dating, but they include a variety of finish and base fragments. All of the light and medium green bottles are probably wine or other alcohol bottles. One insight into the wine bottles comes from an embossed shoulder seal labeled "ST.JULIEN/MÉDOC" (figure 5.10a), which matches one found in Old Sacramento (Schulz et al. 1980:fig. 27c) and probably dates to the 1840s or 1850s. In Old Sacramento, a different Saint Julien shoulder seal was found with the bottle neck and finish still attached, indicating that at least some of these wine bottles had a sheared and fire-polished rim with laid-on lip (Schulz et al. 1980:97–98). This style resembles that found on light green untooled and flat string rims and finishes in the Petaluma collection. Other glass shards display embossing, but they have not been further identified, given their small size (figure 5.10b–d). Their planar shape suggests that they are probably body fragments, which might place their date into the last quarter of the 1800s (Jones and Sullivan 1989:49).

The four aqua-colored finishes are one-part finishes and probably once belonged to preserve bottles. Four base/heel shards also indicate two preserve bottles, one whiskey bottle, and one unidentified form. The brown bottle finishes likely derive from alcohol bottles. The colorless bottles are represented by five finishes: one flanged lip, two flat lip with uneven-string rim, one round, and one threaded. The two flat-lip, uneven-string finishes are a medicine and a bitters bottle. Two colorless heels also occurred: one flat unidentified and one concave Mason jar base fragment. One flat base of a blue bottle also occurs, a rare example of a two-part mold in this collection. Four other indeterminate shards can be attributed to condiment bottles.

In addition to bottles, other glass items are evidenced in the collection, albeit they are few in number. Clear paneled tumblers are represented by one rim fragment, two heel pieces, and one body shard. All but one came from the Midden Trench. Furthermore, a single rim and three body shards of a lamp globe were also discovered in the Midden Trench. Window glass is present, also in the Midden Trench, but as a lone fragment. If this area had contained much post-1850 structural debris, I would have expected more window glass in the site deposits.

Although the glass artifacts represent bottles and other goods that were used on-site, they also offer information on postdepositional processes and the use of glass as a raw material. Many of the glass artifacts from the site are heavily fragmented, flake scarred, and battered, all of which indicate processes other than simple break and discard, but many of these attributes may

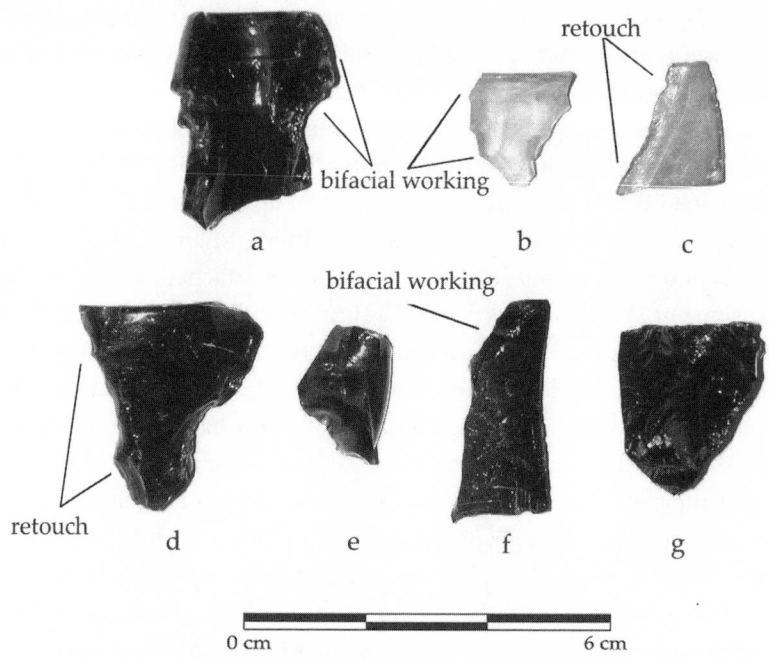

Figure 5.11
Select worked glass: *a*, bifacially worked dark green finish; *b*, bifacially
worked aqua shard; *c*, unimarginally worked light green shard;
d, unimarginally worked dark green heel; *e*, dark green "exhausted core";
f, bifacially worked dark green shard; *g*, dark green glass "core" fragment.
Photo by the author.

relate to secondary or tertiary depositional contexts or to agricultural disturbance. Potentially worked glass specimens number 143, or 4.9 percent of the
total glass subassemblage, but worked glass, or glass with use-wear or retouch, is difficult to identify in the Petaluma glass collection. Of this total, I
am confident of only about 115 (80.4 percent), and I restrict discussion here
to this subset. I do not include any worked glass artifacts from the Stream
Trench.

I describe worked glass artifacts in the same way that I handled lithic artifacts earlier in this chapter. Flakes and flake shatter comprise 63 (54.8 percent) of the 115 examples, and many have numerous dorsal flake scars. Three

excavated fragments seem to be exhausted cores (figure 5.11e), and one artifact from a surface testing unit is a basal fragment with significant evidence of "core" reduction (figure 5.11g). Only three shards—two dark green, one aqua—reveal clear bifacial retouch (figure 5.11a, b, f), but no formed bifaces such as projectile points of any sort are present. Working occurred at all locations on bottles, including finishes, necks, bodies, and bases.

Summary and Synthesis

The high quantity of glass bottle fragments indicates not only their easy breakage but also their great availability to individuals residing in or near the excavated areas. The predominance of dark and other green glass shards, the style of finishes and bases, and the single shoulder seal point strongly toward a large quantity of wine and other alcohol bottles at the site. Although non-Native individuals may have contributed a limited amount of glass bottle refuse to these deposits, it is more likely that these represent acquisition and use by Native people. Whether or not these bottles contained the aguardiente commonly distributed to Native workers on southern California ranchos is unclear, but these artifacts may still represent labor "payment" of alcohol.

The predominance of alcohol bottles is juxtaposed with a small quantity of condiment, bitters, and medicine bottles. Native workers may have received these products as distributions, acquired them through trade or purchase, or scavenged the bottles and contents whenever possible. A limited number may have been dumped here sporadically after the rancho's demise. An even smaller number of glass tumbler fragments and a single shard each of lamp chimney and window glass round out the collection. The paucity of lamp and window glass indicates that these were not common features of the site's architecture.

Individuals, presumably Native, probably used many of these glass items as they were originally designed; that is, wine bottles held wine, and glass tumblers might have been used as drinking glasses. However, this form-to-function relationship should not be assumed across the board, given the non-Western social framework in which Native individuals used them. The clearest example is the use of bottle glass for tool manufacture. Glass reduction and shaping occurred in much lower quantities than in Native deposits at nearby colonial sites such as Colony Ross (Silliman 1997), but it does occur nonetheless. It certainly does not come close to the intensity of use dedicated to actual rock material, yet it should not be overlooked. Individuals modified glass for rather expedient purposes, given the high proportion of unimarginal flaking and the lack of any formal tools. The combination of steep and acute retouch indicates both scraping and cutting tasks (see Wilkie 1996). Still, the low frequency of clearly modified glass artifacts suggests that glass use may have focused primarily on the bottle contents.

Ceramics: Used but Not Made

If there were a material culture mainstay of historical archaeology, ceramics would be a prime contender for the title. Archaeologists have not only produced elaborate classification schemes to understand British, German, Dutch, American, Mexican, Chinese, Russian, and other ceramic vessels found on historic sites all across the Americas, but they have translated them into enriched discussions about gender, status, capitalism, and daily practice. These studies—too many to reference—have shown the great potential of mass-produced ceramics for informing archaeologists about material culture. In many colonial and contact period cases in the Americas, these introduced ceramics help demarcate the lines of cultural accommodation and global incorporation (Cabak and Loring 2000), and they often serve as raw material for Native American production of gaming pieces and tools (Silliman 1997; White 1977). In addition, local or indigenous ceramics also can be used to trace either the continued or transformed activities of Native American groups who had been ceramic producers prior to contact (e.g., Deagan 1996; Johnson 2000) or the adoption of ceramic technology by nonceramic peoples as part of their involvement with the colonial enterprise. The production of Brown Wares in ranchos and mission wares in Franciscan missions by Native American people in southern California is a prime example of the latter, as touched on briefly in chapter 3. Although some ceramic production took place during southern California's precontact periods, the practice rapidly expanded in colonial centers at the hands of Native artisans. The Rancho Petaluma case strikes a different chord.

Vessel Analysis

I classified all ceramic sherds in the Rancho Petaluma collection by paste type, glaze, and decoration (see Silliman 1997). This is relatively standard practice in historical archaeology because it helps to distinguish ceramics by their manufacturing technique, origin, date, and sometimes purpose. Paste

Table 5.5
Frequencies of ceramic types.

Area	Porcelain	Refined Earthenware	Stoneware	Unknown[a]	Total
Stream Trench	5	37	15	0	57
Midden Trench	20	197	78	2	297
Block	0	10	0	0	10
Trench 1	0	3	0	0	3
Trench 2	1	7	0	0	8
Trench 3	0	1	3	0	4
Total	26	255	96	2	379
%	6.9	67.3	25.3	0.5	100.0

[a] Includes one reddish tan porous sherd and one bluish ceramic-like object resembling highly vitrified bone.

type includes three broad categories of ceramic body firing temperature: refined earthenware, stoneware, and porcelain. Glaze assists in further separating these categories, such as dividing refined earthenwares into pearlware, creamware, and whiteware, but some of the clearest distinctions can be made based on transfer-printing colors, design elements, and manufacturer hallmarks, since the gradations in glaze hues make it tricky, if not impossible, to distinguish some whitewares and pearlwares (Majewski and O'Brien 1987; Miller 1980, 1991; Sussman 1977). In this small collection, however, decorations are fragmentary, designs are not easily traceable, and backstamps are rare. General decorative types include underglaze transfer-printed and hand-painted designs on refined earthenwares, underglaze blue painted designs on porcelain, and overglaze painting on stoneware. All counts provided below are sherd counts, since I found nothing close to a complete or conjoinable vessel. For the sake of organization, I also discuss here the other items made of baked clay: kaolin clay pipe fragments and roof tiles.

Ceramics were common but certainly not frequent, with only 379 vessel sherds recovered from the Rancho Petaluma excavations. All ceramics were imports from Britain, the United States, and China, and they fall into the broad categories of refined earthenware, porcelain, and stoneware (table 5.5). Excavation produced no ceramic vessels made on-site of local clays, no wares known to be manufactured elsewhere in California, and no Mexican tin-enameled majolica or lead-glazed *galera* wares. This stands in stark contrast to other rancho excavations from southern and south-central California, where majolica and locally produced Brown Ware ceramics are extraordinarily common. However, the contrast with regard to Brown Ware is not that remarkable, since, unlike several groups in southern California, California's indigenous residents in the North Bay had no history of ceramic production.

The ceramic sherds are predominantly refined earthenware (67.3 percent), with several stoneware (25.3 percent) and relatively few porcelain (6.9 percent) sherds. The majority of ceramics (80.5 percent, or 305) occur in Area A at a peak density of 77.8 sherds per cubic meter in the Midden Trench. Other than one porcelain fragment and three stoneware sherds, all porcelain and stoneware were found in Area A. Interestingly, 5.7 percent (seventeen) of the Midden Trench sherds showed burning. The three refined earthenware sherds in Trench 1 occurred in and around Feature D at the southern end of the trench, five of the eight sherds in Trench 2 occurred in the southernmost contiguous unit, and the four sherds in Trench 3 were randomly distributed.

The refined earthenware ceramics include a variety of pearlware, whiteware, and creamware, plus limited quantities of yellowware and mocha.[5] The most common of these is pearlware (76 sherds, or 29.8 percent) and undifferentiated whiteware/pearlware (108 sherds, or 42.4 percent). Creamware and whiteware follow, with twenty-six (10.2 percent) and twenty-four (9.4 percent) sherds, respectively. Yellowware represents 6.7 percent (seventeen) of the subassemblage, and mocha occurs as only one sherd (0.4 percent). Raw, not minimum, vessel sherd counts for the forty-three classifiable fragments include twenty-four bowls and general hollowware, fourteen plates and general flatware, two saucers, one cup, one serving vessel, and one pitcher.

Decorative types provide better attributes for classification than those offered by the ware distinctions. Yellowware sherds (seventeen) are comprised of fifteen undecorated, one annular blue, and one transferware blue. Unsurprisingly, other refined earthenware sherds reveal more diversity of decoration. Even though more than half (51.8 percent) of the sherds were undecorated portions of vessels, other decorative styles include, in rank order, blue transfer printing, hand-painted polychrome, hand-painted blue, annular brown, blue shell edge, annular blue, green transfer printing, flow blue, annular green, and annular red (table 5.6). I could not identify any of the transferware patterns, other than the few examples of willowware rim sherds.

Table 5.6

Frequencies of refined earthenware types.

Type	Count	%
Undecorated	132	51.8
Blue transferware	81	31.8
Hand-painted polychrome	12	4.7
Hand-painted blue[a]	6	2.4
Blue shell edge	4	1.6
Annular brown	4	1.6
Annular blue	2	0.8
Annular green	1	0.4
Annular red	1	0.4
Green transferware	4	1.6
Flow blue	1	0.4
Indeterminate	7	2.7
Total	255	100.0

[a] Contains one sherd with medium blue slip.

To complement decoration and ware on the earthenwares, I identified the available maker's marks, attempted to locate conjoining sherds, and looked for evidence of ceramic modification. The only identifiable maker's mark occurred on a sherd from the midden surface, "T.WAL——— / TUN——— / ———RO——— / CHI———," printed beneath a garter with tiny leaves on the border (figure 5.12a), indicating an "ironstone china" vessel manufactured by Thomas Walker in Tunstall, Staffordshire, England, between 1845 and 1851 (Godden 1964:643). Only one other partial mark was recovered, the tip of a bird wing (figure 5.12b). This mark resembles but does not match a Thomas Walker backstamp excavated from the 1840s to 1850s Diaz privy in Monterey (Felton and Schulz 1983:fig. 5e). Evidence of conjoining artifacts includes two pairs of blue transfer-print sherds in the midden, each pair from the same respective unit. Two sherds also refit in the Block from units over 3 meters apart. With respect to modification, only one hand-painted polychrome whiteware sherd from the midden displayed short, regular nicks along one side.

The twenty-one porcelain sherds are 76.2 percent white and undecorated, with the clear glaze characteristic of British or American porcelains, and

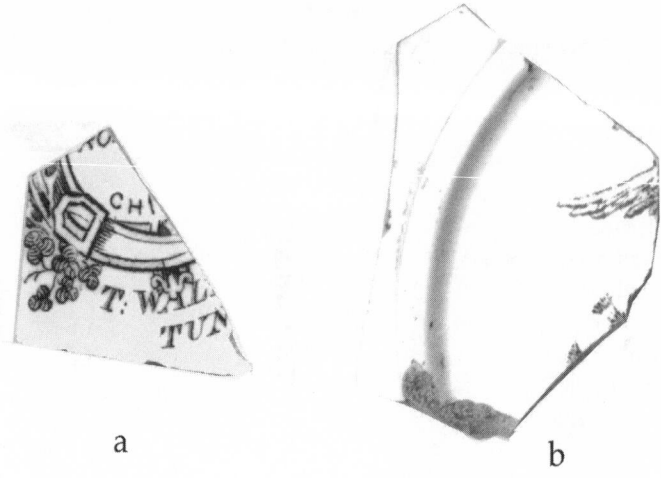

a   b

Figure 5.12
Hallmarks on refined earthenware ceramics: *a*, Thomas Walker semivitreous
ironstone sherd manufactured in Tunstall, Staffordshire, England;
b, pearlware plate base sherd, perhaps also manufactured by Thomas Walker.
Photo by the author.

23.8 percent Chinese, with blue-tinged glaze and underglaze blue painted
designs. Of those identifiable to vessel types, the former sherds represent
one plate, one saucer, and one other general flatware; the latter sherds represent one serving piece, one bowl, and one other general hollowware vessel. I
found no evidence of burning, no hallmarks, and no sherds that could conjoin.

The ninety-six stoneware sherds fall into three main categories: English
brown (41.7 percent), coarse gray Chinese (46.9 percent), and other (11.5
percent). The English brown stoneware sherds have the characteristic brown
exterior, gray paste, and grainy gray interior of this type. The stoneware
collection appears to derive from broken bottles, with only one refit between
a surface and a subsurface sherd approximately 4.5 meters apart.

The coarse gray Chinese stoneware has the following characteristics: grayish yellow exterior glaze with overglaze enameled blue floral or brownish red
annular designs set within black guidelines; coarse gray paste with numerous inclusions; and a variegated, textured brown interior glaze (figure 5.13a–g).

Figure 5.13

Stoneware sherds: *a–b*, body sherd of Chinese stoneware; *c–e*, body sherd of Chinese stoneware showing enameled exterior; *f*, rim sherd of Chinese ginger jar; *g*, base sherd of Chinese stoneware jar; *h–i*, unidentified stoneware with black paint on uneven exterior; *j*, base of bottle with tan glaze and ridged surface on interior; *k*, body sherd with granitelike exterior and ribbed, speckled brown interior glaze–interior view; *l–n*, body sherd with granitelike exterior and ribbed, speckled brown interior glaze–exterior view.
Photo by the author.

The overglaze enamel has deteriorated on several of the sherds, leaving only a remnant design, and several are burned. These sherds appear to be parts of bottles, ginger jars (figure 5.13f), or similar containers based on the shape and diameter of basal sherds. This ceramic type is uncommon in California, and thus far I have found only one type match, which is in a ceramic collection from excavations at the Barracks in nearby Sonoma (Felton 1977:120). The Barracks excavation produced four sherds with the black-lined enamel decorations on the coarse gray body, but only one had the dark brown interior glaze. It may prove to be of consequence that Vallejo controlled both of these locations in the mid-nineteenth century.

The "other" stoneware include the following: three sherds with a brown glaze, dark brown paste, and a raised black design on the rough exterior (figure 5.13h–i); one basal sherd with dark brown glaze on the interior and a gritty tan-glazed ridged surface on the exterior (figure 5.13j); five sherds with a yellow granitelike surface beneath a clear glaze on the vessel exterior (figure 5.13k) and a ribbed and speckled brown glazed interior (figure 5.13l–n); one with a light brown streaked glaze; and one sherd with a reddish brown exterior glaze and no remaining interior surface. The brown sherds with the black designs actually conjoin, even though they were found more than 10 meters apart in the midden. The basal sherd with dark brown interior glaze may be the same ceramic type as the sherds with the yellow granitelike surface.

Pipes and Tiles

Completing the category of fired clay artifacts are the historic pipes and roof tiles. Only six pipe fragments were found during excavation, and all were recovered from the midden. They include five stem fragments and one bowl/ stem fragment (figure 5.14, one not pictured). In addition, twenty-eight fragments of baked-clay tile were retrieved from the site. The relative thinness, typical curvature, gritty underside, orange and brownish red hues, and often incompletely fired "core" in the paste indicate that these are *tejas*, or roof tile, fragments. The Midden Trench contained 46.4 percent of all tile, the Stream Trench held 21.4 percent, Trench 1 possessed 21.4 percent, the Block held 7.2 percent, and Trench 2 had only 3.6 percent. Average fragment weight differed substantially between the Midden Trench (19.7 grams) and Trench 1 (63.3 grams), indicating the much smaller size and, therefore, greater fragmentation found amidst the refuse of Area A.

Summary and Synthesis

Hunter-gatherer groups in northern California did not manufacture or use ceramic vessels in precontact periods. Ceramic technology was known in the greater region, given the presence of fired clay effigies and balls in precontact sites and the distribution of pottery in some southern California hunter-gatherer groups, but individuals in northern California did not direct this technology toward making vessels except in the far northern reaches of the

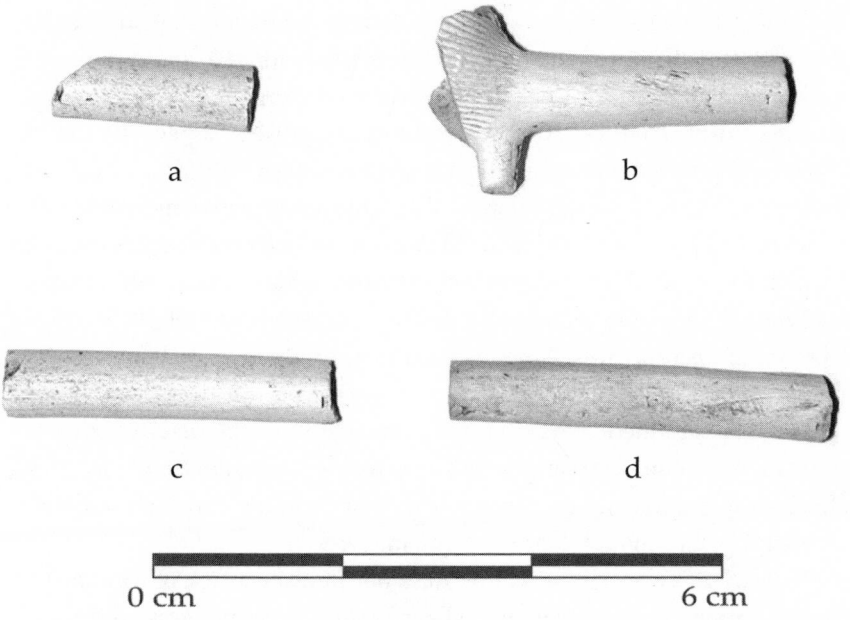

Figure 5.14
Kaolin clay pipe stems and bowl: *a*, pipe stem fragment; *b*, pipe stem and
bowl fragment; *c–d*, pipe stem fragment. Photo by the author.

region (Mack 2003). Tightly woven baskets and boiling stones served cooking purposes well. With the arrival of the Franciscan mission system, many
Native individuals became involved in ceramic production during their participation in colonial labor regimes. Local ceramic production occurred across
California in part from necessity, since supply lines to Mexico were unreli-
able in the first three or four decades of Spanish colonization. Most of the
ceramic needs were met through both legal and illicit trade with British and
American ships along the Pacific Coast, but production of the coarse local
wares continued, even with the increased availability of British and Chinese
ceramics during the expanding international trade in hides and tallow from
the 1810s through the 1840s.

Ceramic artisans, most likely skilled labor brought from Mexico or southern
California missions or newly trained local California Indians, produced earthenwares at northern California missions and perhaps at other colonial sites

such as El Presidio de San Francisco (Skowronek et al. 2001; Voss 2002:app. B). The trajectory of this ceramic production and its use in Native groups that withdrew from the missions and associated colonial communities following secularization in 1834 is unknown. However, a point on one trajectory is available from the Rancho Petaluma assemblage, suggesting that ceramic production did not make its way onto northern California ranchos. At Rancho Petaluma it appears that neither Vallejo nor Native individuals had an interest in ceramic production. I suggest this reflects Vallejo's lucrative economic system of manufacture, agriculture, and livestock, which generated enough money for purchasing necessary ceramics and left little time for laborers to operate kilns. Moreover, ceramic production was never part of the California Indian cultural repertoire in that part of the region anyway. The lack of production was certainly not due to a lack of clay, given the enormous amounts extracted nearby for making the unfired adobe bricks, although it is currently not known if the surrounding clay-rich sediments contain clay fine enough for ceramic manufacture.

The lack of ceramic production does not indicate a lack of ceramic use, for excavation revealed that refined earthenwares, stonewares, and porcelains were part of everyday life for rancho inhabitants. Californio residents set their tables and filled their rooms with these items, but the fact that they occur in refuse deposits across the stream from the main house in Petaluma hints that they also may have been a material component of Native daily practices. The preferred or most accessible ceramics were refined earthenwares, and these seem to have been predominantly bowls or general hollowware and, to a lesser degree, plates. Individuals also acquired fewer stoneware bottles or jars that probably once contained ale, mineral water, or other liquids. Porcelain was relatively scarce and represented mainly by non-Chinese varieties. No majolica ceramics were recovered, indicating both a lack of trade contacts by both Native and Californio residents with traditional Mexican sources and a function of the times, since majolica had dropped out of common distribution by the 1840s. It seems that Vallejo acquired his material goods from vessels and residents in the Yerba Buena (San Francisco) area, which is not surprising, given the settlement's proximity and Vallejo's amount of financial capital.

To make sense of these patterns, these ceramic types can be compared to the limited number found in and around the Petaluma Adobe (Silliman 1999). The majority of ceramics recovered from excavations inside the adobe building postdate the first twenty years of rancho occupation and are dominated by unrefined, coarse, unglazed earthenware fragments. These do not occur in the excavations across the stream. Furthermore, none of the stoneware types recovered from the Son–2294/H site were located inside the adobe building. No majolica was found inside the Petaluma Adobe either, suggesting that the pattern really does indicate its absence from the rancho rather than a case of restricted access by Native American workers at the nearby site. One sherd of black transferware and three of blue transferware refined earthenware were found in the Petaluma Adobe deposits associated with initial construction in the 1830s (Silliman 1999:119).

In general, the recovered ceramics from Son–2294/H are only small portions of their original size, indicating that they may have been subjected to trampling, secondary or tertiary redeposition, or intentional modification. Since only one earthenware sherd shows flaking, the latter is unlikely to account for the generally small sizes. This contrasts with the ceramic modification revealed in the Native living area at Russian Colony Ross (Silliman 1997:147–50), suggesting that fragmentation at Petaluma relates primarily to processes of refuse disposal and redeposition. The lack of significant ceramic modification hints that individuals may have used the ceramics primarily as they were designed—as eating or serving containers—rather than as raw material. The implication is that Native people may have adopted these European goods (e.g., dishes and bottles) into household contexts.

Ceramics can also be useful for bracketing occupation dates at historic sites, but they are equivocal in this regard at the Rancho Petaluma site. Blue transferware is a more common pattern in the 1820s (prior to the establishment of Rancho Petaluma), but the quantity of pearlwares and whitewares points to a date in the second and perhaps third quarter of the 1800s. At the same time, it is unusual to have so few transfer-printing colors represented in the collection, particularly given the production of transferware designs in black, brown, red, and purple from circa 1829 to the late 1840s and in polychrome after 1840 (Godden 1963:115; Majewski and O'Brien 1987:119). At the roughly contemporaneous Colony Ross, these monochrome transfer-printing colors were recovered in both Native and Russian contexts, with polychrome varieties found strictly in Russian deposits (Silliman 1997:166).

Why these do not occur in the Petaluma assemblage is unclear. It is highly unlikely that the ceramics were deposited before Rancho Petaluma was granted, but perhaps the lack of multiple transferware colors denotes some continued use of older ceramics after their decline in popularity near midcentury. The same may account for the lack of many flow blue specimens.

However, the annular yellowware ceramics offer a possible post-1840 date, as does the Thomas Walker hallmark dated between 1845 and 1851. Native workers may have obtained only those ceramics that had been around for several years, not having been allowed access to the newer, more "fashionable" dishes. Much like the clothing, these items may have been hand-me-downs or provisions of cheap goods to pay for workers' labor, but their low quantity suggests that they were not readily available or freely given. Further excavation around the Petaluma Adobe will be necessary to assess ceramic availability for Native workers based on their patterns around and within the colonial building.

More Than Food: Artifacts of Bone and Shell

To continue the discussion of material culture, I turn back to items frequently thought to be associated with Native American people: bone and shell artifacts. The items discussed here were manufactured locally by Native Americans, thus excluding the bone buttons previously mentioned. Bone and shell artifacts are relatively few in number, but they were a unique component of the material repertoire of rancho daily life. Faunal and molluscan remains from Rancho Petaluma represent more than just food intake, which is the topic of the next chapter; they indicate the persistence of indigenous technologies and practices.

Excavation revealed a polished bone tube, a small quantity of incised bird-bone tubes, and miscellaneous modified bone; I discuss only the first two categories here.[6] The large, polished bone tube was recovered from the southern end of Feature E in the Block (figure 5.15). The artifact is 60.6 millimeters long and has a 12.2-by-14.6-millimeter elliptical cross section. The functions of this bone tube are unclear, but it might have served as a gaming piece, part of a pipe, a body decoration, or a "sucking tube" for ritual curing.

The most common bone artifact is the incised bird-bone tube, represented by thirteen specimens (figure 5.16). It is unlikely that birds would have been hunted specifically for their limb bones, but this bone technology attests to the nonsubsistence use of faunal resources at the rancho. The bone tubes have zoned crosshatch designs, meaning that there are areas of no decoration adjacent to bounded zones of intricate incising. Unfortunately, the bird-bone tubes are represented only by small burned fragments, which render accurate interpretation of design patterns impossible. Nonetheless, they bear a strong resemblance to those used by Native Californians at Colony Ross (Wake

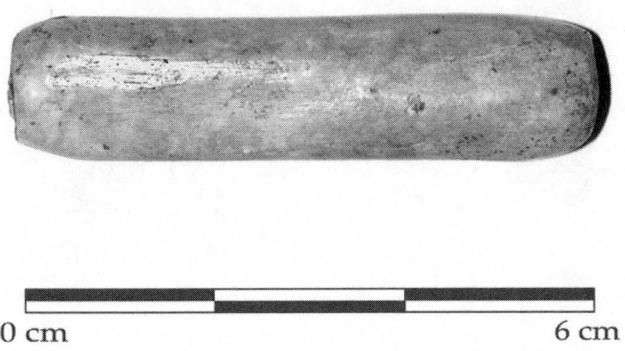

Figure 5.15
Polished bone tube. Photo by the author.

1997a) and those typed as EE2b by Gifford (1940:180, 227) for northern California. These tubes may have been used for gambling, nose or ear decoration, beads, or drinking tubes (Gifford 1940:180; see also Dietz 1976:86). The vast majority (83.3 percent) of the bird-bone tubes occur in the Block, clustered specifically in and around Feature E. The Midden Trench, Stream Trench, and Trench 1 contained only one bird-bone tube fragment each.

The shellfish remains indicate both food and raw material, and I take up the former issue in the succeeding chapter. Fragments of clam, mussel, oyster, and other species are clear indications of food gathering at the bay and along the coast, but gatherers may have sought some of the shellfish, particularly the clam, for raw material. I had expected significant clamshell debris at the site, given the prominence of clamshell disk beads in late precontact, historic, and ethnographic northern California and the location of Rancho Petaluma near the famous Bodega Bay clam beds. Oddly, though, only two clamshell disk beads were recovered, an unexpected scarcity that I return to in the following section.

Beads of Glass

In contact period and colonial sites in North America, glass beads frequently are a telltale sign of Native Americans, and they are numerous at Rancho

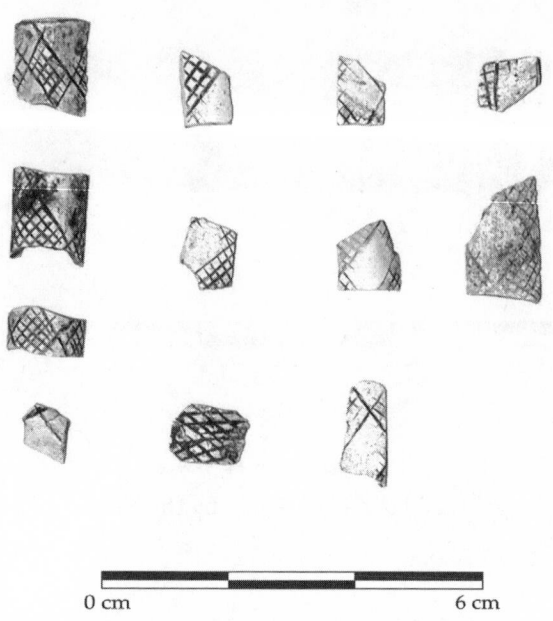

0 cm   6 cm

Figure 5.16
Incised bird-bone tube artifacts. Photo by the author.

Petaluma. One can never assume that all Native Americans had an interest in glass beads or that only Native Americans made use of these decorative glass items.[7] However, glass beads often made their way to the New World from European, Chinese, and other Old World manufacturers for the sole purpose of trade and exchange between Europeans and North America's indigenous people. Moreover, glass beads did not constitute a significant component of Mexican-Californian dress in the nineteenth century, meaning that the beads likely are Native artifacts. Glass beads were significant commodities in North America, readily incorporated by Native people into preexisting exchange and social networks and into community and personal sentiments about comportment and decoration. This phenomenon happened across the continent, often in ways that archaeologists and other scholars have only begun to appreciate. Certainly, most researchers appreciate the quantity of bead exchange and use, but few have explored the quality of that bead use.

Glass beads have been a major research issue on the West Coast for a number of years. From the missions of California (Meighan 1985; Ross 1989) to trade outposts along the Pacific Coast (Ross 1990, 1997), glass beads have been a hot topic for historical archaeologists seeking to unravel the complexities of bead use, display, and trade among Native Americans vis-à-vis their European sources. The Rancho Petaluma case inserts itself into that research agenda with a significant quantity of beads (almost 1,350) found in association with nineteenth-century California Indian material culture.

I analyzed the beads in some detail with regard to measurement, standardized color, manufacturing technique, layering, shape, finish, decoration, diaphaneity, luster, and surface deterioration (Silliman 2000a:349–53). The classification protocol followed the guidelines established by Karklins (1982), Kidd and Kidd (1970), and Sprague (1985), but my methodology had its closest affinity to the work of Ross (1997). This methodology separates beads into "drawn," produced by molten glass being pulled into a long tube and then broken into bead segments; "wound," manufactured by twirling molten glass around an instrument to form a perforated sphere; "wound and shaped," made by further shaping wound beads; and "blown," manufactured using the traditional technique of blowing molten glass to produce a thinner-walled sphere. Some of these bead types, particularly drawn beads, may have two layers of glass of either the same or different colors. At the Rancho Petaluma site, the most common examples were opaque white exteriors on opaque white interiors, opaque red exteriors on translucent light green interiors, and translucent or opaque red exteriors on opaque white interiors. The red-on-green and red-on-white types are often known as Cornaline d'Allepo. Most of the drawn beads at the Petaluma site were cylindrical in shape and had been hot-tumbled, meaning that the glass bead segments had been rolled in hot sand at the factory to round the ends. To categorize diaphaneity, I designated the beads as transparent, translucent, or opaque.

I classified the 1,348 glass beads into 94 varieties, including 64 varieties of drawn beads (1,297), 29 varieties of wound beads (50), and 1 variety of blown bead (1).[8] All raw data can be found in Silliman (2000a), and some of the more unique glass beads are shown in figure 5.17. Rather than delving into complicated glass bead jargon, I can summarize the findings in a manner more attuned to their cultural use rather than their manufacturing technique. Drawn beads predominate at 96.2 percent, which is not uncommon in colonial California (e.g., Ross 1997:fig. 8.12), although the proportion may be

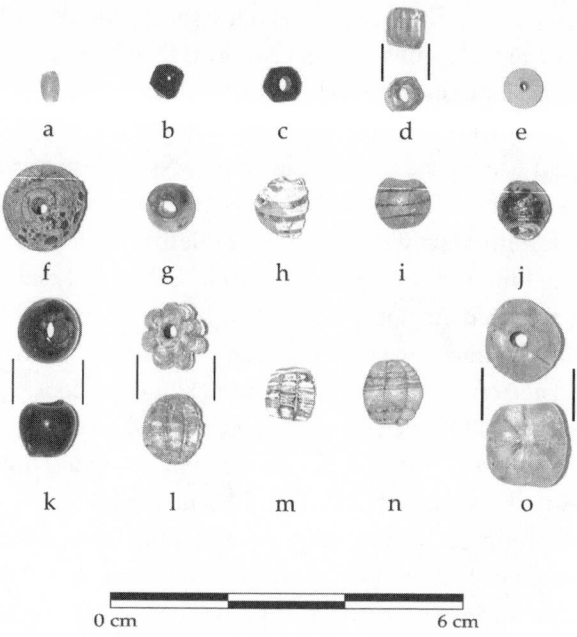

0 cm   6 cm

Figure 5.17
Select glass beads: *a*, variety 36; *b*, variety 38; *c*, variety 41; *d*, variety 42,
two views; *e*, variety 75; *f*, variety 76; *g*, variety 77; *h*, variety 79; *i*, variety
80; *j*, variety 81; *k*, variety 88, two views; *l*, variety 90, two views; *m*, variety
90; *n*, variety 90; *o*, variety 92, two views. See Silliman (2000a:tables 8.8–
8.14) for a full descriptions of bead type varieties.
Photo by the author.

slightly higher in the Petaluma collection. Because drawn beads tend to be
smaller than wound or blown ones, the beads from the site are primarily
(approximately 97 percent) embroidery beads, defined as beads less than 6
millimeters (after Ross 1997:191). Necklace beads occupy the other 3 percent. The continuum of sizes across the 6-millimeter threshold suggests that
this is a somewhat arbitrary distinction, but this does not undermine the
overall trend toward small beads.

Color representation is probably the more interesting aspect of the bead
data because it may represent Native American preferences and practices.
With the exception of red-on-green and red-on-white beads, I here gloss all polychrome beads by their exterior colors for discussion purposes. The combined

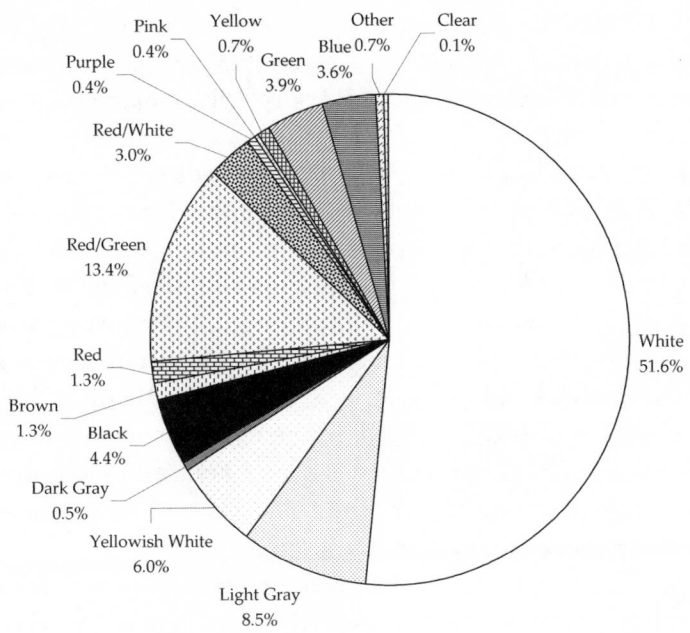

Figure 5.18
Pie chart of glass bead colors.

white (51.6 percent, or 696), light gray (8.5 percent, or 115), and off-white (6 percent, or 81) beads dominate the collection at 66.1 percent (figure 5.18). Red beads occupy the next highest percentage at 17.7 percent (239), a category that includes solid red, red-on-white, and red-on-green beads. The 180 red-on-green beads are the majority (75.3 percent) of this category. Red-on-green beads are common at colonial sites in California such as Fort Ross (Ross 1997), Mission San Buenaventura (Gibson 1976:109), Mission San Antonio (Meighan 1985), Mission Santa Cruz (Allen 1998:tables 7.2, 7.3), and the Ontiveros Adobe (Frierman 1982:table 7). Six of the red-on-white beads have an opaque outer layer, but the other thirty-five specimens have translucent or transparent outer glass. Red-on-white beads occur at Fort Ross (Ross 1997), Mission San Buenaventura (Gibson 1976:109), Mission Santa Cruz (Allen 1998:tables 7.2, 7.3), Mission San José (Dietz 1983), and beneath the Petaluma Adobe on the initial nineteenth-century construction surface (Silliman 1999:119). Black beads are next in proportion at 4.4 percent (fifty-nine), followed by green at 3.9 percent (fifty-three) and blue at 3.6 percent (forty-nine). The remaining 4.1 percent include seventeen brown, ten yellow, ten "other," seven dark gray, five purple, five pink, and two colorless beads.

With the exception of the two heavily burned beads, the "other" beads are typically multicolored with stripes or banding. One is a long black bead with white longitudinal stripes, and another is a large opaque white bead with red and blue bands (figure 5.17h). The latter bead is not uncommon in the West, and it probably dates to the 1830s or 1840s (Roderick Sprague, personal communication, 2000). Another specimen is similar to the previous bead, but the bands are red and gold. Four are "melon" beads of heavily decomposed glass with highly iridized, indeterminate color bands (figure 5.17l–n, one not pictured). Yet another is a large bead with a transparent outer layer, incised panels on the sides, and a blue-and-pink core that may or may not date to the rancho period (figure 5.17o).

Glass beads display a distinct spatial pattern across the five excavated loci. As with most other artifactual materials, the Midden Trench contains the highest bead quantity at 615, percentage at 53.9 percent, and density at 175.7 beads per cubic meter of all excavation loci. The Midden Trench density is over five times the density of the Block, which held the second highest density (36.8 beads per cubic meter); bead density is lowest in Trench 3 (9.7 beads per cubic meter). Color patterns across the site are harder to trace, but they seem to be relatively uniform between site loci, with the exception of the Midden Trench having more red beads (approximately 22 percent) in its locus subassemblage than the other loci (13–15 percent). Not surprising is the larger range of colors in the Midden Trench and Block beads, given the larger sample size therein.

Excavation produced several examples of beads that had melted or fused together from exposure to fire. The most intriguing is a group of at least twenty-one white beads from Trench 2 fused in a semicoiled strand, indicating that a section of a string of beads had fallen into a fire. Six other beads were fused in three pairs, and one yellowish white bead was melted to an unidentified variety of red bead. The white-on-white, yellowish white–on–yellowish white, and red-on-green variety had one fused pair each as well. In addition, one grayish blue bead was fused to another bead. With the exception of the red-white fused pair, these melted segments indicate a stringing pattern of similar colors together as pairs or, in the case of the long strand, as larger sections.

Summary and Synthesis

The high quantity of glass beads points toward a decidedly Native use of nonindigenous material culture, given the strong association of glass beads with California's Native people and the archival evidence suggesting that glass beads were not common accoutrements of colonists and settlers. Native workers may have received beads as payment in kind for labor duties on the rancho, or they may have acquired them through previous or contemporaneous connections with missionaries and traders in the greater North Bay. The large numbers of cheap embroidery beads may indicate daily discard and casual loss, like that hypothesized by Ross (1997:202) for the nearby Native residents at Colony Ross.

As noted above, the glass beads are predominantly embroidery rather than necklace beads. These embroidery beads are relatively inexpensive and could have been used to decorate clothing or basketry. No strong artifactual evidence points to the latter, but many ethnographic baskets in California show an incorporation of glass beads into exterior decoration. Vallejo's son Napoleón gave some insight into the functions of different bead sizes when he recollected that Native people, perhaps after 1850, would use the large glass beads for necklaces and for decorating objects and the smaller ones for embroidering leggings and shoes (n.d.a:2).

Color preferences in the bead assemblage may relate to the importance of the colors of white (marine shell beads, duck and goose feathers) and red (ochre pigment, woodpecker feathers) in traditional crafts in northern California. Yet the high proportion of white or off-white (65.8 percent) and red beads (18 percent) is relatively unique for colonial California. For instance, Native living areas at Colony Ross between 1812 and 1841 had white and red beads as the dominant colors but at only 33 percent and 23 percent, respectively (Ross 1997:fig. 8.12). Mission Santa Cruz had predominantly white in the 242 beads (compiled from Allen 1998:tables 7.2, 7.3) but at a proportion (46.2 percent) still lower than that of Petaluma. On the other hand, Mission San Antonio's 308 beads are weighted toward yellowish brown (35 percent) and blue (25 percent), with only 8 percent white and less than 1 percent red (Meighan 1985).

Only two sites have revealed a similar red or white bead percentage, but they show an even greater preponderance of white. The first is a site at Fort Ross State Historic Park that seems to relate to Native Americans working for the new landowner, William Benitz, in the 1840s and early 1850s. Here, out of 264 beads, Farris (1983) recovered roughly 78 percent white, 17 percent red, and 5 percent all others, including blue faceted, colorless, and black. The second site, the Coast Miwok site of Echa-Tamal in nearby Marin County, produced white and red beads at high proportions of 77 percent and 18.1 percent, respectively, out of over nine hundred beads (Dietz 1976). Given the high numbers of Coast Miwok individuals working at Rancho Petaluma, the similarity may be more than coincidence. The date of the Echa-Tamal site and the Fort Ross Benitz site in the mid-1800s suggests that a predominance of white beads may be a temporal indicator as well. Similar patterns of white beads during later periods are reported for the Sierra Nevada to the east (Shelly Davis-King, personal communication, 2000).

The high frequencies of white and off-white beads and the low occurrence of shell beads noted earlier may be related phenomena. That is, individuals may have incorporated the white and off-white glass beads into embroidery and basketry as a substitute for similarly white shell beads. Given that the Coast Miwok, especially those living at or near Bodega Bay, were the main purveyors of clamshell disk beads and raw material into northern California, the pattern takes on a notable salience. In fact, the Coast Miwok often traded clamshell disk beads much like a monetary currency to the Wappo in the interior for obsidian, at least in ethnographic times (Kelly 1978:418). Perhaps the site pattern reflects a diminution of clamshell disk bead production during the rancho period or the intensified trading of these shell beads outward (for obsidian?) such that few remained on hand for everyday use.

In contrast, perhaps the clamshell disk beads actually were on hand and were kept that way. Individuals may have taken great care to keep the white shell beads around and to preserve them during the upheavals of life on the colonial rancho, meaning that very few shell beads would have been tossed into the midden refuse or accidentally lost without an effort to recover them. On the other hand, the white glass beads might have been remarkably common, easy to acquire, and not a cherished possession. There might have been little effort on the part of wearers or users to retrieve any of these "dime-a-dozen" white beads that broke from their string and scattered on the ground or in the refuse zones of the site.

Nonetheless, it is clear that white glass beads may have been a preferred commodity on the rancho. Perhaps Vallejo purchased primarily white beads, with the archaeological pattern of Native use reflecting simple bead availability. It is difficult to find sufficient clues, but there is some evidence that this is not the case. Vallejo's own writings mention distributing multiple bead colors to

Native people on his arrival in Sonoma in 1835 (1875c:13). In an undated manuscript presumably referring to trading in Sonoma during the early 1850s, Vallejo's son Napoleón notes that Native people "also took *beads* of all kinds, sizes and colors" (n.d.a:2, emphasis in original). Even if Vallejo had purchased bead lots of specific colors, Native color preferences were likely taken into account. A similar "Native request" is also known for Colony Ross (Ross 1997:197–98). This likelihood strengthens the interpretation of bead types as a function of Native choice, however limited it may have been.

Conclusion

The material culture associated with Native American residents at Rancho Petaluma varies with respect to types, purposes, and meanings. Types range across a wide array of nineteenth-century artifacts and include chipped lithic tools, ground stones, and a net sinker; metal sewing items, nails, and silver flatware; glass bottles once filled with alcohol, condiments, or medicines; various imported ceramic wares; white clay pipes and baked-clay roof tiles; worked bone and shell items; and glass beads of numerous sizes and colors.

Artifact purposes are similarly diverse. Chipped stone tools and some worked glass served as cutting and scraping tools, while ground stone tools such as mortars and pestles were used for processing plant foods. Projectile points and bifaces point to a focus on formal tools and to the tipping of arrows. The lithic raw material, especially the obsidian, revealed an intriguing pattern of procurement and use in the nineteenth-century landscape with sources that were both local and distant and both previously known and newly used. Metal artifacts indicated a range of functions, from sewing and clothing accessories to nails and hardware, but they revealed an unexpected absence of knives, cleavers, hatchets, and other heavy-duty tools of the rancho world. The procurement of animal resources is hinted by the stone projectile points, rock net sinker, and ammunition, and these artifacts complement the numerous faunal remains discovered during excavation. Metal buckets and kettles, glass bottles, and ceramic bowls, plates, cups, and jars served as containers for daily food and beverage consumption and storage, and these were seemingly accompanied by the archaeologically ever elusive woven baskets, given the fire-cracked rock and documentary clues. Some glass bottles suggest the potential availability of alcohol among Native workers, but, as previously noted, they also served as a raw material for expedient tools. Perhaps Vallejo also offered the liquor commodity to California Indians in exchange for labor, a practice common in southern California (see Monroy 1990). Bodies were adorned with bone tubes, shell and glass beads, and manufactured clothing that had metal hasps and buckles. Native individuals would have acquired the clothing and glass bead artifacts from direct acquisition, provision payments, trade, and pilfering. The bone artifacts would have been made or traded for on their own.

These interpretations of artifact function and use are grounded in the empirical record, and they offer a textured picture of everyday life and activities on the rancho. I can begin to translate them further into larger issues of cultural identity and indigenous struggles within colonial worlds. On the whole, the artifacts indicate a complex mixture of "traditional" technologies such as chipped and ground stone tools and "introduced" material products such as glass beads, ceramics, and metal. It is not sufficient to talk about these artifact patterns as simple continuity of traditional lifestyles (stone tool production) or as acculturation (adoption of European goods), although a narrow focus on one or two material classes might lead to such a conclusion.

I find a reliance on either acculturation or traditionalism to be insufficient for handling the complex engagements of indigenous people with colonialism. Many Native American attempts to negotiate colonial worlds fell somewhere between these artificial poles, poles that have been circumvented here by an approach that delves into all realms of material culture. One might see both resistance and accommodation in these material culture inventories from Rancho Petaluma, but it seems more appropriate to understand the material items as reflecting complex choices for those residing in colonial circumstances (see Nassaney 1989 for an example in New England). The admixture of "traditional" and "introduced" hinges on the active choices of Native individuals at the rancho. They are not responses of cultural systems, they are not reflections of group adaptation to new circumstances, and they are not easily quantifiable into an index of acculturation. Instead, the artifacts are material clues to the daily practices of social agents, or individuals, making their way through a complex new colonial scene. Much like Pauketat (2001) has argued for the precontact and colonial American Southeast, Native individuals on the rancho were making tradition, not simply clinging to one and abandoning another. Their everyday choices were situated in the conflicted worlds of colonialism and indigenism, of survival and accommodation, and of drawing on the past and working for the future.

Chapter 6

Food and Politics on Colonial Ranchos

The Petaluma Case

The laboring or field Indians about the [New Helvetia] fort are fed upon the offal of slaughtered animals, and upon the bran sifted from the ground wheat.
—Edwin Bryant, *What I Saw in California*

Was beef such an attractive and easily obtainable food source that the Indian ranch hands readily adopted the cattle culture?
—Douglas Monroy, *Thrown among Strangers*

It has been rightly assumed that food can be understood with respect to nutrition and energy, but many archaeologists have argued that food is much more than that. Food is a focal point for how people control one another and how individuals struggle with identity, tradition, and the day-to-day politics of social life. Food marks a critical juncture between inequality, labor, and biological need. Because diet is an important component of daily life, it works in tandem with material practices, for example, as individuals construct and maintain identity (Lightfoot, Martinez, and Schiff 1998), as social agents manipulate the social order (McKee 1999), and as households manage state politics in their domestic space (Hastorf 1991). These types of relations are particularly conspicuous in colonial situations. For instance, food is a major point of interpretive contention among scholars of Spanish missions in California. Some claim that hunter-gatherers joined missions because of food abundance therein (Coombs and Plog 1977; Hornbeck 1989) or because of a food shortage in the native environment (Larson, Johnson, and Michaelson 1994), while others dispute the sufficiency of mission food in terms of abundance and quality and the assumption that hunter-gatherers needed to look for more stable sources of sustenance (Jackson and Castillo 1995:19–26).

Ranchos of nineteenth-century California are no exception. Much like on the New Helvetia rancho near Sacramento highlighted above, food structured aspects of Native life at many levels on Rancho Petaluma. Food production set seasonal schedules, and food distribution structured parts of daily life and movement on the rancho. Moreover, the availability of livestock and agricultural crops may have been a serious consideration for Native individuals deciding when or if to join or leave the rancho labor regime. Perhaps, as hinted in chapter 3, some California Indians opted to work the rancho during part of the summer months to take advantage of the abundant rancho foods, but it would be premature to claim that food was the driving force unless it can be shown that Native people were being driven from their traditional gathering and hunting grounds or showed an interest in abandoning these foodways. Food availability was only one part of a complex process of rancho participation, and despite the compelling evidence for some Native communities in the West actually adopting cattle ranching as a means for survival and for renegotiated identities (Iverson 1994), Monroy's musings about the "cattle culture" seem unwarranted and not attuned to the archaeological and indigenous realities of labor on the California rancho.

These facets point to a number of interesting historical and archaeological questions: What impact did food provisioning by the ranchero have on California Indian attempts to construct a daily menu on the rancho? Were the agricultural and meat products generated on the rancho sufficient for daily sustenance, or were workers expected to secure supplemental foodstuffs? What roles did indigenous foods and food preparation practices have in everyday life for Native workers on the rancho? How can we recognize rancho provisioning versus self-procurement when it comes to introduced crops and livestock?

In what follows, I address these critical issues to shed further light on the experiences of California Indian people engulfed in colonial ranchos. The data presented are specific to Rancho Petaluma, but the implications fan outward to other ranchos in the American West, the Spanish mission regimes across colonial North America, and other institutions like the plantations of the American South and Caribbean. In all of these cases, food occupied a central position in the struggle by the nonelite, nonliterate, indigenous, and enslaved for existence and residence in oppressive social and political worlds. Sorting out how and why individuals acquired, prepared, and consumed certain foods is a critical step in understanding the nature of this struggle.

To set about the task, this chapter discusses the plant and animal remains retrieved from Rancho Petaluma. Although I compare archaeological data to documentary sources, I hope to demonstrate archaeology's vital contribution to unraveling the details of Native daily life on the rancho. Of primary concern is the melding together of straightforward claims of dietary composition based on empirical data on animal and plant remains with theoretical concepts such as gender, identity, and labor. For the sake of time and space, I refer the interested reader to Silliman (2000a:263–328) for the finer details of analysis and identification of these zooarchaeological (faunal) and paleoethnobotanical (floral) data sets, turning here to the substantive results and interpretations.

Summary of Methods

Archaeologists confront the intersection of cultural practices and natural processes when analyzing past diets. Plant and animal remains, often termed *ecofacts*, never reveal everything about subsistence pursuits, much the way that artifacts provide only partial views of material activities. Typical zooarchaeological findings are bones, teeth, claws, and antlers; rarely do archaeologists recover hair or soft tissue because these decompose rapidly in most environments. Frequently, bones can be assigned to a particular animal species or genus, but at other times, the bone is identifiable only to the taxonomic family or order. Common archaeobotanical remains include seeds, starchy segments, woody parts, pollen, and silicate bodies known as phytoliths. With the exception of pollen and phytoliths that are more resistant to decay, most plant remains preserve in archaeological sites only when they have been partially or completely charred or when they have been deposited in very arid or anaerobic environments. Despite preservation biases, ecofacts offer remarkable information about plant and animal use, but what they reveal also depends on the context in which archaeologists recover them. The remains may be evidence of food procurement, processing, consumption, disposal, and any combination thereof, or they might not have been about food at all. Instead, plant and animal remains can indicate past use as fuel, medicine, ritual items, or the source of raw material for manufacturing objects.

A number of techniques and quantification methods can be used to analyze ecofactual data, meaning that archaeological plant and animal remains can be understood only in the context of a particular research methodology. Methodologies determine how data are counted and compared, what proportion or sample of the collection should be studied, and what attributes are necessary to record for each data point, whether bone or seed. The Rancho Petaluma methodology involved a series of research choices and the generous assistance of archaeobotanical and zooarchaeological specialists. For the study of the animal remains, the assemblage was not sampled, meaning that there was no preselection of faunal remains from certain site areas or levels and that every identifiable bone was analyzed. Other than shellfish, all faunal specimens that appeared to be identifiable were selected during laboratory processing and then subsequently identified by specialists at the University of California, Los Angeles, and Sonoma State University. In contrast, the shellfish have undergone only preliminary analysis thus far. Identified faunal remains totaled more than seventy-six hundred bones and bone fragments, but over seventy-two thousand unidentifiable fragments and scrap pieces remained. Bones were identified to genus and species whenever possible, but those fragments lacking discrete identifiable features were sorted into broad size categories by class. Mammal size categories include large, medium, and small, which translate into deer or larger, jackrabbit up to deer size, and smaller than jackrabbit, respectively. For birds, large represents goose size or greater; medium, ducks to jays; and small, robin or tinier.

Counting bones may be somewhat straightforward, but turning these counts into the numbers of actual animals or body parts requires additional steps and assumptions. I followed standard quantification methods of number of identified specimens (NISP) and minimum number of individuals (MNI) to organize the faunal data (see Grayson 1984; Klein and Cruz-Uribe 1984; Lyman 1994; Reitz and Wing 1999; Ringrose 1993). Both are estimates of the number of parts or animals, depending on the technique, that can account for all the bones recovered. To calculate NISP or the number of individual bones present for any given taxon, I summed all identified complete and fragmented bones. Only in cases of known postexposure, postexcavation fragmentation were NISP counts reduced to reflect field observations. I calculated MNI using the most conservative method available: maximum number of specimens of any given element (or element end) per side. This measure determines the minimum number of animals in each taxon required to have produced the available skeletal remains. I did not attempt to pair elements to increase the accuracy of the MNI count, but I did use age to discriminate elements from opposite sides. At best, MNI is a minimum and NISP a maximum estimate of taxonomic abundance in an archaeological assemblage (Klein and Cruz-Uribe 1984:30). The real number of actual animals falls between these two values, with its numerical position dependent on past butchery and consumption practices, the spatial nature of deposits, and preservation conditions. I tabulated MNI by site locus to be consistent with other data classes, despite the chance that the same animal may have had elements represented in these different loci due to butchering or sharing practices.

With the plant remains, the methodological issues differed. During fieldwork, I collected numerous 5-liter soil samples from a variety of feature and nonfeature contexts to be processed through a flotation system to aid in the retrieval of light organic remains. For this discussion, I focus on eighteen samples: (1) six standardized samples taken from the center of the Midden Trench at different arbitrary 10-centimeter levels, beginning at 20 centimeters below the surface; (2) one sample taken from the Midden Trench's Feature A; (3) four samples from Trench 1, including one in Feature B, one in Feature C, and two in Feature D; (4) five samples from the Block comprised of three in Feature E and two in Feature F; and (5) two nonfeature sediment samples taken from the Block. To obtain botanical materials, I processed 3.5 liters of each soil sample through a mechanized flotation system, which was a modified version of the standard Shell Mound Archaeological Project (SMAP) system (Pearsall 1989:52–61). Only one sample from Feature F in the Block could not be floated at this volume, resulting in a 2-liter sample. All plant remains were identified by specialists at the Paleoethnobotany Laboratory at the University of California, Los Angeles. Wood charcoal dominates the flotation samples and indicates significant burning of wood at the site, but I focus exclusively here on the seed, nut, and other plant remains.

To quantify the archaeobotanical results, I use raw counts, percentage ratios, and ubiquity measures (see Popper 1988). I focus primarily on ubiquity, defined as the percentage of samples, or proveniences, with a particular taxon present. To ascertain the ubiquity of a particular plant requires an assessment of independent contexts. For this assemblage, I considered only the six individual features and the aggregated midden lot samples to be independent contexts, bringing the total contexts to seven. To consider the samples from the midden levels as independent would be dangerous, given the predetermined size of the excavation levels and the extent of bioturbation.

Beef: Not the Only Thing for Dinner

Several noteworthy patterns can be extracted from the zooarchaeological data (table 6.1). This data table is an abbreviated version of extensive data tables

Table 6.1
Summary faunal taxonomic list.

			NISP			
Taxon	Midden[a]	Block	Trench 1	Trench 2	Trench 3	Total
Birds[b]						
Medium, large						
(ducks, geese, chicken, raptor)	99	19	6	0	0	124
Small	6	2	0	0	0	138
Unknown	85	24	20	1	0	138
Fish[b]	26	107	7	0	0	140
Large mammals						
Cattle (*Bos taurus*)	267	1,021	171	13	3	1,475
Sheep (*Ovis aries, Capra/Ovis*)	12	18	10	2	2	44
Deer (*Odocoileus hemionus*)	42	42	23	6	0	113
Artiodactyla	37	46	17	6	4	110
Indeterminate	148	429	413	145	7	1,142
Medium mammals						
Rabbits (*Sylvilagus* sp., *Lepus* sp.)	5	1	1	0	7	14
Carnivora	1	0	0	0	0	1
Dog/coyote (*Canis* sp.)	2	2	0	0	0	4
Skunk (*Mephitis mephitis*)	0	1	0	0	0	1
Raccoon (*Procyon lotor*)	0	3	1	0	0	4
Sea otter (*Enhydra lutris*)	0	1	0	0	0	1
Bobcat (*Lynx rufus*)	0	1	0	0	0	1
Seal/sea lion (Pinnipedia)	0	0	1	0	0	1
Indeterminate	6	19	0	1	1	27
Small mammals						
Rodents, insectivores[b]	33	56	41	7	2	139
Woodrats (*Neotoma* sp.)	1	0	0	0	0	1
Mammalia, general	114	170	40	4	1	329
Reptilia/amphibia						
Serpentes	0	1	0	0	0	1
Amphibia, general	1	1	0	0	0	2
Vertebrata	11	12	1	0	0	24
Total	1,449	3,467	785	253	26	4,838

[a] Includes only the Midden Trench sample and not the Stream Trench.
[b] See text for particular species classified here.

divided by site loci available in Silliman (2000a). No faunal remains have yet been identified from the Stream Trench, but these specimens would do little to refine site patterns, since the remains were highly fragmented and few in number (Silliman 2002:47).

Cattle (*Bos taurus*) dominate the faunal collection.[1] Cattle bones are at least thirteen times more numerous than deer and over thirty-three times more numerous than sheep or goat. Cattle also outnumber deer and sheep or goat in the category of MNI counts across the site, but some areas, such as the midden, have equal numbers of minimum individuals in categories of both cattle and deer. I suspect that these numbers actually underestimate the enormous amount of beef consumed at the site, since much of the beef was stripped and dried as *tasajo*. These strips would have been prepared by Native laborers, stored, and easily provisioned by Vallejo to rancho workers. Archaeologists have documented a similar focus on cattle in Native deposits at other California colonial sites: Mission Santa Cruz (Allen 1998:56–58), Mission San Antonio (Langenwalter and McKee 1985), and Mission San Juan Bautista (Farris 1991). A predominance of cattle is also true for Californio deposits at nineteenth-century southern California ranchos (Gust 1982, 1987). Only in the Native residential area at nearby Russian Colony Ross are cattle and sheep subordinate to deer (Wake 1997b).

Given Rancho Petaluma's focus on raising cattle and butchering them for hides, tallow, and meat, the abundance of cattle is not unexpected.[2] The question is whether the cattle remains indicate Native acquisition of beef and secondary products such as leather for household consumption or whether they reflect required rancho butchery tasks such as a matanza that took place near Native residential quarters. The evidence points solidly to household consumption with near- or on-site butchery rather than large-scale processing for the hide and tallow trade. The strongest evidence that these cattle remains represent Native domestic and subsistence practices is their association with other consumed faunal species such as deer, fish, and birds and with residential material culture such as ground stones, lithics, ceramics, glass, and metal. This type of mass slaughter was unlikely to have occurred on top of a Native American living area or away from the corrals constructed on the promontory next to the Petaluma Adobe. Additional evidence that the deposits do not reflect a matanza event includes the lack of numerous articulated elements, no complete carcasses, and many more artifacts and ecofactual remains than would be found in the primary deposit of a mass cattle slaughter (see Gust 1982:120). In fact, fewer groups of still-articulated bones occur in the Petaluma assemblage than in the Ontiveros Adobe collection, where Gust has argued strongly against interpreting it as a matanza event (1982:table 16).

Element distribution suggests that individuals butchered at least eleven but probably many more cattle carcasses on-site rather than brought back only particular cuts of meat, tasajo strips aside, obtained elsewhere.[3] All skeletal segments—cranial, vertebral, forelimb, forefoot, ribs, pelvic girdle, hind limb, hind foot—are represented, except for horn cores, which are absent from the sample (Silliman 2000a:269–77). The relatively equal representation of skeletal elements suggests, in part, that Native individuals exhibited no preference for beef cuts, choosing low-meat parts such as feet and toes as often as meaty ribs. This may not be surprising if the majority of beef entered Native meals as dried strips already removed from the bones. Alternatively, the equal representation of body parts may indicate sporadic availability of meaty cuts during provisioning and the need for individuals to fill dietary gaps with less meaty elements. Simpson documented Native consumption of potentially poor cuts of beef on his 1841 visit to one of Vallejo's worker camps when he commented that Native people ate "the worst bullock's worst joints" (1847:77).

Yet the data suggest that entire cattle carcasses were processed and dumped in the site deposits, with no bias toward less meaty elements. The recovery of articulated lower limb and foot elements in the Block and Trench 1 excavations indicate the discard of still-fleshed lower leg segments without subsequent butchery and consumption.[4] At least during the particular butchery and depositional episodes represented in these areas of the site, Native workers did not need or seek to extract meat from every skeletal part. Lower limbs were discarded with other residential debris. Perhaps this meat "waste" occurred during an off-site matanza, when cattle were slaughtered in vast numbers for hides and tallow and meat was plentiful, but it is unlikely that individuals would drag back entire carcasses instead of select portions from such an event.

No specific age determinations were attempted on the remains, but general patterns suggest a dietary focus on young cattle. The high proportion (83.3 percent) of juvenile elements among femora, humeri, radii, tibiae, and ulnae with age determinations (thirty) may point to the rancho practice of killing young steers, or novillos (Davis 1929:138). Beef would have been available in enormous quantities during these times, since thousands of cattle were dispatched, and there is little evidence other than Simpson's observation that Vallejo or his ranch overseer prohibited Native access to the meat once Vallejo had acquired all that his operation and family required. As previously noted, rancheros had cattle butchered primarily for secondary products of hides and tallow, not meat, despite the prominent role of the latter in ranchero and worker diets.

Although site residents discarded some skeletal elements without subsequent processing, other cattle remains show evidence of butchery. Butchery evidence does not occur in high proportions due, in part, to the fragile surfaces of the 150-year-old bones in this soil environment. Intact butchery marks were found on a variety of skeletal parts, ranging from several ribs and long bones to carpals, phalanges, and mandibles. Native people worked over these elements for either meat or hide removal. The cut marks suggest the predominant use of metal knives for cutting and filleting, some use of stone tools for cutting, and the probable use of metal cleavers for chops at bone ends. In addition, several shafts and articular ends show signs of smashing for possible marrow extraction.

Deer (*Odocoileus hemionus*) and sheep or goat (*Capra/Ovis* sp.) remains round out the large mammal aspect of the collection, and in noticeable quantities. Compared to cattle, the deer and sheep reveal different aspects of subsistence at the rancho. Historical records note the presence of sheep in Petaluma (Bancroft 1885:720; Boggs 1913; Davis 1929:31), but there is no current evidence for goats, hinting that the *Capra/Ovis* specimens probably are domestic sheep. Sheep, especially those imported by Vallejo, served primarily as a source of wool rather than meat (McKittrick 1944:174); therefore, their presence is intriguing, especially given the butchered limbs and burned limbs and tarsals. Native individuals obviously consumed mutton in their daily meals, although its low relative number suggests that it may not have fed them as consistently or as abundantly as beef. Compared to cattle, sheep elements of humerus, radius, femur, tibia, innominate, and carpal occur in higher proportion than other elements, but, unlike cattle, so do phalanges. The pattern of disproportionate elements suggests that less than entire sheep carcasses may have been present or that certain cuts of meat were provided or desired. Since 86–92 percent of the eighteen sheep bones aged in the sample are adult, most of the sheep had reached or perhaps surpassed good wool-producing ages before being butchered.

To complement the meat provided by domestic cattle and sheep, Native Americans continued to hunt deer. Deer hides may have been valued commodities at the rancho (Alvarado 1845; Boggs 1913; Vallejo 1875c:252), but their main use would have been as food. Deer would have resided in the general Petaluma area in high numbers, and Native hunters used either stone-tipped projectiles, firearms, or nets to dispatch them, as evidenced by the obsidian points and gun accessories found in the excavations. Bones of black-tailed deer occur in association with cattle and sheep bones in all loci but Trench 3. Burning is present on 20–25 percent of deer bones regardless of locus, which exceeds the proportions for all other taxa except for high proportions of burned sheep bone in Trench 1. The pattern reflects different, perhaps higher intensity, cooking or disposal practices for deer. Butchery marks on deer are present but in low proportions, and one articulation unit of metatarsal, cuneiform, and naviculocuboid was recovered in the Block. As with the cattle, this remnant foot indicates that individuals discarded potentially less savory meat parts. Despite the numerous postcranial bones, skeletal elements from the head were underrepresented. Numerous teeth were recovered, but the remainder included only two mandibles and not a single antler.

Birds were also important constituents of Native worker diets, although their densities in the archaeological record diminish rapidly outside of the Midden Trench, Block, and Trench 1. Birds are the second most abundant group of animals at the site next to artiodactyls (even-toed ungulates such as cattle and deer), and they denote different food procurement practices in the rancho setting, despite their proportionately smaller meat contribution. Other than the single domestic chicken (*Gallus gallus*) bone in the Midden Trench, the vast majority of identified bird remains reflect the hunting and trapping of wild avifauna. The species representation indicates a strong focus on marsh, bay, estuarine, and coastal settings, and many of these contexts occurred on the large Rancho Petaluma along Adobe Creek, Petaluma River, and Sonoma Creek southward into San Pablo Bay. The waterfowl species include a variety of ducks such as widgeon (*Anas americana*), gadwall (*A. strepera*), mallard (*A. platyrhynchos*), scaup, redhead, canvasback (*Aythya* spp.), and those unidentifiable below the *Anas* genus as well as Canada goose (*Branta canadensis*), white-fronted goose (*Anser albifrons*), and snow goose (*Chen caerulescens*). Ducks and geese would have been available almost year-round but in their highest abundance from September to April (Bolander and Parmeter 1978), and they would have been captured with nets, decoys, or perhaps rifles with bird shot. Bones classified only as medium or large Aves probably also represent these taxonomic groups. It is of particular significance that no shorebirds are present, suggesting that waterfowl may have been hunted and trapped in the immediate riverine settings rather than at San Pablo Bay proper or that Native groups had no interest in them. American robin (*Turdus migratorius*) and songbirds (Passeriformes) elements are also present, but only as three specimens. In addition, the Midden Trench contained a single accipiter (raptor) second phalanx, but it is unclear what significance this toe bone holds.

The procurement of wild avifauna is not novel for a rancho setting, given the presence of ducks and geese in the faunal assemblage of the Ontiveros Adobe (Gust 1982:141) and the Aros-Serrano Adobe (Gust 1987) in southern California. However, when coupled with the other evidence at the site for predominantly Native American habitation, the bird remains reveal decidedly Native practices at Rancho Petaluma. Wild birds served to fill out the nineteenth-century Native menu on the rancho, much as they did for Native residents at Colony Ross (Simons 1997) and Mission San Antonio (Langenwalter and McKee 1985), but some species may have been chosen for their material value. Duck feathers were prized by some Pomo-speaking groups (Gifford 1967:18; Loeb 1926:156), and raptors seem to have been used solely for feathers or whistles in ethnographic contexts in the greater North Bay (Barrett 1952:102; Gifford 1967:18–19; Loeb 1926:167). White duck feathers were important for Coast Miwok basketry (Kelly 1978:418) and for ornamentation in the hair of Chief Solano (N. Vallejo 1890:7) and other Suisun warriors during battle (Sanchez 1930). If Native women (and men) continued to make baskets at the rancho, then feathers would have been critical materials, but the absence of skeletal elements from woodpecker and quail, the primary source of basket feathers, does little to evidence basket decoration.

Much like birds, fish occupied an important place in the menu for Native people, and the identifiable fish species also reflect a predominantly stream, estuary, and bay focus. Based on NISP, the Native fishery at Rancho Petaluma focused primarily on minnows (Cyprinidae, Cypriniformes) such as Sacramento blackfish (*Orothodon microlepidotus*) and pikeminnow (*Ptychocheilus grandis*). Other fishes include suckers (*Catostomus occidentalis*), herrings (Clupeidae), topsmelt or jacksmelt (Atherinidae), and surfperch (Embiotocidae). Cyprinid minnows are primarily freshwater species, although Sacramento blackfish and pikeminnow can inhabit slightly saline waters; the same is true for suckers. Herring and jacksmelt or topsmelt are coastal marine and estuarine families that can be found in Tomales Bay and San Pablo Bay, especially during spawning season (Miller and Lea 1976; Moyle 1976), but differentiating species within these two families usually does little to refine interpretation of Native American fishing practices (Gobalet 1997:320). Although herring may indicate some ocean capture, the surfperch (Embiotocidae) elements point more strongly to this possibility; however, it is possible that the surfperch remains are from the single freshwater species (tule perch, *Hysterocarpus traski*) or from one that often frequents the calm bay waters of San Pablo Bay. Additional species likely captured in fresh water include sturgeon (*Acipenser* sp.) and salmon (*Oncorhyncus* sp.), although they are represented by only three dermal ossicles and one vertebra, respectively. The primary method of capture for all of these fishes would have been lines, weirs, or nets, some deployed from balsa rafts. Evidence for processing or cooking is minimal on the fish elements. The majority of remains are vertebrae, and the only burned element is a minnow vertebra.

Medium-size mammals of both terrestrial and marine origins made a small but noticeable contribution to the activities of Native people on the rancho. The main representatives are raccoon (*Procyon lotor*) and canids (*Canis* spp.), but single elements of bobcat (*Lynx rufus*), skunk (*Mephitis mephitis*), seal or sea lion (Pinnipedia), and sea otter (*Enhydra lutris*) are also present. The canids and bobcat could represent a minor food resource (Loeb 1926:170) or a source of clothing material (Gifford 1967:17; Loeb 1926:154). In spite of their rarity in the assemblage, the single pinniped and sea otter elements demonstrate a link to the coast. It is unclear whether these sea mammals were traded to indigenous groups at Rancho Petaluma from coastal villages or whether some Native individuals at the rancho made forays to the coast for hunting, fishing, and gathering shellfish. The latter suite of activities is suggested by many of the shellfish remains as well as the bones of surfperch, if actually belonging to coastal varieties. Compared to the numbers of large mammals, birds, and fish, these medium-size mammal species did not contribute significantly to the Native diet. In fact, some of the elements may have been prized for nonfood reasons. According to Maria Copa, the Coast Miwok in the Point Reyes area to the west used raccoon bones in poisons (Collier and Thalman 1996:362).

Small mammals, primarily rodents, occur in notable numbers at the site and indicate a diversity of subsistence pursuits for rancho residents. Rabbits seem to have been a part of the nineteenth-century rancho diet, but they occur in small numbers overall (an NISP of eight). These animals, primarily black-tailed jackrabbit (*Lepus californicus*) but also Audobon's cottontail (*Sylvilagus audobonii*), represent local species that inhabited the general area around the Petaluma Adobe, and they could have been easily obtained. Like bird taxa, the rabbit elements may point to consumption as well as to the use of skins for blankets and clothing (see Gifford 1967:17; Loeb 1926:170–71).

Many of the small mammals (especially mouse, vole, and mole species) seem to be intrusive, given their condition and the prevalence of rodent burrows at the site, but the single burned gopher (*Thomomys* sp.) pelvic bone suggests that small mammal utilization can be recognized in the assemblage. It was common for northern California Native groups to consume gophers, ground squirrels, woodrats, and other small mammals (Gifford 1967:17; Loeb 1926:170), but the frequent practice of crushing the bodies with rocks before consuming them might weigh against good bone recovery. The burned gopher bone provides a provocative possibility. The single woodrat (*Neotoma* sp.) bone may also denote a food resource, since woodrats probably did not live in the immediate vicinity of the Petaluma Adobe and would have been transported to the site, potentially from nearby hills, by humans.

The presence of certain faunal species makes even more sense when compared to those species that are absent. One must be careful not to overinterpret absences in the archaeological record, since many factors, including sheer chance, could account for the pattern. However, certain circumstances give patterned absences some interpretive value. The faunal data here offer such an opportunity, since two species are conspicuously absent: pig (*Sus scrofa*) and horse (*Equus caballus*). Although the unit that we never excavated may have contained both of these taxa, it is worth considering their absence from the current sample.

One of the most conspicuous absences is pig. Excavations beneath the floor of several Petaluma Adobe rooms had revealed pig remains, but these bones were found in stratigraphic layers that appeared to postdate the initial construction and use of the adobe (Silliman 1999:119). Yet pigs may have been kept on the rancho during the 1830s or 1840s, according to Salvador Vallejo's claim that his brother maintained a small drift of hogs (United States District Court 1852:14). Elsewhere, pig remains occur in small quantities in nineteenth-century colonial sites in the West such as the Russian colony of Ross (Wake 1997b), Mission San Juan Bautista (Farris 1991:39), the Ontiveros Adobe (Gust 1982:138), and the Aros-Serrano Adobe (Gust 1987). Only the latter two contexts are associated with Californio rather than Native families. The absence of pig in the Petaluma faunal assemblage may be a function of sample size, or it may indicate their unavailability or undesirability to Native workers, at least those residing in the investigated area.

Horse bones were also not recovered, but this does not in any way reflect their absence from the rancho. On the contrary, horses were plentiful at

Table 6.2

Identified plant taxa and distributions.

Scientific Name	Common Name	Total	Burned	Site Locus[a]
Amaranthus sp.	amaranth	1	1	BL
Arctostaphylos sp.	manzanita	4	4	MT,T1
Asteraceae	sunflower family	4	4	BL
Brassicaceae	mustard family	1	1	T1
Calandrinia sp.	redmaid	270	0	MT, T1, BL
Caryophyllaceae	pink family (silene?)	2	2	BL, T1
Cereal, cultivated		31[b]	31	T1, BL
Cheno-ams	goosefoot/amaranth	15	14	BL, MT
Chenopodium sp.	goosefoot	28	20	MT, T1, BL
Deschampsia sp.	hairgrass	1	1	MT
Erodium sp.	filaree	72[c,d]	72	MT, BL, T1
Fabaceae	legume family	3	3	MT, T1
Festuca sp.	fescue	1	1	MT
Hordeum sp.	wild barley	8	7	Bl, MT, T1
Hordeum vulgaris	cultivated barley	14	14	MT, T1
Juncus sp.	rush	2	1	MT, BL
Madia sp.	tarweed	5	5	T1, MT
Malvaceae	mallow family	265	222	MT, BL, T1
Medicago sp.	alfalfa, California bur-clover	6	5	MT
Melilotus/Trifolium sp.	sweet clover	7	7	MT, BL, T1
Phacelia sp.		1	1	MT
Phalaris sp.	canary grass	5	5	MT, BL
Poaceae #1	grass family	756[e]	756	BL, MT
Poaceae, small	grass family	54	53	MT, T1, BL
Poaceae, large	grass family	15	13	MT, T1, BL
Poaceae, fragments	grass family	33	33	MT, BL
Poaceae (embryo, floret/rachis)	grass family	36	36	MD, T1
Polygonaceae	knotweed	2	2	MT, BL
Quercus sp. (nutshell)	oak	60	60	MT, BL, T1
Ranunculus sp.	buttercup	1	1	BL
Rhus integrifolia	lemonadeberry	1	0	BL
Rumex sp.	dock	11	9	MT
Salvia sp.	sage	10	0	BL, T1
Scirpus sp.	bulrush	2	1	MT, BL
Triticum sp.	wheat	79[f]	77	MT, T1, BL
Umbellularia californica (nutshell)	California laurel	63	63	MT, BL, T1
Zea mays (kernel)	maize	8	8	MT
Zea mays (cupule)	maize	2	1	MT

Table 6.2 *cont.*

Scientific Name	Common Name	Total	Burned	Site Locus[a]
Amorphous	starches	41	41	MT, T1
Anther		3	3	MT
Nutshell		32	32	MT, BL, T1
Unidentifiable plant parts		27	27	MT, BL, T1
Unidentifiable seeds		250	250	MT, BL

[a] Ordered from highest to lowest quantity. MT, Midden Trench; BL, Block; T1, Trench 1. No flotation samples taken in Trench 2, Trench 3, or Stream Trench.
[b] 23/26 (88.5 percent) in Trench 1 from Feature B.
[c] 19/20 (95 percent) in Block from Feature E.
[d] 15/19 (78.9 percent) in Trench 1 from Feature D.
[e] 688/689 (99.9 percent) in Block from Feature E.
[f] 23/24 (95.8 percent) in Trench 1 from Feature B.

Rancho Petaluma as the focal point of vaquero life and livestock herding. Vallejo owned four to five hundred horses around 1836 (United States District Court 1852:12), increased these to three to six thousand in the late 1830s (Davis 1929:31; United States District Court 1852:14), and may have retained two to three thousand in 1846 (Boggs 1913). Horses were highly valued on all Mexican-Californian ranchos, and the killing and consumption of them by Native workers would not have been tolerated. Native groups throughout California often expressed their resistance to colonial intrusion by stealing horses for both transportation and consumption (Davis 1929:63; Monroy 1990:130; Osio 1996:134), but such acts of resistance appeared not to take place on the grounds around the Petaluma Adobe, at least not in the areas excavated for this project. An unbutchered juvenile horse tibia was found on the original construction surface beneath the Petaluma Adobe dating to 1834–36 (Silliman 1999:76), but because it was deposited during supervised building episodes of the Petaluma Adobe, the bone may reflect the convenient disposal of a recently deceased horse. Equid bones were also found dumped in a ranchero trash feature at the Ontiveros Adobe in southern California (Gust 1982:138).

Lastly, a brief comment should be made about the enormous quantities of unidentified bone scrap (more than seventy-two thousand) found at the site.

Without belaboring a list of weights, densities, and counts, I provide a brief example. The Midden Trench alone had over 42,000 individual pieces counted in the laboratory with a density of 13,241 bone fragments per cubic meter and a weight of almost 8 kilograms. Although the Midden Trench far surpassed other areas in producing highly fragmented bone, fragments reached a total weight of 13.9 kilograms across all site loci, excluding the unweighed specimens from the Stream Trench (Silliman 2000a:table 7.12). These patterns, particularly those in the Midden Trench, are significant. They indicate that animals were heavily processed (skeletal elements were crushed intentionally for other reasons, perhaps boiling them for fat), that the bone refuse underwent notable trampling or damage between butchery and final deposition, or that the preservation conditions caused in-the-ground bone breakage prior to excavation. The presence of largely intact and often fragile skeletal elements across most areas of the site suggests that this fragmentation primarily occurred while they were being used and deposited rather than after being buried, compacted, and burrowed. The fact that the highest fragmentation and density occur in the midden is not surprising, since this area would have received refuse after it had been through a variety of cultural uses and modifications.

Seeds, Grains, Nuts, and Greens: The Plant Diet

When interpreting paleoethnobotanical data, it is imperative to recognize that archaeobotanical remains may represent several aspects of production, processing, and consumption (Hastorf 1988; Pearsall 1989:224–31) and various depositional contexts (Miksicek 1987). The Rancho Petaluma excavations did not recover any floor surfaces, which precludes a straightforward assessment of processing or consumption debris. Instead, all archaeobotanical samples come from layers within a dense sheet midden or from individual features. This reality complicates the deciphering of consumption debris, plants burned in general refuse, or the use of floral products as fuel. Site locus variation at Rancho Petaluma seems to denote differences in activity and refuse disposal rather than differences in as-of-yet-undetected "household" consumption practices. The represented plant species are diverse (table 6.2).[5]

Wheat (*Triticum* sp.), barley (*Hordeum vulgaris*), and corn (*Zea mays*) were used by Native cooks in the preparation of meals. By far, wheat was the most abundant and widespread cultigen, dominating other domesticated plants in all flotation samples. Currently, it is unclear what wheat varieties are present, but Vallejo had both common wheat and beardless wheat planted at the rancho (Alvarado 1849), and other rancho deposits in southern California have revealed club wheat (*Triticum aestivum compactum*) (Honeysett 1982). Barley was more sporadic in the Petaluma samples, occurring in the general midden, Feature A in the Midden Trench, and Feature B in Trench 1. Corn occurs only in the Midden Trench, where it is associated primarily with Feature A, which suggests that its low ubiquity may be a function of the larger sample of floral materials from that excavation area that permits detection of this rare taxon. However, it is more likely that the midden represents generalized dumping of everyday household cooking and consumption refuse, while the features in Trench 1 and the Block reflect specific dumping and processing activities. For instance, Feature B contained a dense collection of cultigens but not corn. A related explanation is that corn may have been ground into meal elsewhere and brought into Native households in that form, whereas wheat may have been obtained as whole grains.

At minimum, these three cultigens reflect the active incorporation of rancho agricultural crops into Native diets. The predominance of wheat parallels that seen in Native American deposits well to the south at Mission Santa Cruz (Allen 1998:46–47) and perhaps Mission San Juan Bautista (Farris 1991:40), and the ubiquity of wheat mirrors the significance of the crop in production on this particular rancho (Alvarado 1849; Davis 1929:136; Vallejo 1941:2). Although one might speculate that Native families tended small garden plots with wheat plants, these are usually grown as field rather than garden crops. There is also currently no evidence that Native people at Rancho Petaluma, many of whom had practiced a hunting-and-gathering lifestyle prior to joining the rancho, developed or were even permitted garden areas. It is more likely that Vallejo and Alvarado distributed wheat and perhaps barley and corn as part of the laboring agreement (Davis 1929:136). Provisioning of plant foods may have been only partly supervised, given that Alvarado (1839) could not account for 135 *fanegas* (8,084 kilograms) of wheat after he had provided large portions to the *Limantour* schooner and various individuals in the winter of 1839. In California wheat and barley generally were used to make the soupy grain dish known as atole, and it is believed to have been a staple food offered to Native workers in Petaluma in prepared form (Hoopes 1965:36). Well after the rancho period, in the 1930s, Maria Copa remembered mixing wheat, corn, and other plants together with pinole, or native seeds parched and ground into flour (Collier and Thalman 1996:146).

Since wheat, barley, and corn were toasted before being ground into atole or pinole flour, the likelihood of charring and thus archaeological recovery is high.

Despite a strong focus on cultigens, Native individuals made active efforts to use indigenous tree and shrub species in their subsistence practices. Oak (*Quercus* sp.) as acorns, bay (*Umbellularia californica*) as nuts, and manzanita (*Arctostaphylos* sp.) as berries were staple tree or shrub crops for the precontact and ethnographic Native American societies surrounding San Francisco Bay, and botanical evidence discovered at Rancho Petaluma confirms their continued use in the colonial period. Acorns and bay nuts dominate the Petaluma samples with high ubiquity, but the chaparral species, manzanita, occurs intermittently as berry pits in the Midden Trench and in Feature D (Trench 1). These wild food taxa are densest in the midden, again suggesting that this locus served as a major location for dumping household food preparation and consumption debris. Since acorn hulls and manzanita berry pits are not subjected to fire during preparation or consumption, their presence as charred remains indicates that they were probably burned in general refuse or accidentally dropped into open flames.

Intermixed with the cultigens and wild tree and shrub resources is a variety of native and introduced grasses and related taxa. Many of the species such as goosefoot (*Chenopodium* sp.), wild barley (*Hordeum* sp.), tarweed (*Madia* sp.), buttercup (*Ranunculus* sp.), and dock (*Rumex* sp.) are probably food remains, given their widespread occurrence in precontact sites in northern California (see Wohlgemuth 1996:table 5), in Native-associated deposits at Mission Santa Cruz near Monterey Bay (Allen 1998:43–47), and in ethnographic accounts of the Coast Miwok in the Point Reyes area (Collier and Thalman 1996).[6] Some species such as goosefoot might have been used in poultices (Bocek 1984:249) or as seeds in food dishes (Collier and Thalman 1996:43).

At a general level, the Poaceae grass specimens probably reflect the invasion of the Petaluma landscape by several European grasses. Precise identifications are not possible, but the tentative assignments offered by Meyer (2000) indicate that many of the smaller caryopses are not likely to be from indigenous taxa but rather from *Poa annua*, an introduced variety. The specimens identified only to the general Poaceae family may have been edible grass seeds, although the high numbers in some contexts (such as Feature E) might suggest that they were used for fuel. However, given the high quantities of wood charcoal that filled the burned pit features (Features A, B, C), lined the base of Feature D, comprised Features E and F, and occupied all of the Midden Trench, it seems likely that wood rather than grass was the primary fuel source. Yet Maria Copa during her interviews with Isabel Kelly stated that hot rocks and grass were necessary for any earth oven cooking (Collier and Thalman 1996:149). The tentative evidence for such cooking features at the site makes this an attractive explanation. At the same time, since seeds are parched and roasted (see references in Mead 1972) before being ground to form pinole, their incorporation into burned features is not surprising. These may have been accidental losses or burning of unprocessed seeds and other plant parts after disposal.[7]

Some plant species recovered in the Rancho Petaluma excavations are not clearly cultural in origin or dietary in purpose. The lack of charred redmaids (*Calandrinia* sp.) in the deposit is striking, given the presence of this floral resource in precontact sites in the region (see Wohlgemuth 1994:3, 1996) and the abundance of unburned redmaid seeds at the site. According to Maria Copa, its flowers were also used as a rouge for make-up among Native women (Collier and Thalman 1996:39). I have to interpret the numerous uncharred redmaid seeds in the Petaluma collection as modern intrusions through rodent activity, but site residents may have used some of the seeds in the nineteenth century.

The abundant charred mallow (Malvaceae) seeds are more enigmatic. Its use as food is uncertain, as is its status as native or introduced, but some indigenous groups in northern California are reported to have used one species, *Malva parviflora*, as a medicinal plant (Bocek 1984:250; Mead 1972:129–30). Some mallows such as *Sidalcea* were also reputed by Maria Copa to be good ingredients for pinole (Collier and Thalman 1996:121). Whether or not these mallows were food or just accidental incorporations in the cooking process or refuse debris is currently indeterminate. Interestingly, the Malvaceae taxon has also been recovered from Native neophyte deposits at Mission Santa Cruz (Allen 1998:table 5.2) as well as in sheep feces and other deposits at the Ontiveros Adobe (Honeysett 1982). Similar discoveries of mallow have occurred in a colonial household and midden at El Presidio de San Francisco, but the function of these plants, as potential food or medicine, remains elusive (Voss 2002:476–77, 551).

The charred sweet clover (*Melilotus* or *Trifolium* sp.) seeds, although perhaps introduced taxa, may reveal the use of clover in the Native diet. Maria Copa and Tom Smith of the Coast Miwok were clear with regard to the importance of this food resource (Collier and Thalman 1996:120–21; see also Johnson 1978:255 for Patwin).

Filaree (*Erodium* sp.) seeds are a large component of the Petaluma floral samples, and they are likely to be one or more introduced varieties. Although two species of filaree are native to California's natural landscape, they are restricted to southern California (see West 1989:341 for references). The abundance and high ubiquity of filaree at Petaluma strongly suggest the establishment of European plants in the northern California landscape by the 1830s and 1840s. Few would deny that this broad weedy intrusion probably occurred much earlier (Hendry 1931; West 1989), and the invasion resulted in severe, if sometimes regionalized, disruptions in native vegetation and fauna. Yet filaree leaves and seeds have been reported ethnographically (Mead 1972:89) and archaeologically (Heizer and Hester 1973) as a food resource in some areas of Native California. In addition, red-stem filaree (*Erodium cicutarium*) has been reported from the Ontiveros Adobe excavations in southern California but often embedded in sheep feces rather than associated with any human consumption (Honeysett 1982). A limited quantity of filaree seeds was also recovered from a late-eighteenth-century midden and an early-nineteenth-century household at El Presidio de San Francisco that are unlikely to have been associated with California Indians (Voss 2002:478). The dominance and complete ubiquity of *Erodium* in the Petaluma floral collection may point toward focused exploitation, given the striking parallel to the similar ubiquity of unambiguous food resources such as wheat and nutshell (acorn, bay), or toward widespread landscape takeover to the point of being unavoidable in household burning. I suspect the latter is more likely. There is no evidence from Petaluma to support an alternative hypothesis that people used livestock manure full of filaree and other grasses as fuel. Wood served as the primary fuel source, and California Indians were not known to make use of dung as fuel. However, they may have used filaree plants as kindling for their wood fires or as earth oven fuel.

At a general level, the plant taxa offer insights into seasonality at Rancho Petaluma. The taxa identified at least to genus indicate plant collection during spring, summer, and fall with no winter-collected species (e.g., *Brodiaea* bulbs).[8] The grass and herb taxa found in the site deposits have seeds available from the late spring through the summer, depending on the particular species, and the tree (oak, bay) species have nuts that ripen in the fall. Manzanita berries are available in the summer and sometimes into the fall (Munz 1968). Whether or not the presence of these taxa indicates consumption only during these seasons is uncertain, especially since acorns and other seeds were frequently stored through the winter in Native California. In addition, some of the wetland species in the floral assemblage are often collected and consumed in the summer, for example, rush (*Juncus* sp.) and bulrush (*Scirpus* sp.). These may denote procurement for use in basketry instead of or at least in addition to possible consumption.

The cultigens also correspond to summer harvesting: barley in May or June and wheat in July or August (Lugo 1950:28). This would have been a critical time for Native participation at the rancho not only from Vallejo's perspective of completing agricultural tasks but also from a Native point of view to acquire additional foodstuffs. Yet the abundance of wheat in the floral remains does not necessarily indicate simply late summer occupation or consumption by Native workers, since wheat was stored for long periods of time in the Petaluma Adobe itself (Boggs 1913). From there it could be distributed to workers, traded to Russians at Colony Ross, or marketed in the burgeoning San Francisco area. It likely served as an almost year-round commodity for permanent Native workers residing on the rancho.

Finally, like the faunal collection, the absence of other plant taxa in the Rancho Petaluma assemblage deserves attention. Given the chance nature of preservation, not too much can be made of floral absences (Pearsall 1989:228), but a comparison of the recovered assemblage from Petaluma with that from other nineteenth-century Mexican or Spanish settlements in California and with that expected from documentary evidence in Petaluma heightens the interpretive potential. Compared to archaeobotanical data from the Ontiveros Adobe on the Rancho de los Nietos in early-nineteenth-century southern California (Honeysett 1982), the Rancho Petaluma floral assemblage lacks a variety of agricultural and garden products such as bean (*Phaseolus vulgaris*), pepper (*Capsicum* sp.), watermelon (*Citrullus lanatus*), tomato (*Lycopersicon lycopersicum*), rice (*Oryza sativa*), and peach (*Prunus persica*). Many similar species also recovered at Mission Santa Cruz did not appear in Petaluma: bean, watermelon, peach, olive (*Olea* sp.), pea (*Pistum sativum*), fava bean (*Vicia faba*), squash (*Cucurbita* sp.), bottle gourd (*Lagenaria* sp.), and cherry, plum, or apricot (*Prunus* spp.) (Allen 1998:46–47). Farris (1991:40) also recovered fava beans at Mission San Juan Bautista. Recent excavations at El Presidio de San Francisco in deposits dating to the late eighteenth and early nineteenth centuries similarly reveal a variety of cultivated legumes such as fava bean and pea (*Pisium* sp.) (Voss 2002:524, 582).

The broad comparison might be of limited use, since the colonial contexts differ and existed many miles apart, were it not for the fact that *many of these taxa were grown on Rancho Petaluma*. Vallejo claimed to have grown wheat, barley, beans, peas, lentils, and "vegetables of all kinds" at Rancho Petaluma and to have had them in "superabundance" in 1843 (Vallejo 1941:2). A similar agricultural list for Vallejo's operation at Petaluma is echoed in the U.S. land case court depositions (United States District Court 1852:10). Archival sources mention wheat, beans, barley, tomatoes, and peppers stored at the Petaluma Adobe (Boggs 1913), and Davis reports that Vallejo had Indian workers plowing for wheat, barley, beans, oats, garbanzos, and *lantejas* (lentils) (1929:136). Generally speaking, North Bay ranchos are reputed to have grown wheat, barley, beans, corn, onions, peas, cabbages, *calabazas* (pumpkins), lentils, and melons (Davis 1929:34). In fact, some of these crops, including beans, chili peppers, corn, and wheat, were grown in quantities large enough on the rancho to supply schooners (Vallejo 1875c:293).

Although these products filled plates on Californio tables (see Simpson 1847:174–75 for an example), they undoubtedly made their way into some Native meals in the region as well. For instance, at the nearby Sotoyome Rancho owned by Carlos Fitch on the Russian River, Native laborers in 1849 were reputedly fed a stew of "beans or peas, seasoned with peppers and rich with beef bones" (Tuomey 1926:123). At Sutter's New Helvetia near Sacramento in 1846, Edwin Bryant saw Native people coming to the settlement with watermelons and muskmelons (1985:265). He also witnessed a ranchería in Suisun, the likely "homeland" of the Southern Patwin workers on Rancho Petaluma, growing corn, beans, and melons (Bryant 1985:322).

However, no cultigens other than wheat, barley, and corn were recovered during excavations at Rancho Petaluma. An obvious possibility is that they may await discovery in unexcavated areas of the site. Another explanation is preservation based: many of these plants such as watermelon and peach were not cooked, thereby reducing their chances of being burned. Similarly, the boiling of beans causes little charring, leading to slim chances of survival in the archaeological record. Nevertheless, the discovery of these taxa at Mission Santa Cruz and the Ontiveros Adobe suggests that they *can* be recovered in archaeological contexts. The likelihood that many of the plants actually recovered at Petaluma were burned as refuse should not have selectively precluded certain taxa.

Therefore, one plausible explanation is that these products were not available to Native workers. Perhaps Vallejo and his overseer did not distribute these plant foods to Native families or individuals, or perhaps Native people had no interest in or access to them. At minimum, the absence of these taxa strongly indicates that Native Americans did not maintain personal gardens at Rancho Petaluma, at least in the general area investigated. Tomatoes, peppers, and fruits—not wheat and barley—would have been products raised in such plots. Instead, California Indian individuals and families supplemented the primary crop products of wheat, barley, and corn, which they received as provisions, with wild flora in the form of grasses, nuts, and berries.

Conclusion

The animal and plant remains from Rancho Petaluma serve to clarify many aspects of California Indian life in this colonial setting. Both data sets attest to a mixture of native and introduced species in the diet of rancho workers. Cattle provided the bulk of meat either as full or partial carcasses or as meat strips that left no archaeological signature, but individuals consumed mutton or lamb and also procured deer, fish, birds, and medium and small mammals to complete the meaty portion of their subsistence routine. In addition, some of these animals, such as rabbits and birds, may have offered raw material for clothing and personal adornment.

Native people complemented meat with a variety of vegetal foods. Wheat dominated the cultivated part of the diet, but barley and corn were also available and consumed. Corn may have been a more significant component than currently recognized if it were ground into meal away from the living areas excavated for this project (see Voss 2002:558 for a similar conclusion from El Presidio de San Francisco). Native workers living in this area of the Petaluma site seem to have used no other crop or garden products, meaning that all agricultural products would have been provisions. Although consumed in high quantities, the introduced cultigens did not replace indigenous interests in or need for wild foods, particularly acorns, bay nuts, and manzanita berries. In addition, Native individuals, probably women, continued to gather and process wild grass seeds, but they may have done so slightly less often than in late precontact and protohistoric contexts, given the availability of cultivated plants.

The continued reliance on wild plant and animal foods may suggest that laborers did not receive sufficient food rations on the rancho and had to seek nutritional or caloric sufficiency elsewhere or that they actively sought to reaffirm their social worlds in part by their choice of diet. The former scenario seems unlikely, given the large quantities of beef wasted after the matanza slaughtering and the high volume of agricultural crops produced and stored on the rancho for yearlong consumption. The matanza was a short period of time when individuals gorged on beef, but Simpson noted for the similar mission slaughters that "meat enough to supply the fleets of England is annually either consumed by fire or left to the carrion-birds" (1847:166). The ranchos would have offered an even more conspicuous case. Although rancho foods were most accessible during and immediately following harvesting and slaughtering in the late summer, stored dried beef strips and ground wheat and other crops were used year-round at the Petaluma Adobe.

Therefore, the acquisition of wild foods was more likely a choice and a preference. Native individuals sought to create a menu that included more than the meat and grains handed to them as part of their work payment. A combination of explicit restrictions on Native burning of grasslands for environmental management and the severe ecological impacts by colonial livestock grazing, farming, and unintentional weed introductions would have made indigenous wild foods all the more difficult to obtain. The presence of summer-ripening grasses and shrubs and fall-ripening tree products indicates that Native people sought these wild foods precisely when rancho food availability would have been at its highest. Although they may have been stored for later use, these wild plants were certainly gathered during the busy, at least from Vallejo's point of view, summer months.

The conflict between rancho labor and Native seasonal subsistence practices was probably severe, but individuals devoted considerable time and effort to secure wild flora and fauna. They may have sought these wild foods as a self-conscious attempt to assert their "Native" identity in the rancho milieu, or they may have pursued these resources as a less political but no less active effort to maintain long-standing food traditions and create new ones. Dietary habits often fall into the realm of the routine and mundane, but they take on a different valence in colonial cases. It would be difficult to characterize the subsistence choices of Native Americans in Petaluma as "automatic" when they were faced with novel foods, alternate modes of obtaining nourishment, provisioning protocols, and social control. Rancho workers may not have used food to actively resist Vallejo's operation, particularly since Vallejo probably cared as little about what foods Native people ate as he did about what they worshiped so long as the labor duties were completed, but the food remains represent attempts by California Indians to reside in the rancho world, to carve a place that drew from the past but worked in the present.

Chapter 7

Colonial Worlds, Indigenous Practices

Interpreting Rancho Petaluma

Borne to the earth by the toils of civilization superadded to the privations of savage life, they [Vallejo's Native workers] vegetate rather than live, without the wish to enjoy their former pastimes or the skill to resume their former avocations.

—George Simpson, *An Overland Journey round the World during the Years 1841 and 1842*

On the rancho, Indians lived their pastoral customs, little influenced by ideas of personal ambition or material progress. Isolated from the main currents of Mexican social life, the rancho took its tone from the simple life of its Indians.

—Chad Hoopes, "The Petaluma Adobe"

Studies of stone tools, mass-produced colonial goods, bone artifacts, animal bones, shellfish, and plant remains for Rancho Petaluma have begun to clarify the social and cultural web of the rancho, a web that both supported and entangled Native American people. Archaeological information has revealed the blatantly unsatisfactory nature of Sir George Simpson's views of Vallejo's Native workers and Chad Hoopes's historical assessment of Rancho Petaluma life. Simpson's portrayal of California Indian workers, although addressing the difficulties endured by Native Americans in the thralls of forced labor and economic hard times and the ways that some individuals might express that burden, reflects a lack of intimate, sustained contact with them during their daily lives. The archaeological record has counteracted that unfamiliar view, revealing instead people trying to uphold cultural practices and forge new ones. Hoopes's portrayal is equally deficient by casting Native Americans as simple, passive, and unaffected by the broader colonial world of California. These Native workers actively used, manipulated, endured, and died on Rancho Petaluma—they were in a colonial world that was *not* isolated from the "currents" of Mexican California. In many ways, this rancho epitomized colonialism and the complexity, not simplicity, of social life for the many people wrapped up in it. To baldly claim that rancho life adopted its stride from the lifestyles of Native workers denies the hardships, labor regimes, and structural inequalities that defined its very character.

Set alongside historical documents, archaeological studies have disclosed the labor relations that structured indigenous participation in and experience of rancho life. Native Americans responded to this colonial rancho world in a variety of complex ways. Their diets contained a mixture of wild and domestic plants and hunted and herded large mammals as well as a diverse assortment of fish, birds, and mollusk species taken from the local environs. California Indians acquired rock raw material, crafted stone tools, and used lithic artifacts in the material world of the rancho. Metal, glass, and ceramic goods entered the repertoire of daily life for Native people—glass beads traded and worn, wine bottles emptied and broken, metal tools used and discarded, and ceramic vessels filled and cast off.

The preceding lines of evidence each advance a clearer view of Rancho Petaluma and indigenous participation therein, both in sorting through the local contexts and offering a point of comparison to other California ranchos. But the fullest picture—the true "big picture"—of Native American interactions with colonial ranches becomes visible only when these archaeological and historical elements are considered in tandem. Doing this requires retying the knot that opened the book. I characterize this as a retying since the knot of past lives and colonialism cannot be entirely reconstructed or completely described from all possible perspectives. The past is real, but the remnants are fragmentary, the experiences recorded in it are highly diverse, and the interpretation of it has developed completely in the present. My version is not the only one possible, but I feel that it solidly integrates and accounts for the available information from material culture, dietary remains, and archival sources. It is attuned to the politics of history and to the lived experience of indigenous people on the rancho.

The integration of material culture, food remains, and documentary data offers guideposts for tracking Native American life and labor at Rancho Petaluma. Material and social practices comprised part of the constant negotiation of life on the rancho, and many of them were political in nature. I do not mean the politics of states and nations but the infrapolitics of everyday life (after Scott 1985, 1990) in which individuals grapple with structures of domination, the possibilities of resistance, and the necessities of "making do." Like Michel de Certeau (1984) and his approach to everyday life, I see these daily activities not as free from overarching systems of domination or as grand strategies that seek to overtake positions of power. Instead, they are social tactics, actions that "trace out the ruses of other interests and desires that are neither determined nor captured by the systems in which they develop" (Certeau 1984:xviii). Tactics may or may not end up being revolutionary, but they are creative practices, ones that arise and perhaps thrive in spaces that are already disciplined and colonized (Certeau 1984:30). Typically, Certeau's "tactics are not liberatory in the material sense of the word: the little victories of everyday life do no more (but, also, no less) than disrupt the fatality of the established order" (Buchanan 2000:104–5). Unlike Certeau, however, I recognize the possibilities of seeing identity within and between these social tactics and the ways in which they manifest in material culture. With this perspective in mind, I synthesize the book along three major themes: foodways, stone tools, and labor.

Foodways

The predominance of food-related items—charred animal and plant remains, mortar-and-pestle and other ground stone technology, obsidian projectile points, a net sinker, thermally affected rocks—in the archaeological record parallels the importance of food in everyday life on the rancho. Importance here is a two-part phenomenon. First is the obvious need for people to eat and the archaeological capacity to track dietary practices. The list of relevant material items given above is testament to that capacity. Second are the ways that dietary practices implicate daily politics. Relevant factors include the regimentation of daily activity through scheduled food distribution, the system of food provisions exchanged for labor, and the possible relationship between food availability and some Native individuals' decisions to join or leave the rancho. The evidence suggests that these foodways also may mark individuals' attempts to express identity.

As chapter 6 details, provisioned foods comprised the bulk of animal and plant remains. Numerous cattle and sheep bones, charred wheat and barley, and a few burned corn fragments were recovered at the site. Cattle and wheat were the dietary heart of these rancho-based foods based on archaeological quantities and historical documents, even despite the likely archaeological underrepresentation of beef due to the practice of stripping and drying boneless meat on California ranchos (see Gust 1982:122–23). Food remains were discarded in large refuse piles such as Feature E in the Block, in general scatter as found in all excavation units, and in discrete pits such as Feature A in the Midden Trench and Features B and C in Trench 1. Some of these food products were charred during processing; others seem to have been burned as refuse.

The evidence is clear that livestock and cultigens were provisions rather than household-generated foods. In other words, Native individuals more frequently acquired these foods as part of the labor agreement rather than kept and maintained them in their households for residential use. Despite the secularization protocol that directed missionaries to give agricultural tools and livestock to neophytes when they left the mission, the likelihood of California Indians maintaining personal plots and livestock at the center of Vallejo's operation is slim. Vallejo had taken charge of many ex-neophytes' livestock and other resources in exchange for their labor, and he would never have allowed the commingling on his grazing lands of his own cattle acquired, in part, from ex-neophytes with livestock still owned by Native Americans. Individuals may have obtained meat as relatively complete carcasses at times, based on the faunal data, but workers probably received entire cattle carcasses during the late summer matanza rather than tended their own small herds.

One might speculate that pigs and chickens, not cattle and sheep, would have been more likely husbanded by Native people on Rancho Petaluma, given their smaller space and easier food requirements and their presence, at least that of domestic fowl, in some Indian living quarters at missions (Margolin 1989:90) and at postmission Native communities in the 1840s (Lugo 1950:210). Again, the Petaluma archaeological data resoundingly eliminate this hypothesis with the recovery of only one chicken bone and not a single pig skeletal element. The archaeological evidence for household gardens is similarly meager. No typical "garden" products such as tomatoes, peppers, and melons were recovered in the household debris, nor were any horticultural tools. George Simpson contrasted Native people working on a rancho in the Santa Barbara region with those on Vallejo's North Bay rancho: the Santa Barbara workers "appeared, however, to be, on the whole, more comfortable than General Vallego's [sic] serfs, possessing enclosures of land with a few cattle and horses" (1847:216–17). The contrast illuminates the uniqueness of the Petaluma case and hints perhaps at the result of at least four additional decades of colonialism in the Santa Barbara region when compared to the North Bay. Yet time alone cannot explain the difference, since such a perspective inherently has to presume gradual, yet directional, acculturation. I resist that presumption.

Although provisioned foods filled many stomachs and regimented daily schedules, Native workers were not bound solely to these foods. If Vallejo's statement is accurate that he gave "freely to the Indians" from his storerooms of superabundant grains (1941:2), workers perhaps could have subsisted solely on these supplies.[1] The same goes for the matanza carnage: beef would have been plentiful, since the slaughter typically generated so much waste in the pursuit of hides and tallow that carcasses were discarded and burned as refuse or left out in the open for vultures and grizzly bears. Estimates of Vallejo's sheep herd are consistently high as well. Instead, like many mission neophytes at Santa Cruz (Allen 1998) and San Antonio (Langenwalter and McKee 1985), individuals and families at Rancho Petaluma complemented beef, mutton, wheat, barley, and corn from rancho provisions with the wild plant and animal resources of the region. Individuals and families designed their own menus within the array of available resources. Rather than cattle marking acculturation or acorns marking vestigial conservatism, I interpret this information as people constructing their diets within the complexities of rancho life. Beyond asking whether the wild foods were a necessity or luxury, I query their position in the negotiation of identity and social position.

Charred floral remains reveal that acorns, bay nuts, manzanita berries, and grass seeds remained important food resources. From ethnographic and historical sources, we know that Native Californians, typically women, leached acorns, pounded them into meal, and then cooked the flour as mush, breads, and other foods. Manzanita berries were typically made into cider, and grass seeds were often toasted and then boiled to make pinole. Aside from entire families gathering acorns in the fall (e.g., Wilkes 1845:192), women probably gathered and processed almost all of these plants. Bay laurel and oak trees may have grown near the site but would have been more common a few kilometers from the Petaluma Adobe. Manzanita definitely required treks to higher chaparral slopes. Native grasses may or may not have been locally available, given the alterations in the landscape caused by livestock grazing and agriculture. Copious seeds of filaree, introduced grasses, and mallows in the archaeobotanical record attest to this disturbance. In addition, Native individuals made limited use of rush, bulrush, mustard, and clover. All four probably served some food purposes, but the former two may also indicate the acquisition of these wetland resources for basket making. In total, the patterns indicate significant "logistical mobility" and efforts to secure the plants. Like the cultivated crops, these plant species also indicate harvesting between late spring and fall. This may correspond to the influx of seasonal workers and the subsequent need to feed more people or the transport of these foods with workers as they rotated into the rancho, but the pattern may also suggest the importance of storage of acorns and other wild plants for year-round consumption by the permanent Native residents.

Individuals hunted the neighboring hills, valleys, and plains with bow and net for deer, and they hunted and trapped rabbits, woodrats, and perhaps gophers in the vicinity. They netted nearby streams and rivers for fish using rock-weighted nets, and they also fished the bay or ocean shore or at least traded for such fish products. The fish represent mainly freshwater cyprinid minnows, but other freshwater-capture species (suckers, sturgeon, salmon) and bay species (topsmelt or jacksmelt, herrings) were retrieved as well. Birds primarily consisted of ducks and geese that Native people hunted along nearby waterways, although songbirds and a raptor were present as well. Individuals sought out shellfish beds in San Pablo Bay and Bodega Bay, or they maintained exchange relations with those who did for marine food as well as bead-making raw material. One or more individuals even acquired a pinniped and a sea otter (or at least a part of each) while residing at the site. With the exception of shellfish gathered by both women and men, the hunting, trapping, and fishing were probably done by men, as documented ethnographically and historically.

Native cooks likely prepared food in the Petaluma Adobe quadrangle for the ranchero household and for communal distribution (Hoopes 1965:36), but the archaeological evidence confirms that cooking for Native consumption also took place in Native households, outside Vallejo's purview. Yet cooking practices for the plant and animal foods are hard to track. Despite the possible use of iron kettles for cooking, individuals seem to have relied heavily on stone boiling in baskets for atole and pinole, given the large number of thermally affected rocks with contraction fractures. In 1842 Edward Vischer noted stone boiling being used by migrant Native workers a few miles south of the Petaluma Adobe (Gudde 1940), and Vallejo described it for the specific Native groups of Suisun, Sonoma, Napa, Licatiut, and Satiyomi (1875a:12), many of whom must have filled his roster of rancho workers. According to observations made by Vallejo's son Platon, meat also may have been boiled this way, at least with the Suisun (1914:14), but it was typically roasted over coals or baked in an earth oven. The latter may have been the function of the two baked-earth pit features discovered during excavation, given the amount of unburned bone, expansion-fractured rocks, and charcoal in the nearby refuse features. The lack of significant burning on the surfaces of these bones indicates that they were not roasted over an open flame, but they very well may have been cooked in a pit over hot rocks.

Based on archaeological inference, individuals at Rancho Petaluma processed wild and cultivated plant foods primarily using mortars and pestles with some limited use of manos and (extrapolated) metates. This pattern contrasts with the noticeable presence of the latter in the missions (Allen 1998:63–64; see also Cook 1976:92; Margolin 1989:86).[2] Napoleón Vallejo, son of the rancho owner, recollected that Indian women were required to pound a certain amount of corn flour pinole in mortars (N. Vallejo 1890:4), and George Simpson remarked on the pounding of nut foods (1847:177). If the wheat or corn were ground rather than pounded in a mortar and pestle, these grains may have been processed off-site, perhaps before provisioning, given the paucity of milling tools such as metates recovered in excavation. The paucity of manos and metates and the lack of many charred corn remains may support this off-site processing hypothesis, but the same does not apply to wheat. The presence of unprocessed wheat seeds in the floral remains means that they had not yet undergone the transition to flour. The predominant ground stone technology to convert them to flour, based on the archaeological evidence, was mortar-and-pestle technology. From an archaeological standpoint, the association of acorns and mortar-and-pestle technology is not surprising, but the high number of charred grass seeds, the presence of corn and wheat, and the lack of many manos and any unambiguous metate fragments echo the growing concern that the technology-to-resource correlation may not be as strong or as exclusive as once believed (Basgall 1987; Wohlgemuth 1996:84). That is, mortars and pestles are perhaps best viewed as multipurpose processing tools, possibly used to grind acorns, grass seeds, and cultigens at Rancho Petaluma. However, grinding tools often have very long use-lives, and the short duration of the Rancho Petaluma enterprise may weigh against them having been discarded very often. This would account for the overall low quantities in the excavated collection but not the disproportionate recovery of mortars and pestles versus manos and metates.

Stone Tools

The continuity and form of stone tool technology trace out other kinds of daily practices at Rancho Petaluma. They do so primarily because they represent clearly the contours of Native American activities and struggles in the colonial world of the California rancho. Very few classes of artifacts at Rancho Petaluma offer such clarity, since they are products only used, rather than both made and used, by indigenous social actors. To understand stone tool production and use requires juxtaposing lithic artifacts with other classes of material culture at the site. Stone tools and associated manufacturing debris can be analyzed and interpreted in their own right, but they offer clearer insights when contextualized as they would have been during their use—as part of everyday life, as a choice among other material technologies, and as a meaningful practice (Silliman 2001a, 2003b).

Although California Indians undoubtedly contested stylistic or raw material aspects of lithic production in precontact times, stone tool technology was the accepted way to manufacture hard, durable, and sharp tools. The arrival of the colonial period and the involvement of California Indians in the rancho system changed that, as numerous material and technological alternatives were introduced. Yet in spite of exposure to nineteenth-century industrial and mass-produced items such as metal and glass, Native laborers at Rancho Petaluma remained focused on lithic technology. The choice was both a political and a functional one (Silliman 2001a).

One potential explanation for the continuity of stone tool practices could be the lack of Native access to metal or other European tools at the rancho. However, the assemblage suggests otherwise, with metal tools such as scissors, files, iron pot fragments, flatware pieces, and various other items. This suggests that various forms of metal were available to site residents, much like the ceramics, glass, and glass beads. In fact, metal artifacts supplied by Vallejo through his contacts around the San Francisco Bay area were probably the backbone of rancho labor but not of Native household labor. The available evidence suggests that Native individuals selectively introduced metal objects into their households and that the process may have been a gendered one, focusing on tools directly related to female activities.

An alternative explanation of lithic use could be that there simply were not enough metal tools for everyday tasks or even for rancho duties required by the overseer. In other words, perhaps the large numbers of Native workers present during the late summer matanza taxed even the wealthy Vallejo's ability to equip them for the task at hand. If true, individuals would not have made formal bifacial tools for these jobs, since retouched flakes and steep-sided scrapers generally work very well for cutting and scraping, respectively, and can be repaired or discarded as needed. Yet formal bifacial implements were major components of the stone tool collection. Further complicating the scenario is the fact that many of the butchered animal bones have V-shaped cut marks more characteristic of metal knives than stone ones, but the archaeological record provides virtually no examples of such metal tools. Perhaps Native men produced stone projectile points to hunt wild game because guns were in restricted supply, but this would still explain only a small component of the lithic assemblage (i.e., projectile points and associated manufacturing debris).

With these alternatives offering less than satisfactory accounts for the continuity of lithic technology, I argue that stone tool technology was practiced as part of the active daily involvement in colonialism (Silliman 2001a, 2003b). The fact that lithic artifacts occur in refuse characterized more by residential activity than rancho tasks further accentuates their use in Native household practices, despite the evidence that metal tools may have been used to butcher the animals found in residential trash deposits. These stone tools may or may not have been conscripted into rancho duties, but they certainly held strong currency in the space of domestic and off-work life and may have had strong implications for gender relations in the context of procurement, manufacture, and use.

As a social tactic, lithic working and use may have done little to subvert rancho labor, but it was an active way for individuals to stake a claim in the colonial world. This claim may not have been an overtly political or resistant one but rather an active attempt to craft a stable place of residence, figuratively speaking, in the nineteenth century. Given the control of space and time exerted by labor regimentation, stone tool manufacture would have occurred primarily during off-work hours, those times when friends and families regrouped during an early afternoon siesta or at the end of the workday. The prevalence of lithic production and use at the site suggests strong Native control over the residential sphere and widespread interest in these tools across the site. Contrary to models of "acculturation," individuals conscripted these stone artifacts as active materializations rather than passive symbols of Native practice.

The raw material used in stone working offers additional insight, especially given the roughly equal amounts of obsidian and chert raw materials.

The critical point is that stone tool production was not simply a decision of convenience, since lithic sources were not located in the immediate vicinity of the living quarters on the rancho. Some chert and igneous stones were available somewhat locally, but the nearest obsidian sources—both primary and secondary deposits of Annadel, Franz Valley, Napa Valley, and Oakmont— were at least 23–35 kilometers away, with two other artifacts of obsidian obtained from even farther afield (Borax Lake, Mount Konocti). None of these occur within the bounds of the vast Rancho Petaluma. The presence of common sources such as Napa Valley and Annadel is not surprising, given their prevalence in the archaeological record for the general area and their geographical proximity, but the array of more localized and little-recognized sources such as Franz Valley and Oakmont in the obsidian collection bespeaks a pattern very different from that of precontact groups in the region. The difference means either that rancho workers tapped into obsidian sources that very few individuals in precontact times had ever utilized or that previous attempts by archaeologists to assign sources to obsidian artifacts based only on macroscopic characteristics have overlooked the unexpected sources. I have argued that the "truth" is probably a combination of the two (Silliman 2000b, 2005).

The source identifications indicate that Native people at Rancho Petaluma maintained trading relationships with nonrancho groups controlling the obsidian sources or made forays to these localities to obtain raw material during either work times or off-season mobility. At some level, disparate sources may reflect the geographical origin of Native workers and/or their seasonal mobility. Perhaps the single arrow point from Borax Lake denotes the capture of a Native man from the Clear Lake region who carried the weapon on his person or the presence of a seasonal worker who arrived at the rancho from a region outside of Vallejo's immediate landholdings. Alternately, Native laborers may have traded rancho or indigenous products to outlying villages for lithic raw material or finished products along the lines recorded in Pomo, Coast Miwok, and Wappo ethnographies (Barrett 1908; Collier and Thalman 1996; Driver 1936). Either way, time, effort, and connections were necessary for individuals to access these lithic raw materials, variables that underscore the significance of lithic technology in the rancho period. Obsidian may have served a common material and symbolic "currency" that linked Native people ensnared in the rancho system with those outside of its reach.

Maintaining access to lithic sources seems even more significant when contrasted with the worked bottle glass assemblage. As was the case at many other colonial sites, Native individuals at Rancho Petaluma used techniques of lithic technology on glass bottles. Bottle fragments were struck with rocks or other knapping equipment to produce usable flakes, to reduce the glass mass into a functional shape, or to sharpen a glass edge by removing flakes on one or both sides of a margin. Yet unlike other contact period assemblages in the West such as Colony Ross (Silliman 1997) and Mission San Antonio (Hoover and Costello 1985), the modification and utilization of bottles at Rancho Petaluma involved primarily expedient use rather than formal tool manufacture. That is, no glass projectile points or other bifacial tools were discovered, although some shards display bifacial retouch. This modest use is notable, since glass bottles were numerous and readily available for tool manufacture, and they are a "superior" raw material for controlled flaking in contrast to some of the microcrystalline silicates (e.g., chert) and igneous rocks found in the Petaluma lithic collection. Nevertheless, Native laborers at Rancho Petaluma sought actual rocks for the majority of expedient and formal tool production, despite the distance and presumed effort involved.

To complete the discussion, the prevalent lithic technology can be juxtaposed with the relative lack of substantial bone, shell, and other stone technology. The incised bird-bone tubes, a larger bone tube, several miscellaneous bone artifacts, and two clamshell disk beads represent the only unequivocal organic artifacts in the assemblage. The lack of more clamshell disk beads is perplexing, given the proximity of the site to Bodega Bay and their frequent co-occurrence with glass beads in Napa Valley (e.g., Heizer 1953) and at Colony Ross (Silliman 1997). Gone are the common bone and shell artifacts of late precontact and historic sites in the North Bay region such as scapula saws, bone awls, abalone pendants, and *Olivella* beads of various sorts (e.g., Beardsley 1954; Bennyhoff 1994; Dietz 1976; Fredrickson 1984; Heizer 1953; Moratto 1984:218–83). Steatite beads, magnesite pipes, and charmstones are also missing from the Petaluma site assemblage, despite their common occurrence prior to contract in sites across the North Bay. The lack of charmstones is particularly intriguing in light of the large quantities found approximately 6–7 kilometers southeast of the Petaluma Adobe in precontact sites (Elsasser 1955), in a probable contact period site near Lake Tolay (Phebus 1990:128), and in the adjacent Napa Valley to the east (Heizer 1953).

The lack of these bone, shell, and other stone items at Rancho Petaluma is intriguing vis-à-vis the continuity of lithic technology. Many of these organic and stone artifacts typically have been found as burial goods, suggesting that their absence from Petaluma may relate directly to the lack of mortuary contexts. Yet Bennyhoff (1994:53) noted that historic burials in the Napa region are also marked by a lack of abalone artifacts, although they commonly contain magnesite pipes and painted stone tablets. Ultimately, the social context of use (e.g., trade, ritual, ceremony, gender) for many of these goods may have shifted significantly in the rancho context and in the historic period more broadly. Context certainly changed for chipped stone lithic technology, but the change was one that individuals apparently negotiated with continued practice.

Labor

The underlying theme throughout this work has been the significance of labor in the Native experience of the California rancho. As historical sources make very clear, labor was the primary node of interaction between indigenous people and Californio and other rancheros. Except in rare instances of actual rancho ownership or interethnic marriage, California Indians participated at ranchos solely as workers. They prepared and served food; herded, branded, and butchered cattle; processed and hauled hides and tallow; made bricks, candles, shoes, and blankets; plowed, planted, and harvested crop fields; and performed household chores for ranchero families. For these labors, Native individuals and families typically received provisions of food, clothing, and shelter rather than monetary payment.

Historical sources outline this broad labor structure for Rancho Petaluma, but what historical records do not relay are the ways that labor translated into social relations and daily lives for California Indians. What did these tasks mean to Native workers? How did this labor impact household life and identity? Archaeology provides some tantalizing clues, which I combine with archival data to make three points: (1) the types of mass-produced goods reveal that site occupants were primarily those individuals who worked in and around the Petaluma Adobe rather than in the fields and herding camps; (2) some of the material goods may reveal the expression of identity along the lines of gender and worker "occupation"; and (3) the labor regime rigidly structured daily life, but individuals did not surrender completely themselves or their traditions to it.

Site Residents and Material Goods

My first point regarding site occupants and their association directly with the Petaluma Adobe hinges on the discovery of specific material items rather than on the silent historical record. Colonial labor served as the primary venue for indigenous people at Rancho Petaluma to use and acquire mass-produced European goods. For instance, cooks and household servants handled silverware, plates, bowls, glasses, and bottles, while field hands worked with plows and harvesting tools. Vaqueros rode horses with saddles, bridles, and spurs, while butchers and hide processors worked with knives, kettles, and other implements for preparing the cattle carcasses, tallow, and hides. Native artisans used looms, needles, thread, and leather to make woven and other goods. Many of these items could have been stolen, scavenged, or acquired through payment in kind for labor services.

In that light, the Rancho Petaluma artifacts have produced an ambiguous yet telling collection of objects tied explicitly to rancho labor. The ones retrieved relate strongly to tasks that would have occurred inside the adobe rather than in the fields. For example, the site produced sewing artifacts such as thimbles, needles, and scissors, but not a single mass-produced artifact could be attributed unambiguously to the duties of planting and harvesting crops or herding, branding, and butchering cattle. Only one metal buckle may indicate a harness of some sort. All recovered knives and utensil handles were tableware and not the heavy-duty tools of cattle processing, and the rasps and kettles may have been used in and around the adobe quadrangle. Absent are the large metal knives, cleavers, and axes used for butchery and the bridles, brands, and spurs used in vaquero tasks. Plows were probably primarily wooden with perhaps an iron piece at the end for breaking the soil and therefore may not have offered much in the way of preservable artifacts or space for storage in Native living areas. Yet hand sickles would have probably been used for harvesting (Hoopes 1965:39).

Given that agricultural and livestock tasks were the timepiece and economic center of rancho activity, at least from the manager's or owner's perspective, the associated material goods should have been numerous. That is, they "should have been" discovered in excavations if individuals from all types of rancho work lived at the site and brought these items home. Certainly, some of these material objects would have been too bulky to pilfer, too expensive to be let out of an overseer's sight, or too specific in function to be useful in a Native household. However, I would not expect these conditions to apply to tools such as metal knives, cleavers, and spurs.[3] To account for the restricted array of colonial tools and the spatial location of the site in close proximity to the Petaluma Adobe, I argue that the evidence suggests instead that site residents were primarily individuals involved in the day-to-day activities of the adobe rather than those involved in livestock herding and butchery. Residents would have included workers such as household servants, cooks, and artisans who lived on the rancho for much of the year rather than the seasonal influx of people during agricultural or matanza seasons. Native herders, who often came from unmissionized communities, more typically lived in field camps near livestock watering holes for convenience (Híjar 1988:20; G. Vallejo 1890:185), and such sites have not yet been located on Rancho Petaluma. As workers inside and around the Petaluma Adobe, these site residents probably comprised the more "trusted" workers in the eyes of Vallejo and Alvarado. Many were probably ex-neophytes from Mission San Francisco Solano or Mission San Rafael who had been trained in the mission trades.

The involvement of site residents in activities in and around the Petaluma Adobe may have granted Native individuals the opportunity to acquire colonial household goods such as the ceramic vessels, glass bottles and tableware, and flatware evidenced in the deposits. These were the items that servants and cooks used to set the Vallejo table and serve food at Petaluma; they formed the material base of required labor. Vallejo probably did not give many ceramic plates, bowls, and other vessels to Native workers as part of his provisioning system, since the standard fare was clothing and food. However, he may have paid workers in kind, as was often done with glass beads and alcohol-filled bottles, a practice that would account for the abundance of these two artifact types in the archaeological record. Native people obtained no currency from Vallejo to purchase ceramics from him or anyone else, but they may have acquired the goods as trade goods, hand-me-downs, or scavenged items.

The trade possibility is unlikely, for labor provisioning arrangements would have overshadowed any trading relationships between site residents and Vallejo. Furthermore, beads, blankets, clothes, and tobacco were more typical trade goods between Vallejo and neighboring groups (e.g., Vallejo 1875c:13, 252; Vallejo n.d.a:2). The more than thirteen hundred beads at the site indicate their popularity among Native workers, regardless of how they obtained them. Southern California rancheros such as Manuel Nieto also offered tools or "whatever else struck an individual Indian's fancy" in exchange for labor

(Mason 1993:181), and a similar deal might have been worked out between Native workers and Vallejo.

The high fragmentation of the glass, ceramic, and metal objects could support the scavenging hypothesis if ceramics or bottles rarely entered Native hands as whole vessels. However, as discussed earlier, the processes of secondary or tertiary deposition seem a more likely cause of the grossly incomplete artifacts. The pattern does parallel the high fragmentation of both glass and ceramic items at a Native living area at Fort Ross, which has been forwarded as evidence of the use of these industrial goods as raw material in Native hands (Farris 1997:130; Silliman 1997:170–71). However, the relatively low incidence of glass working and the very low frequency of ceramic modification at Rancho Petaluma suggest that individuals did not seek these goods, at least initially, as raw material. Only the presence of a few weathered glass specimens indicates possible scavenging.

A more convincing interpretation is that Native individuals used ceramics and glass as vessels and bottles and not primarily as sherds and shards, regardless of how they actually procured them. Glass shards are ubiquitous across the site, many as fragments of alcohol bottles. This suggests a widespread availability of the commodities, both glass and alcohol, among the Native community. Similarly, the ceramic sherds may point to the use of ceramic vessels in some cooking and eating practices in their households, but the small quantity of ceramic artifacts suggests that such practices were not widespread or were restricted to very specific uses. Many of the European and Asian ceramic containers made of porcelain, stoneware, and earthenware would not have functioned as direct-heat vessels for cooking. If used as designed, they would have been storage containers for solid or liquid food or as serving and eating vessels for prepared food. Without additional analysis or excavation, ascertaining their actual function, meaning, and symbolism for site residents remains difficult.

Occupation, Gender, and Identity

The conclusion that many of the site residents spent their laboring time around the Petaluma Adobe sets the parameters for my second point, that individuals at Rancho Petaluma used these artifacts in part for statements about identity. Although the site excavations may not cross-section anywhere near the full variability of the Native workforce, they do offer keen insights into these particular individuals' negotiations of identity and labor in the material world of the Native household. Material items associated with colonial tasks obviously served their functional purpose in daily duties and in household activities, and they were perhaps assigned by a labor overseer to complete required tasks. However, the material culture of colonial labor may have taken on a different meaning in Native social worlds. Individuals could have introduced some objects of labor into Native households as a way to alter "off-work" activities and social relations or as a way to affiliate symbolically with a task-based identity that brought them status on the rancho. At the same time, household members may have excluded some items from the residential space as a way to distance the home from colonial labor. Consequently, to find an artifact of colonial labor in a Native archaeological context is to find something other than simple "acculturation."

The likelihood that site residents were involved in tasks at the Petaluma Adobe itself opens a window for gender and identity issues. The adobe-based workforce was a strongly but not exclusively female one centered around activities such as spinning, weaving, cooking, and processing food (see, however, Alvarado n.d. for males listed as loom workers). All are the colonial duties represented in the artifacts of the site. Many of these Native women would have had spouses or been relatives of men who worked the fields and tended the livestock, and they would have coresided at this site. This recognition expands the perspective slightly from my previous point to include the presence of potential field workers living on the site. However, the lack of artifacts associated with most men's required activities on the rancho is striking. The discrepancy suggests that women materialized certain aspects of their identities with colonial goods, whereas men negotiated theirs in other ways, perhaps with lithic access and use or hunting. Identity politics may have played out as much in the "workplace" as they did in the household, although the latter is the only one that I can address here.

Native women spent many hours in cloth- and leather-working activities inside the Petaluma Adobe, and the recovered pins, scissors, and thimbles suggest that individuals, probably women, introduced these objects into their households because of the presumed usefulness of such items in residential activities such as repairing tailored clothing or sewing embroidery beads. There is no evidence to suggest that Native women did home piecework—labor based on quotas such as making a certain number of shoes or blankets rather than on time. Simultaneously, women may have used the artifacts to affiliate actively with their rancho task despite being in their own domestic spaces. Vallejo's spouse, Francisca Benicia, illuminates this possibility: "Indian women are not much inclined to learn many things. For this reason, she who is taught cooking will not hear of washing clothes, and, on the other hand, a good washerwoman will regard herself insulted if she were to be compelled to sew or spin" (Engelhardt 1915:136; see also chapter 4). Although Francisca Benicia referred to her home in Sonoma, the same issues undoubtedly played out at the more populous Rancho Petaluma.

Rather than a lack of inclination or trainability on the part of female workers, the pattern intimates that Native women frequently used their labor tasks to stake an identity claim. They may have made this claim in their working lives and in their home worlds. In addition to being California Indians, women, and mothers, some were also seamstresses. The expression of each was probably highly contextual, but actively affiliating with a labor task may have been a way for women to reside in as much as resist colonial labor. The presence of sewing items such as scissors and thimbles in neophyte residential areas at Missions Santa Cruz (Allen 1998:88), San Antonio (Hoover and Costello 1985:65), San Juan Bautista (Farris 1991:35), and La Purísima (Deetz 1963:184) may indicate a similar phenomenon.[4] These "occupations" probably entailed differences in status as well, perhaps demarcating trusted household servants and adobe workers with better access to living quarters and food than field hands and unmissionized gentiles. Furthermore, refusing to be trained in other tasks may have allowed women more time for other preferred activities, since they could not be called upon for multiple duties. Their image as untrainable in multiple tasks provided them with a certain freedom to not be overextended in their tasks, and they may have promoted this stereotype to their own benefit. This ability to choose (or what some might call "passive resistance") demonstrates a particular power, albeit circumscribed, held by Native women in the colonial world.

This interpretation in no way implies that Native women abandoned "traditional" practices when they allied with colonial labor roles, nor should the data be construed to address all women at the site but rather the subset who may have been responsible for these particular material remains. The grass, nut, and berry remains demonstrate great effort in obtaining them on foraging trips, and visitors to the area noted the continued focus on grinding plant foods (e.g., Simpson 1847). The mortars and pestles recovered archaeologically provide additional support. The mixture of "Native" and "Western" foods and material objects suggests instead a complex material world and identity.

In contrast, Native men spent much of their time herding cattle, riding horses, plowing fields, and butchering and skinning livestock, yet their "tools of the trade" did not make it into the residential deposits. Some women spent considerable time processing hides and harvesting crops as well. Several explanations for the paucity of these field and livestock items are possible: (1) Vallejo held tightly to the essential commodities involved in such duties, and Native people were not allowed to take them into their own living quarters; (2) items such as knives, axes, and spurs may have been not as easily broken or discarded as thimbles, pins, and scissors; and (3) men discarded their broken tools such as knives and cleavers where they were mainly used, which may have been activity areas outside of the excavated site. All three are potentially applicable explanations, but these reasons are also equally valid for the "adobe-focused" tools actually recovered. In fact, butchery knives and cleavers should be just as likely to break under typical workloads as would thimbles and scissors. Therefore, another factor underlies the discrepancy.

With the intensity of cattle butchery at the rancho and the numerous cattle bones found during excavation, the lack of metal cutting tools in the refuse deposits requires additional consideration. How were these carcasses processed? Could stone tools have been the primary tool for butchery and its widespread occurrence an index of laboring tasks? The numerous stone tools, both formal and expedient, may have been occasionally used to skin and butcher livestock and thereby to bring colonial labor duties into material familiarity. Deetz advanced a similar argument for the tanning vats at Mission La Purísima (1963:172). However, not all and perhaps not even most butchery at Rancho Petaluma was performed with stone tools, which begs the question of why no metal knives made it into the refuse deposits. Since non-Native residents in nineteenth-century California would not have thought of bifaces and flakes as "knives," most historical accounts imply that the knives used to remove hides and strip meat were metal. As noted earlier, my preliminary examination of cut marks on the excavated bones also indicates that butchers commonly employed metal knives, since relatively few show the wider cut marks characteristic of stone tool butchery. Native butchers also used large metal cleavers or axes, given the deep and wide cuts-to-break on ribs and other elements. A similar pattern of metal knife butchery (Wake 1997b) with few such knives recovered in archaeological deposits (Silliman 1997) characterizes the Native Alaskan neighborhood at Russian Colony Ross.

A possible interpretation is that individuals involved in these field tasks did not incorporate their common rancho tools into residential practices. That is, butchers may have used metal implements on the slaughtering ground but not back at home. The pattern contrasts sharply with uncritical expectations that Native Americans would have quickly adopted metal knives in contact or colonial cases to replace stone tools. Neither components of this process—adoption or replacement—can be seen in the Rancho Petaluma data. These rancho laborers, primarily men, may have had notions of identity different from the women and adobe-focused workers described above. Since only men could be vaqueros, the lack of horse equipment may signal their lack of interest in claiming a vaquero identity in the daily realm of the household, despite the fact that riding horses and herding cattle formed the core of many Native men's experiences of Rancho Petaluma. Native groups were famous for raiding colonial settlements in California for horses, both to ride and to consume (e.g., Davis 1929:63; Wilkes 1845:174). Yet it seems that little of this took place in Native living quarters just outside the adobe, given the lack of horse remains and riding materials. To find Native American men distancing themselves from the vaquero lifestyle is perhaps unexpected, given the research that suggests that Native Americans in many parts of the Spanish, Mexican, and then American West adopted ranching as a unique way to remain "Indian" in the face of European and Euro-American settlement (Iverson 1994). The difference in the Petaluma case may lie in the ways that individuals chose *not* to use ranching material culture as an element of identity in the rancho setting, despite the intense and sustained activities of livestock herding and butchering, and in the lack of reservation land and community autonomy for Native Americans living on the Rancho Petaluma. That is, unlike the Native American communities in Iverson's study, indigenous people at Rancho Petaluma were not adopting cattle ranching as a "symbol for a new day" (1994:14), since it was a labor choice made under duress rather than a community or family effort anchored in a tenuous but defendable land base. In addition, I contend that the adoption and expression of identity in this rancho setting, as in most other social contexts, was contextual and gendered.

The implication is that Indian men chose to forge or negotiate their identities outside of rancho life, perhaps through other means such as hunting, trading, and flint knapping. These three activities are strongly represented in the assemblage and are traditionally the realm of Native California men, as recorded in ethnographic and historic texts. Alternately, men may have cultivated their connection to labor through the acquisition of crop and livestock products for meals. That is, beef rather than metal cutting tools might have been their material connection to labor tasks, but the data cannot be used to address such a subtlety. The affiliation with labor for its ends (e.g., food) rather than its means (e.g., tools) could be a critical distinction between the strategies of men and women on Rancho Petaluma.

Complementing the gender differences, the dissimilar presence of labor tools in this excavated area may also point to disparities between the missionized, "trusted" workers at the Petaluma Adobe and the unmissionized gentiles who worked seasonally in the fields and herds. That is, workers living near the adobe may have had more permanent, closer ties with Vallejo's provisions and supplies. This social and spatial proximity might have provided opportunities to acquire industrially produced goods or the contexts in which to display or use them.

Scheduling

My final point concerns the impact of colonial labor on the scheduling of daily life. Historical archives hint at the ways that required daily labor occupied many waking hours for rancho workers. For instance, Native workers were called into the quadrangle of the Petaluma Adobe at dawn, given a breakfast of atole, and assigned their daily tasks (Hoopes 1965:36).[5] Vallejo himself states that "every morning the laborers met to call the roll, before dispersing for their various occupations" (1941:2). After a siesta break of approximately two hours around noon, work probably continued until dusk, although this is only an educated guess based on broader work patterns in Spanish America. How this work schedule played out on a weekly or monthly basis is unknown.

Similarly unknown is how Vallejo and Alvarado assigned individuals to labor tasks. If it was at all like its labor cousins, the missions and plantations, Rancho Petaluma may have had a combination of task and gang labor. In task systems, individuals worked on certain activities until finished; in gang systems, individuals worked for a certain amount of time during the day on a long-term project. Examples of the former might include weaving blankets and making candles; examples of the latter might include plowing fields and slaughtering cattle. As some plantation archaeologists have shown, the differences in labor type have significant effects on social life and the endurance of enforced labor (e.g., Singleton 1985; Young 1997), and this would be a fruitful topic for rancho studies.

It is currently impossible to ascertain the severity of the work schedule for Native Americans at Rancho Petaluma because the available documents are simply too coarse-grained, but we can be sure the schedule was strict and consistent. However, the archaeological record reveals that Native individuals and families had time to pursue other practices. If individuals were tethered too tightly, they would not have been able to procure obsidian, to gather manzanita berries from the chaparral slopes away from the adobe, to hunt deer and waterfowl, to gather shellfish and other resources in coast and bay settings, and to maintain trade relations with outlying groups to acquire these products. They would have eaten only those foods (e.g., beef, wheat, corn) provided and/or readily available and used only those raw material and tools (e.g., precontact obsidian on the surface, broken glass bottles) near at hand.

I discuss this latitude in opportunity only to illustrate the resilience of Native individuals involved in Rancho Petaluma and their dedication to other pursuits outside the colonial core. I do not mean to deny the hardship that many people endured at the rancho or the difficult times that led them to it. The varieties of recruitment methods were often severe, and Vallejo had a tendency to run his operations with a heavy hand. As Charles Brown, a resident in the area during the late 1830s, stated, Vallejo's "will was law, and no one dare[d] gainsay it" (1878:8). Native individuals having or perhaps making the opportunity to pursue practices outside of those required in a labor regime does not lessen the burden of colonial labor. What the pattern does indicate are many individuals' interests in holding tightly to some traditional practices and in using them in novel ways to live in and through the rancho labor regime. In parallel ways, archaeologists have shown that enslaved Africans on plantations in the American South and Caribbean could seek resources and relationships outside the plantation despite the known hardships of slave labor (e.g., Reitz, Gibbs, and Rathbun 1985; Thomas 1998; Wilkie and Farnsworth 1999).

Conclusion

To investigate social aspects of nineteenth-century Native American life at Rancho Petaluma required placing Native archaeological remains in a spatial and temporal context. Diet, stone tool technology, and labor formed key aspects of the archaeological record at Rancho Petaluma, much as they did in the everyday lives of Native Americans working at the rancho during the 1830s and 1840s. Food, rocks, and European and Asian goods were part of a complex social scene played out in daily activities. Earlier chapters related the specifics of activities that Native people participated in on a regular basis: finding food, grinding plants, butchering animals, preparing meals, making stone implements, working bone and shell raw materials, decorating themselves with beads and bird-bone tubes, and using ceramic, glass, and metal items. This chapter situated these activities in broader theoretical arenas.

More than simply subsistence, dietary remains denote a Native negotiation of practical politics on the rancho. Individuals accepted Vallejo's provisions, but they sought out acorns, grass seeds, deer, rabbits, and other foods to complete their meals. They felt the pressure of controlled food distribution, as many of them had witnessed in the Franciscan missions, but they managed to subvert its domination of their menus. More than simply an "old habit," lithic technology served as a node of practical politics on the rancho. Individuals procured raw material from a variety of sources (or trade networks connected to them), made these rocks into particular tool forms, and used them in a range of tasks. They did this in spite of the availability of metal tools for at least some tasks, the colonial "preference" for mass-produced goods, and the abundance and workability of glass bottles. Finally, more than simply the economic impact of labor, Native individuals felt the regimentation of their daily lives, household arrangements, and gender relations under the heavy hand of rancho labor. The hold was frequently tight, but individuals managed to reside within it. This "residence" provided access to food and goods, and it may have served as a site of identity negotiation between California Indian men and women. Some opted to introduce their labor duties and its associated toolkit into the household, whereas others did not.

The evidence, both archaeological and archival, suggests that Native people forged new identities in the colonial world of Rancho Petaluma. They held tightly to some traditional practices amidst new political and material choices, but they also adopted European items and perhaps associated practices. The glass, ceramic, and metal artifacts hint that these items may have been used, at least initially, in their designed forms. That is, Native people may have used ceramic bowls, glass bottles, metal containers, and manufactured clothing. Interestingly, the most prevalent practices were those surrounding stone tools, glass beads, and the creative mixture of wild and domesticated foods in the diet. This amalgamation comprised the material parameters of nineteenth-century Native American life and set the stage for Native persistence, changes, struggles, and identities in the latter half of the nineteenth century and well into the twentieth century.

Chapter 8

Conclusion

Stepping Back and Moving Forward

Exploring the entanglement of colonial worlds and indigenous practices on nineteenth-century California ranchos required an integrated suite of theoretical and methodological approaches and a focused case study. Notions of labor, agency, and practical politics provided unique entry points for chasing the various historical and social strands that held Rancho Petaluma together. As the results show, some strands were bound tightly, reining in and holding California Indians on the rancho, while others were wrapped more loosely, allowing Native people to control various aspects of their lives and relationships within or despite the labor regime. Some strands were anchored to the larger colonial system spread over the region, while others grew out of everyday interactions and goals in the local setting.

To study the past, we must study the actions of individuals within larger social and cultural settings. Even though certain individuals may be under severe domination and control, they still act with meaning and purpose. Classic cases are Native Americans swept up in colonial expansion, a process that archaeologists and historians have studied diligently for many decades. In this milieu, Native people frequently forged both a residence in and a resistance to the colonial world of the rancho, and they did so in very material ways. Illuminating these actions is possible only through the interplay of numerous archaeological and historical methods.

A multifaceted approach is the backbone of historical anthropology and archaeology. Each data source offers a way to evaluate the accuracy of another, and a multitude of data sources permits one to fill gaps left by others (Deagan 1991; Deagan and Scardaville 1985; Leone and Potter 1988; Wylie 1992). More importantly, the varieties of information provide an opportunity to explore the nuances, intricacies, and plurality of experiences within any given setting. As Matthews adeptly stated: "To situate what we recover from the archaeological record in history is not just the application of these rich historical data to archaeological findings, but the articulation of all our data in a dialectical fashion which restores the integration of cultural life originally found in our subjects' lives" (1999:269). In other words, doing archaeology without history or history without archaeology moves us away from enriched and inclusive histories of colonialism. This perspective informed my study of Rancho Petaluma. To try to study the Rancho Petaluma case without considering as many artifact classes as possible, without consulting available archival records, and without probing ethnographic sources would have been an injustice to those lives that I wanted to study. More than necessary to sort out the local issues in northern California, the resulting richness of information for Rancho Petaluma has implications for studies of archaeology, anthropology, and history in California and in colonial cases across North America.

California Historical Anthropology

This project follows in the tradition of those that study the multiethnic colonial history of western North America during the eighteenth and nineteenth centuries (e.g., Cook 1976; Greenwood 1989; Haas 1995; Hackel 1998; Hurtado 1988; Jackson and Castillo 1995; Lightfoot 1995; Lightfoot, Martinez, and Schiff 1998; Lightfoot, Wake, and Schiff 1993; Monroy 1990; Phillips 1974, 1975, 1980, 1993; Rawls 1984). Much like these scholars, I have tried to show that Native people were active players on the historical fleld, despite the hardships surrounding them. Yet I find that Phillips's assessment made over twenty-five years ago still rings true for the rancho period and the role of Native Americans: "Seldom has the historian viewed them as anything more than passive spectators of their own destruction, doing nothing to solve the problems created by invading white men and thereby playing only an insignificant role in the historical process" (1975:4). Not only should scholars focus more on Native social agency, but those who do should also acknowledge as much social agency in those individuals who sought a place in the colonial world as in those who resisted it outright (Hackel 1998:124). The latter forms of resistance—stealing horses, avoiding colonial settlements, battling colonial militias—often generate the most public attention, but they were frequently not the chief ways that indigenous people resisted or sought their own way through colonial worlds. Many indigenous people lived alongside, if not in, colonial contexts, and we must examine those lived lives, daily practices, and on-the-ground experiences. To study this phenomenon adequately, material evidence gathered through archaeology is critical. The nineteenth century is an important and volatile period when Native and colonial histories intertwined in California, but the interface has not received enough attention. Yet, the interface has direct consequences for ethnographies recorded in the late nineteenth and early twentieth centuries and for contemporary politics and culture.

This project was neither an exhaustive summary of rancho archaeology nor an attempt to characterize all possible responses by California Indians to Spanish and Mexican colonization. Instead it sought to explore the intricacies of Native American lives on California's ranchos by emphasizing a case with significant archaeological and historical potential. Despite its usefulness for this endeavor, the Rancho Petaluma example in nineteenth-century northern California should not be overgeneralized. It should not be taken to represent Native experiences on all Mexican-Californian ranchos until other rancho sites have been thoroughly examined, nor should the interpretations about this particular site, likely the residence of "trusted" workers attached to the Petaluma Adobe, be extrapolated to other as-of-yet-undiscovered sites on the historic Rancho Petaluma related to herder camps and outlying work spaces. Very different people, labor duties, and social relations may have been present in these localities.

That said, the Rancho Petaluma case still can contribute to anthropological, archaeological, historical, and Native American studies of the American West. Its uniqueness resides in the large numbers and diversity of indigenous people who worked the rancho; the enormous scale of productivity in livestock, crops, and manufactured goods; the influence of the rancho owner, Vallejo, in California politics and history; and the position of the rancho at a geopolitical nexus of Russians, Californios, American and British trappers, and numerous Native political groups across the region.

The Rancho Petaluma project not only offers its own particular framing of colonial and Native histories during California's early years but also provides a comparative case for refining interpretations of other colonial institutions. The most pertinent comparison lies with other ranchos across the region. At one level, the Rancho Petaluma project offers compelling views of everyday life for Native people on a Californio rancho that have not yet been available to historians or archaeologists. Brief glimpses have been offered for over forty years (Evans 1969; Greenwood 1989:460–61; Hurtado 1988; Monroy 1990; Wallace and Wallace 1958), and I hope that this project helps to fill the lacunae by contributing an in-depth treatment of a particular case. The project reveals the continuity of Native American stone tool technology and other crafts, the creative mixture of wild and domestic foods to complete the diet, and the incorporation of some mass-produced industrial goods into everyday life. It is worth pondering these same patterns for other rancho contexts to see if Rancho Petaluma was an anomaly on the far northern frontier of Mexican California.

At another level, the Rancho Petaluma project elucidates the potential of archaeology to draw out Native workers from the colonial shadows. It reveals the need to investigate other ranchos with an eye for studying Native workers through a combination of archaeological and historical data sets. We simply cannot rely solely on archival sources to understand the complex ways that Native people adapted to and struggled in rancho labor regimes. Historical archives pinpoint John Sutter's New Helvetia, the Yorba ranchos in southern California, and Salvador Vallejo's and George Yount's properties in Napa County as ripe for sustained archaeological study. Preliminary archaeological research at Vallejo's mother-in-law's rancho near Santa Rosa also holds promise (Beard 1993).

Another comparison for Rancho Petaluma is the Franciscan mission system. The two contexts possessed similar labor and supervisory regimes but vastly different religious, sexual, and residential attributes (see Cook 1976:302–8; Jackson and Castillo 1995). In addition, many ranchos succeeded the missions after secularization began in 1834, and Native people often left the mission confines to work for rancheros. Studying ranchos will give a longer-term perspective to mission studies by exploring what happened next in the story of Native American culture change and continuity during the historic period. Archaeological studies by Allen (1998), Costello (1989a, 1989b, 1990), Deetz (1963), Farnsworth (1989, 1992), and Hoover and Costello (1985) provide a solid template for comparing the effects of colonial labor, material goods, food availability, and social control on Native populations (see Silliman 2001b). Many of the material practices and items noted for Rancho Petaluma have parallels in earlier Native mission households: continued use of stone tools; adoption of ceramic and glass items for various purposes, including raw material; and the incorporation of domesticated crops and livestock into the diet without the full replacement of native species. Yet compared to the missions, the Rancho Petaluma excavations revealed more lithic practices tied into the regional landscape, more task-specific adoption of metal tools, and less diversity of introduced ceramics.

A further point of comparison for Rancho Petaluma is the Russian settlement at Colony Ross, established in 1812 (Farris 1989b; Lightfoot, Martinez, and Schiff 1998; Lightfoot, Schiff, and Wake 1997; Lightfoot, Wake, and Schiff 1993). The colonial outpost overlapped with Rancho Petaluma between 1834 and 1841, and Russian residents interacted and traded with Vallejo, other colonists, and Native Americans in the Sonoma-Petaluma region. Colony Ross and Rancho Petaluma both used Native labor extensively and may have had similar recruitment and provisioning practices. Differences between the two include the presence of a company store at Ross, the Russian "importation" of Alaskan Natives to the Sonoma Coast for sea otter hunting, and the extensively documented intermarriage between California Indians and Native Alaskans (Lightfoot, Schiff, and Wake 1997). Some of the more profitable comparisons between Colony Ross and Rancho Petaluma might concern the greater reliance on wild foods at Colony Ross, the differences in bead color preferences between the sites, the greater connection of Rancho Petaluma workers to obsidian trade networks, and the related lack of formal tools made from bottle glass and ceramics in Petaluma relative to Ross.

Archaeology of Colonialism and Culture Contact

In addition to addressing regional historical and anthropological issues in California, Rancho Petaluma has implications for studies of culture contact and colonialism elsewhere in North America. Much of this relevance concerns theoretical and methodological issues more than empirical ones, since material culture and historical trajectories differed between various regions, periods, and colonizing groups.

By framing the book around the juxtaposition of colonial worlds and indigenous practices, I sought to counteract the implicit assumption that ranchos are worthy of study only from the perspective of their owners, the rancheros. Native workers far outnumbered rancheros and their families on the larger rancho properties, but they have received very little scholarly attention. I also wanted to subvert the notion that colonial worlds directly and rigidly channel their participants toward colonial practices. Like their counterparts in missions, forts, and other settlements, indigenous workers and residents at ranchos were not automatons with proscribed reactions or passive recipients of colonial domination. This does not mean, however, that they were equal participants in the colonial system or that they were not severely subjugated beneath legal, political, economic, and physical coercion. Only archaeology, combined with written or oral history, can hope to reveal the subtleties.

One can term these communities multiethnic or perhaps even pluralistic, but these terms should not conjure up images of equal opportunity coexistence between different cultural or social groups. Rather, they should illuminate the diversity of experiences (e.g., ethnicity, gender, class) that permeated the rancho setting and the relations of power that structured the domains in which these played out. Studying indigenous people in colonial communities requires remembering—a very political and public process—that they were there. One must recognize their participation, contribution, and lives in these settings before there is any hope of finding the evidence for them. These are not pioneering observations, since many archaeologists and historians have focused much of their careers on unraveling the Native aspects of post-Columbian North America (and Central and South America). However, scholars outside of this research realm and a vast majority of the public are not yet aware of the indigenous aspects of colonial worlds. When they think of ranchos or haciendas, they do not "remember" that California Indians worked them or that ranchos were instruments of colonialism.

The study of Native people in colonial communities also requires viewing their activities in the context of their own cultural traditions and the colonial world that surrounded them, a dual process that can take place only in the interplay of different kinds of historical information. This represents more than a demonstration to nonarchaeologists of the role of archaeological information for historical studies. It serves also as a reminder to archaeologists to be wary of the disciplinary divide between "history" and "prehistory" and the assumptions packed into it (Lightfoot 1995). My concern is that contact period and postcontact Native American sites are misidentified on the West Coast and elsewhere because of assumptions about what an "Indian" site should look like. Greenwood correctly stated that it would be difficult to identify a rancho period Native American site because of the mixing of material culture and food practices from Native and European cultures (1989:462), but, as undoubtedly she would agree, difficulty is not impossibility. The implicit assumption of what "Indian" material culture looks like in the archaeological record of colonialism before we even begin looking at it can be detrimental to culture contact and colonial studies. No Native American was "indigenous" to a rancho or, similarly, to a mission, fort, or colonial town, even though ranchos would have been the only such institution with a size large enough to potentially encompass somewhat autonomous Native villages. Despite the high likelihood that individuals involved in these colonial settings would have drawn on their prerancho (or fully precontact) cultural practices and material culture, we cannot assume that stone tools mean "traditional" or that metal tools mean "acculturated." Stated generally, we cannot assume that the way that something is made or the person responsible for manufacturing it determines its ultimate use and meaning. Colonial settings entail immense complexity, with individuals vying for resources, identities, power, and survival.

Much like the need to recognize the social and cultural plurality of the rancho, the role of labor in structuring and experiencing colonialism requires direct attention. To sort out the practices of daily life at Rancho Petaluma required explicit considerations of colonial labor: how it structured everyday activity, how it impacted social relations, how it was endured, how its materiality impacted the household, and how it might be used or rejected in identity politics. Much of this was possible only through considering a variety of archival, spatial, faunal, floral, and artifactual data. Framing social questions around labor revealed distinctive aspects of Rancho Petaluma. For instance, diet was more than an index of acculturation; it marked the interplay of labor provisions and off-work food procurement. Metal objects were more than reflections of Native adoption of new technology; they were intimately tied to labor duties on the rancho and users' perceptions of and access to them. Stone tools meant more than a continuity of traditional practice; they revealed Native attempts to bring colonial labor into material familiarity, to make stone tool use meaningful in the nineteenth century, and to retain the social access to raw material sources in the indigenous landscape.

Rancho Petaluma serves as only one case among many where colonial settlements involved the employment, conscription, or enslavement of indigenous people for colonial labor. Because of the centrality of labor in many Native American experiences of colonial communities, labor must be admitted into the center of scholarly attempts to interpret them. No simple formula can track labor, since it can be oppressive and subduing, mundane and routine, opportunistic and productive. Labor can be all of these at once, given the variety of individuals and institutions involved in any colonial setting. Even though labor can usefully be considered as an economic structure, a quantifiable property, or an index of social stratification, it is much more than these. Labor is a critical ingredient in the negotiation of social relationships and everyday life for those involved in it, particularly in the realm of colonialism in Native North America. The Rancho Petaluma study offers an example of how to track such labor on the ground, within the everyday lives of indigenous people and their interactions with colonialism, and in the ground, within the diverse and rich archaeological record.

Notes

Preface

1. I use the term "Mexican California" throughout the book to refer to a period after what would be appropriately termed "Spanish colonial California." The former term better captures the political scene of the second quarter of the nineteenth century than would broader monikers such as "Hispanic California" or "colonial California." However, this nomenclature should *not* imply that Mexican-Californians, or Californios as they came to be called, thought of themselves as "Mexican." Although a former Spanish colonial territory falling under the jurisdiction and governance of Mexico following that region's independence from Spain in 1821, California developed its own regional identity and, at times, attempted to institute its own provincial government and commerce, particularly in the mid-1830s and 1840s. Later sections in the book briefly outline this process.

2. Throughout this work I refer to indigenous groups of California as both California Indians and Native Americans. The former is the term preferred by many Native people who claim that heritage, although the latter is considered the more appropriate appellation on the national level to refer to America's indigenous populations. I alternate between them only to vary writing style while respecting the indigenous communities' rights to name themselves.

3. "North Bay" refers to regions fringing and beyond the northern edge of San Francisco Bay in the counties of Marin, Sonoma, Napa, and Solano; "South Bay" refers to regions along the southern edges of San Francisco Bay.

Chapter 1. Native Americans and Colonialism: An Introduction

1. The epigraph and text quotations by Engelhardt regarding Francisca Benicia Carrillo de Vallejo are quotations drawn from Manuel Torres, who visited the Vallejos in Sonoma in 1844, and his recounting of her statements.

2. *Nondirected contact* is a term used by some scholars to refer to instances where "there is interaction between members of the different societies . . . but there is not control of one society's members by the other" (Spicer 1961:520). Its opposite would be *directed contact*, a situation more appropriately termed *colonialism*.

3. For alternate applications of similar theoretical frameworks, see Dobres (1995, 2000), Dobres and Hoffman (1994), Dobres and Robb (2000), Johnson (1989), and Meskell (1998).

4. California's indigenous people can be called hunter-gatherers because of their sole reliance on food products obtained through gathering, fishing, and hunting. Yet invoking the term often conjures up a suite of assumptions about social organization that homogenize the variability seen in many hunter-gatherer societies, especially those that resided in California for several thousand years. Although this project has ramifications for studies of the impact of colonialism on hunter-gatherers (as opposed to agriculturalists), I do not explicitly engage this issue here. Native entry into the rancho system or any other context in colonial California altered subsistence pursuits such that few California Indians remained strictly "hunter-gatherers," but these social and material predecessors are crucial to understand their adaptations in the colonial world.

5. When using information drawn from Sherburne Cook, I have chosen to refer to the 1976 compilation of his 1940s *Ibero-Americana* articles, since the book version is the more widely available. Readers seeking the context of information and quotations used in this book should note that within the 1976 volume, page numbers 1–194 belong with Cook (1943a), page numbers 197–251 belong with Cook (1943b), page numbers 255–361 belong with Cook (1943c), and page numbers 449–507 belong with Cook (1941).

Chapter 2. Native Life and Labor: A California Rancho Perspective

1. Of course, sixty years have not passed since the 1976 compilation volume but since the first publication of Cook's articles in *Ibero-Americana* in the early 1940s.

2. In California, aguardiente (Latin *agua ardens*, or "fire water") referred to a cheap wine brandy often made in southern California vineyards (Phillips 1980:435 n. 30).

3. Costello (1994:5) has also discussed archaeological results from two ranches associated with Mission San Antonio de Padua. Worked by Native neophytes at the mission, these sites contained *tejas* (roof tiles), *ladrillos* (floor tiles), ceramics, and stone tool debitage.

Chapter 3. Revisiting History: Native Americans at Rancho Petaluma

1. For instance, the translated diary of Father Altimira mentions "the large *Laguna de Tolay*, so named for the chief of the Indians who formerly populated this vicinity," "the beautiful plain of the aforesaid *Napa*, so called by the Indians who formerly lived here," "the famous Plain of *Suisun* which was the name of the Indians previously settling at this place," and "the small water of the *ranchería* of the *Petalumas* who in former times lived there" (Smilie 1975:6, 8, 10). Although a view only through colonists' eyes, the picture is of a relatively depopulated landscape immediately north of San Francisco Bay. Native Americans accompanying the expedition

with Altimira were knowledgeable of the terrain, having once been residents there (Smilie 1975:6, 8, 11), but the only indigenous inhabitants seem to have been those in the Suisun Valley area at the far eastern edge of the North Bay (Smilie 1975:8–9). Altimira did, however, meet a band of Petaluma warriors along Adobe Creek (see note 7 below).

2. In a 1956 interview, Alice Adams of Petaluma noted that this location across Adobe Creek from Petaluma Adobe "seemed about right" for the locations of Vallejo's California Indian workers (Issler 1956).

3. Native American youth, both girls and boys, may have entered positions of servitude on ranchos as part of treaty making. For instance, Vallejo received as part of the 1837 treaty forged with Succara, a leader of the Satiyomi who remained in conflict with Vallejo for years, six young Native women and Succara's brother and two sons (Vallejo 1875c:251–52). However, Vallejo turned the women over to Chief Solano and treated Succara's kin as he would have "Russian soldiers" at Sonoma. What this entailed is unclear.

4. The document cited is undated with no author attributed to it. However, comparison of the handwriting style for specific letters and entire words between this document and others penned by Miguel Alvarado attest that the same author wrote all of these. Since Alvarado was responsible for managing Rancho Petaluma and its workers, this discovery is not at all surprising, and it suggests that Alvarado probably compiled the roster sometime between 1839 and 1849. I am very grateful to Rose Marie Beebe of Santa Clara University for her generous assistance in deciphering the list.

5. Even though this number has often been cited as a direct reference to the number of Native workers (Hoopes 1965:20), Vallejo's wording cannot be taken at face value. He very well may have referred to the number of Native workers on the rancho at any one time, or he may have alluded to the total number of Native people who had worked the rancho and received supplies over the fifteen or more years of operation or to the number of Native people off the rancho with whom he had maintained trading relations in exchange for military and political peace. Despite being a statement by Vallejo himself, I find this population estimate the most suspect.

6. All direct quotations from Alvarado's notes are translations of the original Spanish, provided in a typewritten document entitled "A Series of Letters from Miguel Alvarado to General Vallejo, 1839–1849" on file at the History Room, Petaluma Regional Library, Petaluma, California. Based on notes by Anne Issler, the translator is presumed to be George Tays. Note also that all Native Americans baptized at Franciscan missions were given Spanish names.

7. This is a variant of the Coast Miwok name Livantolomi for the Konhomtara Southern Pomo group near Sebastopol (Milliken 1995:246). Father Altimira situates the Libantiloyomi approximately 3.5 leagues, or over 10 miles, to the northwest of their camp. The "wandering warriors" joined the Altimira encampment on Arroyo Lema, or Adobe Creek, in a location perhaps not far from the future Petaluma Adobe site or, according to Smilie's (1975:12) speculations, right on it. The expedition party left the camp the next morning, barely twelve hours later, and they returned to

this campsite approximately one week later for another night of rest (Smilie 1975:6, 10).

8. The Licatiut (Lekahtewut) were called Pet-a-loo-mah-che by the Cainamero (Merriam 1907:355, 1977:139), and the name Petaluma translates as "flat back" (Barrett 1908:310). Maria Copa claimed that Coast Miwok at the Petaluma village may have called themselves Leka-tiwüt, meaning "cross-ways willow" (Collier and Thalman 1996:9).

9. See McLendon and Oswalt (1978:279) and Merriam (1977:62–63). This is the group called Gallinoméro by Powers (1976:174–85). Their Coast Miwok name and possible Wappo affiliation make this Southern Pomo affiliation uncertain, but the geographical location places them in that territory. It is still possible that the Satiyomi were a displaced Wappo group (Heizer 1978:701; McClellan 1953:235), and given the antagonism between the Cainamero and the Satiyomi, there is a chance that the Satiyomi were related to the Ashochimi Wappo mentioned by Powers (1976:174, 196–203; see also Kroeber 1925:219). Yet Vallejo and others made no mention of the Ashochimi chief Colorado in treaties or battles, even though he was a prominent leader (Powers 1976:198; see also Revere 1849:143).

10. Atole in California appears to have consisted of ground wheat (Cook 1976:93; Hoopes 1965:36), barley (Hoopes 1965:36; Margolin 1989:85), acorns (Bryant 1985:268; Vallejo 1875a:12), and, undoubtedly, corn. This is a considerable divergence from its usage in Mexico, where it refers strictly to a cornmeal gruel. It is unclear whether the expansion in word meaning is due to different food preferences in California or to some non-Hispanic visitors' inability to distinguish "real" atole from other gruellike dishes such as *pinole* made from ground seeds (traditional) or corn (Mexican) or traditional acorn mushes.

11. The limited 1967 edition of Davis's book contains this passage at the end of chapter 7. Interestingly, this text is absent from the original 1929 John Howell edition and from the original 1889 *Sixty Years in California* that gave rise to the expanded *Seventy-Five Years in California* published after Davis's death. The publisher's preface to the 1967 edition provides the following clarification: "This third edition, edited by Harold A. Small, is issued by Warren R. Howell, who continues at the same address the business founded and so long conducted by his father. By kind permission of the California Historical Society, which in 1937 acquired from Ralph H. Cross of Berkeley, Davis' own marked copy of the first edition, the corrections and additions handwritten therein by the author are included in the present text; they have been inserted at the proper places by Linda Peterson."

12. *Pinole* is not a term normally associated with corn flour, and it is unclear why Napoleón Vallejo employed it. The term usually refers to flour ground from wild or domesticated seeds. Napoleón was born in 1850, after the decline of the Mexican period and the heyday of Rancho Petaluma, so he speaks either of activities in the 1850s or of stories that he heard about the 1840s. His observation does suggest, however, that individuals may have ground corn in a designated workplace, perhaps accounting for the lack of significant corn in the archaeobotanical record of Native American living areas on his father's rancho (see chapter 6).

13. Yet recollections of a Petaluma resident in the 1950s mentioned that the Farleys, who resided in the Petaluma Adobe sometime around 1854, had Vallejo's "Indian retainers" working occasionally for them "driving wild cattle" (Issler 1956).

Chapter 4. Lost Laborers in Northern California: Search and Recovery

1. The data from these streamside excavations have been incorporated throughout the book, rendering counts and percentages different from those first reported in Silliman (2000a).

2. Four 1-by-1-meter test units were also excavated in the field, but unless noted otherwise, I exclude their artifacts, except for glass beads, from all tabulation and discussion, since they contributed little to overall site interpretation (see Silliman 2000a:138–43).

3. Obsidian hydration analysis involves the width measurement of water absorption bands that form on an exposed surface of obsidian as a function of time. The method is common in California as a chronometric tool, but controversy surrounds its accuracy as a dating method. As I detail elsewhere (Silliman 2005), the Rancho Petaluma obsidian hydration data are extremely useful for identifying the use(s) of the site over time and the intensity of lithic production in the nineteenth century.

Chapter 5. Things of Everyday Life: Material Culture on Rancho Petaluma

1. I reiterate that these are the items that survived the ravages of time (i.e., they are largely inorganic) and that happened to be discovered during excavation. The list is only a subset of the full repertoire of material culture made, used, and discarded by Native Americans in the nineteenth century, but this subset can be compiled into a rich story of Native life on Rancho Petaluma.

2. A flake is defined as chipping debris showing evidence of a platform where the core was struck to detach the flake, an identified dorsal (outside) and ventral (inside) surface, and a terminus (end) where the force that had entered from the platform found its exit from the rock. Flake shatter refers to debitage pieces that are missing either the platform or the terminus but are still clearly flakes. Those missing only the terminal end are called proximal flakes. Angular shatter refers to debitage that has no flake characteristics and has shattered from the core during knapping. My analysis closely follows Andrefsky (1998).

3. Further details are provided elsewhere (Silliman 2000b, 2005). This is an interesting but complex issue that I cannot detail here. Note that the Oakmont source is not shown in figure 1, but it is probably located near Franz Valley (see Silliman 2000b).

4. For instance, Felton, Lortie, and Schulz (1984:fig. 17) classified these larger varieties as harness buckles. They are also reminiscent of two buckles recovered by Dietz (1976:fig. 12b–c) at a Coast Miwok site in Marin County.

5. Some of the ceramics classified as whiteware may be the semivitreous ironstone of the nineteenth century. The only good way to distinguish these wares is

through either a hallmark or a test of paste hardness, since ironstone is vitrified and will pass a "scratch test." Other methods such as visual appearance, body thickness, and decoration are not reliable (Paul Farnsworth, personal communication, 2003). Having realized this problem late in the research, I opted not to redo my ceramic analysis to distinguish these two wares, since the distinction would not have altered the book's interpretations. Ironically, though, the only truly identifiable ceramic hallmark at the site (described in the second paragraph following this one) does belong to an ironstone vessel, at least according to the printed words. Since I originally believed this to be a whiteware, I imagine that fine-tuning the Rancho Petaluma ceramic classification may be necessary in the future. Fortunately, such a reclassification would likely affect less than 5 percent (approximately twenty sherds) of the entire ceramic assemblage.

6. Seven other bone artifacts were recovered: (1) a burned incisor with circumferential scoring in the Block; (2) two refittable burned bone items with shallow cut marks on the outer surface and an approximately 1.4-millimeter hole drilled into the ends found in the Block; (3) a fragment of a burned, gently serrated bone artifact in the Block; (4) a long bone shaft fragment of a large mammal with coarse serrations recovered in the Midden Trench; (5) a portion of an object with parallel rows of perforations and a central hole, perhaps of non-Native manufacture; and (6) a long bone shaft fragment with irregularly spaced but angled notches along one side found in Trench 1.

7. For example, recent excavations from El Presidio de San Francisco retrieved glass beads in midden and floor deposits from a late 1700s to early 1800s colonial household (Voss 2002:451–53, 540). No California Indians are believed to have been associated with this apartment and residential trash area, a pattern that hints at the possibility that Spanish colonial residents in the San Francisco Bay area made some use of glass beads. However, Voss recovered only twenty-eight beads out of over fourteen thousand items of artifactual material culture from the household floor and midden contexts, suggesting that they played only a minor role. In stark contrast to the Rancho Petaluma site and others that denote significant California Indian residence, not a single opaque white bead was found in the very darkly colored bead collection.

8. Note that this is the only category of artifacts that include items found in the four test units excavated away from the core of Area B and in the surface testing units (see Silliman 2000a:138–43, 349). I simplified the glass bead classification by assigning a unique variety number based on the assemblage. The classification combined variables of color, shape, and size to produce a variety unique to this particular bead assemblage. The drawn beads included 693 specimens in 20 varieties of opaque, monochrome, cylindrical, undecorated beads; 83 specimens in 14 varieties of translucent, monochrome, cylindrical, undecorated beads; 2 specimens in 2 varieties of transparent, cylindrical-molded, undecorated beads; 9 specimens in 8 varieties of the combination of monochrome ovoidal-molded-spheroidal-toroidal beads; and 509 specimens in 20 varieties of opaque

and translucent, polychrome, cylindrical, undecorated beads. One additional drawn bead is included in the site total, but its condition is too poor for categorization. The wound beads include 14 specimens in 9 varieties of monochrome beads of ovoidal, pyramidal, and bipyramidal shapes; 31 specimens in 17 varieties of spheroidal beads that range from opaque to translucent and from undecorated to banded; 4 specimens in 2 varieties of large "melon beads" with heavily decomposed, banded glass; and 1 specimen of 1 variety of a possible wound-and-shaped bead, which is a large bead with a transparent exterior overlaying a pink-and-blue core.

Chapter 6. Food and Politics on Colonial Ranchos: The Petaluma Case

1. Although not reliably identifiable, the vast majority of indeterminate large mammals shown in the tables compare favorably to cattle with respect to size and shape, further emphasizing the prominence of this livestock species.

2. Vallejo also procured tule elk from Mare Island, near the modern city of Vallejo, for tallow (Davis 1929:31; Robinson 1891:72; N. Vallejo 1890:6), and Native people made strings of these elk spinal cords for their manzanita bows (N. Vallejo 1890:6). However, no elk bones were recovered during excavation.

3. Such an element comparison is viable, since there appears to be little attrition due to differences in bone density.

4. Specific articulated units include one each of (1) astragalus, calcaneus, tarsals, metatarsal, and sesamoids; (2) tibia and tarsals; (3) radius and ulna; (4) radius, distal ulna, and carpals; and (5) phalanx 1, phalanx 2, and sesamoids.

5. See Silliman (2000a:tables 7.14–7.19) for all raw counts.

6. The dock could be an introduced variety.

7. The latter might be evidenced by the charred Poaceae embryos and floret/rachis pieces in the Midden, especially in Feature A.

8. Maria Copa and Tom Smith both claim that these bulbs were collected in the spring (Collier and Thalman 1996:46).

Chapter 7. Colonial Worlds, Indigenous Practices: Interpreting Rancho Petaluma

1. Vallejo (1941:2) may have been referring only to the Native people "who lived in the surrounding country, and in peace" with him rather than to workers, but it is likely that his workers had similar access to food.

2. Metates had been in use at Petaluma before the construction of a grinding mill, but the reference is unclear (Fitch 1874:43).

3. For instance, these very categories of metal artifacts have been recovered in presumed Native contexts at Spanish mission sites such as Mission San Antonio (Hoover and Costello 1985).

4. However, these artifacts often co-occur with male laboring tools such as axes and plows, suggesting different types of social and material relations in mission households.

5. Hoopes may have taken a bit of literary license when describing the specifics of the daily labor schedule. I have tracked most of the references in his unpublished manuscript that he completed for the California Department of Parks and Recreation, but they do not offer the kind of detail that he suggests. As a result, I use his reconstruction only tentatively.

References Cited

Allen, Rebecca S.

1992   The use of shellfish and shell beads at Santa Cruz Mission. *Pacific Coast Archaeological Society Quarterly* 28(2):18–34.

1998   *Native Americans at Mission Santa Cruz, 1791–1834: Interpreting the archaeological record.* Perspectives in California Archaeology, vol. 5. Los Angeles: Institute of Archaeology, University of California.

Almaguer, Tomás

1994   *Racial fault lines: The historical origins of white supremacy in California.* Berkeley: University of California Press.

Alvarado, Miguel

1839   Letter to Mariano G. Vallejo from Petaluma, December 6. In Documentos para la historia de California, 1769–1850, compiled by Mariano G. Vallejo, 1874. BANC MSS C–B 32:334, Bancroft Library, University of California, Berkeley.

1844a   Letter to Mariano G. Vallejo from Petaluma, September 23. In Documentos para la historia de California, 1769–1850, compiled by Mariano G. Vallejo, 1874. BANC MSS C–B 34:60, Bancroft Library, University of California, Berkeley.

1844b   Letter to Mariano G. Vallejo from Petaluma, December 3. In Documentos para la historia de California, 1769–1850, compiled by Mariano G. Vallejo, 1874. BANC MSS C–B 34:80, Bancroft Library, University of California, Berkeley.

1845   Letter to Mariano G. Vallejo from Petaluma, January 9. In Documentos para la historia de California, 1769–1850, compiled by Mariano G. Vallejo, 1874. BANC MSS C–B 13:131, Bancroft Library, University of California, Berkeley.

1848   Letter to Mariano G. Vallejo from Petaluma, February 29. In Documentos para la historia de California, 1769–1850, compiled by Mariano G. Vallejo, 1874. BANC MSS C–B 12:334, Bancroft Library, University of California, Berkeley.

1849   Letter to Mariano G. Vallejo from Petaluma, February 10. In Docu-mentos para la historia de California, 1769–1850, compiled by Mariano G. Vallejo, 1874. BANC MSS C–B 13:6, Bancroft Library, University of California, Berkeley.

n.d.   List of inhabitants at Petaluma. In Documentos para la historia de California, 1817–1850: Alviso Family Papers. BANC MSS C–B 66:163, Bancroft Library, University of California, Berkeley.

Amaroli, Paul E., and Thomas M. Origer

1984   *Salvage excavation of a human cremation at CA–Son–1281, Petaluma Adobe State Park, Petaluma, California*. Report on file, Northwest Information Center, Sonoma State University, Rohnert Park, Calif.

Andrefsky, William, Jr.

1998   *Lithics: Macroscopic approaches to analysis*. Cambridge Manuals in Archaeology. Cambridge: Cambridge University Press.

Archibald, Robert

1978   Indian labor at the California missions: Slavery or salvation? *Journal of San Diego History* 24(2):172–81.

Arnold, Jeanne E.

1993   Labor and the rise of complex hunter-gatherers. *Journal of Anthropological Archaeology* 12(1):75–119.

1996   Organizational transformations: Power and labor among complex hunter-gatherers and other intermediate societies. In *Emergent complexity: The evolution of intermediate societies*, edited by Jeanne E. Arnold, pp. 59–73. International Monographs in Prehistory, Archaeological Series 9, Ann Arbor, Michigan.

Arnold, Jeanne A., and Ann Munns

1994   Independent or attached specialization: The organization of shell bead production in California. *Journal of Field Archaeology* 21(4):473–89.

Bakken, Gordon Morris

1997   Rancho Cañon de Santa Ana. In *Rancho days in southern California: An anthology with new perspectives*, edited by Kenneth Pauley, pp. 207–23. Studio City, Calif.: Westerners, Los Angeles Corral.

Bamforth, Douglas B.

1993   Stone tools, steel tools: Contact period household technology at Helo'. In *Ethnohistory and archaeology: Approaches to postcontact change in the New World*, edited by J. Daniel Rogers and Samuel M. Wilson, pp. 49–72. New York: Plenum Press.

Bancroft, Hubert Howe

1885   *History of California, volume III: 1825–1840*. San Francisco: History Company.

1886   *History of California, volume IV: 1840–1845*. San Francisco: History Company.

1888   *California pastoral*. San Francisco: History Company.

Barrett, Samuel A.

1908   *The ethnogeography of the Pomo and neighboring Indians.* University of California Publications in American Archaeology and Ethnology, vol. 6, no. 1. Berkeley: University of California Press.

1952   *Material aspects of Pomo culture.* Bulletin of the Public Museum of the City of Milwaukee, vol. 20, pts. 1–2.

Basgall, Mark E.

1987   Resource intensification among hunter-gatherers: Acorn economies in prehistoric California. In *Research in economic anthropology,* vol. 9, edited by Barry L. Isaac, pp. 21–52. Greenwich, Conn.: JAI Press.

Bates, Robert L., and Julia A. Jackson, editors

1984   *Dictionary of geological terms.* 3rd edition. New York: Doubleday.

Bauer, Helen

1953   *Early rancho days.* Garden City, N.Y.: Doubleday and Company.

Beard, Vicki R.

1993   Let the world draw closer together: Sociocultural aspects of the Carrillo Adobe Site. Master's thesis, Sonoma State University, Rohnert Park, Calif.

Beardsley, Richard K.

1954   *Temporal and areal relationships in central California archaeology.* University of California Archaeological Survey Reports 24, 25. University of California, Berkeley.

Becker, Robert H.

1964   *Diseños of California ranchos: Maps of thirty-seven land grants [1822–1846].* San Francisco: Book Club of California.

Bennyhoff, James A.

1994   The Napa district and Wappo prehistory. In *Toward a new taxonomic framework for California archaeology,* edited by Richard E. Hughes, pp. 49–56. Contributions of the Archaeological Research Facility 52, University of California, Berkeley.

Binford, Lewis R.

1981   *Bones: Ancient men and modern myths.* New York: Academic Press.

1984   *Faunal remains from Klasies River mouth.* New York: Academic Press.

Black, E. B.

1975   *Rancho Cucamonga and doña Merced.* Redlands, Calif.: San Bernardino County Museum Association.

Bocek, Barbara

1984   Ethnobotany of Costanoan Indians, California, based on collections by John P. Harrington. *Economic Botany* 38(2):240–45.

Boggs, William M.

1913   An interesting letter regarding "The Old Adobe," 1907, courtesy of Robert A. Poppe. *Northern Crown* 5(5).

Bolander, Gordon L., and Benjamin D. Parmeter

1978   *Birds of Sonoma County, California: An annotated checklist and birding gazetteer.* Napa, Calif.: Grape Press Printing.

Bourdieu, Pierre
1977   *Outline of the theory of practice.* Cambridge: Cambridge University Press.
1990   *The logic of practice.* Cambridge: Polity Press.
Bowman, Jacob N., and George W. Hendry
1940   The Spanish and Mexican adobes and other buildings in the nine San Francisco Bay counties, 1776 to about 1850, vol. 2. Bancroft Library, University of California, Berkeley.
Brack, Mark L.
1991   Domestic architecture in Hispanic California: The Monterey style reconsidered. In *Perspectives in vernacular architecture, IV,* edited by Thomas Carter and Bernard L. Herman, pp. 163–73. Columbia: University of Missouri Press.
Brown, Charles
1878   Statement of recollections of early events in California. BANC MSS C–D 53, Bancroft Library, University of California, Berkeley.
Brown, Madie D.
1956   General Vallejo's Petaluma Adobe . . . A house of the past. *Argonaut,* July 20, 8–9.
Bryant, Edwin
1985   *What I saw in California.* 1848. Reprint, Lincoln: University of Nebraska Press.
Buchanan, Ian
2000   *Michel de Certeau: Cultural theorist.* London: Sage Publications.
Cabak, Melanie, and Stephen Loring
2000   "A set of very fair cups and saucers": Stamped ceramics as an example of Inuit incorporation. *International Journal of Historical Archaeology* 4(1):1–34.
Carlson, Pamela McGuire, and E. Breck Parkman
1986   An exceptional adaptation: Camilo Ynitia. *California History* 65(4):238–47.
Carrico, Richard L., and Florence C. Shipek
1995   Indian labor in San Diego County, California, 1850–1900. In *Native Americans and wage labor: Ethnohistorical perspectives,* edited by Alice Littlefield and Martha C. Knack, pp. 198–217. Norman: University of Oklahoma Press.
Carriger, Nicolas
1874   Autobiography. BANC MSS C–E 65:6, Bancroft Library, University of California, Berkeley.
Carrillo, Julio
1877   Statements of Julio Carrillo. BANC MSS C–E 67:8, Bancroft Library, University of California, Berkeley.
Cassell, Mark S.
2003   Flint and foxes: Chert scrapers and the fur industry in late 19th- and early 20th-century North Alaska. In *Stone tool traditions in the contact era,* edited by Charles Cobb, pp. 151–64. Tuscaloosa: University of Alabama Press.

Castillo, Edward D.

1978 The impact of Euro-American exploration and settlement. In *California*, edited by Robert F. Heizer, pp. 99–127. Vol. 8 of *Handbook of North American Indians*, William Sturtevant, general editor. Washington, D.C.: Smithsonian Institution Press.

1989a The assassination of Padre Andrés Quintana by the Indians of Mission Santa Cruz in 1812: The narrative of Lorenzo Asisara. *California History* 68(3):116–25.

1989b The native responses to the colonization of Alta California. In *Archaeological and historical perspectives on the Spanish Borderlands West*, edited by David Hurst Thomas, pp. 377–94. Vol. 1 of *Columbian consequences*. Washington, D.C.: Smithsonian Institution Press.

Certeau, Michel de

1984 *The practice of everyday life*. Berkeley: University of California Press.

Chace, Paul G.

1969 The archaeology of Cienaga: The oldest structure on the Irvine Ranch. *Pacific Coast Archaeological Society Quarterly* 5(3):39–70.

Chesnut, V. K.

1902 Plants used by the Indians of Mendocino County, California. *Contributions of the National Herbarium* 7(8):295–422.

Cleaveland, Alice Mae

1932 The North Bay shore during the Spanish and Mexican regimes. Master's thesis, Department of History, University of California, Berkeley.

Cleland, Robert Glass

1941 *The cattle on a thousand hills: Southern California, 1850–1870*. San Marino, Calif.: Huntington Library.

Clemmer, John S.

1961 *The corrals at Vallejo's Petaluma Adobe State Historical Monument*. Report on file, California Department of Parks and Recreation, State Archaeological Collections Research Facility, West Sacramento.

Collier, Mary E. T., and Sylvia B. Thalman, editors

1996 *Interviews with Tom Smith and Maria Copa: Isabel Kelly's ethnographic notes on the Coast Miwok Indians of Marin and southern Sonoma counties, California*. 2nd printing. MAPOM Occasional Paper no. 6. San Rafael, Calif.

Colton, Walter

1854 Don Mariano Guadalupe Vallejo. BANC MSS 76/79c, box 3, Napoleón Vallejo "Notes and Drafts," Bancroft Library, University of California, Berkeley.

Comaroff, John, and Jean Comaroff

1991 *Of revelation and revolution: Christianity, colonialism, and consciousness in South Africa, vol. 1*. Chicago: University of Chicago Press.

Cook, Sherburne F.

1941 The mechanism and extent of dietary adaptation among certain groups of California and Nevada Indians. *Ibero-Americana* 18:1–59.

1943a The Indian versus the Spanish mission. *Ibero-Americana* 21:1–194.

1943b   The physical and demographic reaction of the nonmission Indians in colonial and provincial California. *Ibero-Americana* 22:1–55.

1943c   The American invasion, 1848–1870. *Ibero-Americana* 23:1–115.

1976   *The conflict between the California Indian and white civilization.* Berkeley: University of California Press.

Coombs, Gary, and Fred Plog

1977   The conversion of the Chumash Indians: An ecological perspective. *Human Ecology* 5:309–28.

Costello, Julia

1985   Ceramics. In *Excavations at Mission San Antonio 1976–1978,* by Robert L. Hoover and Julia G. Costello, pp. 20–48. Monograph 26, Institute of Archaeology, University of California, Los Angeles.

1989a   *Santa Inés Mission excavations, 1986–1988.* Salinas, Calif.: Coyote Press.

1989b   Variability among the Alta California missions: The economics of agricultural production. In *Archaeological and historical perspectives on the Spanish Borderlands West,* edited by David Hurst Thomas, pp. 435–50. Vol. 1 of *Columbian consequences.* Washington, D.C.: Smithsonian Institution Press.

1990   Variability and economic change in the California missions: An historical and archaeological case study. Ph.D. diss., Department of Anthropology, University of California, Santa Barbara.

1992   Not peas in a pod: Documenting diversity among the California missions. In *Text-aided archaeology,* edited by Barbara J. Little, pp. 67–81. Boca Raton, Fla.: CRC Press.

1994   *The ranches and ranchos of Mission San Antonio de Padua.* Keepsake Volume, California Mission Studies Association.

Costello, Julia, and David Hornbeck

1989   Alta California: An overview. In *Archaeological and historical perspectives on the Spanish Borderlands West,* edited by David Hurst Thomas, pp. 303–32. Vol. 1 of *Columbian consequences.* Washington, D.C.: Smithsonian Institution Press.

Crowell, Aron

1997   *Archaeology and the capitalist world system: A study from Russian America.* New York: Plenum Publishing.

Cusick, James

1998   Introduction. In *Studies in culture contact: Interaction, culture change, and archaeology,* edited by James G. Cusick, pp. 1–20. Center for Archaeological Investigations, Occasional Paper no. 25, Southern Illinois University, Carbondale.

Dakin, Susan

1939   *A Scotch paisano: Hugo Reid's life in California, 1832–1852, derived from his correspondence.* Berkeley: University of California Press.

Dana, Richard Henry

1980   *Two years before the mast: A personal narrative of life at sea.* 1911. Reprint, New York: Macmillan.

Davis, William Heath

1929　*Seventy-five years in California 1831–1906.* San Francisco: John Howell.

1967　*Seventy-five years in California 1831–1906.* Limited edition, edited by Harold A. Small. San Francisco: Lawton and Alfred Kennedy.

Deagan, Kathleen

1991　Historical archaeology's contributions to our understanding of early America. In *Historical archaeology in global perspective,* edited by Lisa Falk, pp. 97–112. Washington, D.C.: Smithsonian Institution Press.

1996　Colonial transformation: Euro-American cultural genesis in the early Spanish-American colonies. *Journal of Anthropological Research* 52(2):135–60.

1998　Transculturation and Spanish American ethnogenesis: The archaeological legacy of the Quincentenary. In *Studies in culture contact: Interaction, culture change, and archaeology,* edited by James G. Cusick, pp. 23–43. Center for Archaeological Investigations, Occasional Paper no. 25, Southern Illinois University, Carbondale.

Deagan, Kathleen, and Michael Scardaville

1985　Archaeology and history on historic Hispanic sites: Impediments and solutions. *Historical Archaeology* 19(1):32–36.

Deetz, James

1963　Archaeological investigations at La Purísima Mission. *UCLA Archaeological Survey Annual Report* 5:163–208.

Delle, James A.

1998　*An archaeology of social space: Analyzing coffee plantations in Jamaica's Blue Mountains.* New York: Plenum Press.

Dietz, Stephen A.

1976　Echa-Tamal: A study of Coast Miwok acculturation. Master's thesis, San Francisco State University, San Francisco, Calif.

1983　*Final report of archaeological investigations at Mission San José (CA–Ala–1).* Report distributed by Archaeological Consulting and Research Services, Santa Cruz, Calif.

Dobres, Marcia-Anne

1995　Gender and prehistoric technology: On the social agency of technical strategies. *World Archaeology* 27(1):25–49.

2000　*Technology and social agency: Outlining an anthropological framework for archaeology.* Oxford: Blackwell.

Dobres, Marcia-Anne, and Christopher R. Hoffman

1994　Social agency and the dynamics of prehistoric technology. *Journal of Archaeological Method and Theory* 1(3):211–58.

Dobres, Marcia-Anne, and John E. Robb, editors

2000　*Agency and archaeology.* London: Routledge.

Donley-Reid, Linda W.

1990　A structuring of structure: The Swahili house. In *Domestic architecture and the use of space,* edited by Susan Kent, pp. 114–26. Cambridge: Cambridge University Press.

Driver, Harold

1936   *Wappo ethnography.* University of California Publications in American Archaeology and Ethnology, vol. 36, no. 3. Berkeley: University of California Press.

Ellison, William H., and Francis Price

1953   *The life and adventures in California of don Agustín Janssens, 1834–1856.* San Marino, Calif.: Huntington Library.

Elsasser, Albert

1955   *A charmstone site in Sonoma County, California.* University of California Archaeological Survey Report 28. University of California, Berkeley.

Emparan, Louisa Vallejo

1968   *The Vallejos of California.* Gleeson Library Association, University of San Francisco.

Engelhardt, Zephyrin

1915   *Upper California.* Vol. 4 of *The missions and missionaries of California.* San Francisco: James H. Barry Company.

Evans, William S., Jr.

1969   California's Indian pottery: A Native contribution to the culture of the ranchos. *Pacific Coast Archaeological Society Quarterly* 5(3):71–81.

Farnham, Thomas Jefferson

1947   *Travels in California with map.* 1855. Reprint, Oakland, Calif.: Joseph A. Sullivan.

Farnsworth, Paul

1989   The economics of acculturation in the Spanish missions of Alta California. In *Research in economic anthropology*, vol. 11, edited by Barry Isaac, pp. 217–49. Greenwich, Conn.: JAI Press.

1992   Missions, Indians, and cultural continuity. *Historical Archaeology* 26(1):22–36.

Farris, Glenn J.

1983   Archeological excavations related to the construction of the Fort Ross Visitors' Center, Fort Ross SHP, Sonoma County, California. Draft report on file, California Department of Parks and Recreation, State Archaeological Collections Research Facility, West Sacramento.

1989a   A peace treaty between Mariano Vallejo and Satiyomi Chief Succara. Paper presented at the 5th California Indian Conference, Arcata, Calif.

1989b   The Russian imprint on the colonization of California. In *Archaeological and historical perspectives on the Spanish Borderlands West*, edited by David Hurst Thomas, pp. 481–97. Vol. 1 of *Columbian consequences*. Washington, D.C.: Smithsonian Institution Press.

1991   *Archeological testing in the neophyte family housing area at Mission San Juan Bautista, California.* Report on file, California Department of Parks and Recreation, State Archaeological Collections Research Facility, West Sacramento.

1997   Historical archaeology at the Native Alaskan Village Site. In *The Native Alaskan Neighborhood: A multiethnic community at Colony Ross,* edited by Kent Lightfoot, Ann Schiff, and Thomas Wake, pp. 129–35. Vol. 2 of *The archaeology and ethnohistory of Fort Ross, California.* Contributions of the Archaeological Research Facility 55, University of California, Berkeley.

Faulkner, Alaric

1986   Maintenance and fabrication at Fort Pentagoet, 1635–1654: Products of an Acadian armorer's workshop. *Historical Archaeology* 20(1):63–94.

Felton, David L.

1977   Sonoma Barracks: Archeological and historical investigations, 1976. Draft report on file, California Department of Parks and Recreation, State Archaeological Collections Research Facility, West Sacramento.

Felton, David L., Frank Lortie, and Peter D. Schulz

1984   *The Chinese Laundry on Second Street: Papers on archeology at the Woodland Opera House Site.* California Archeological Reports no. 24, Department of Parks and Recreation, Sacramento.

Felton, David L., and Peter D. Schulz

1983   *The Diaz collection: Material culture and social change in mid-nineteenth-century Monterey.* California Archeological Reports no. 23, Department of Parks and Recreation, Sacramento.

Finley, Ernest Latimer

1937   *History of Sonoma County: Its people and its resources.* Santa Rosa, Calif.: Press-Democrat Publishing Company.

Fitch, William

1874   Narrative of William Fitch. BANC MSS C–E 67:3, Bancroft Library, University of California, Berkeley.

Foster, John M., Gwendolyn R. Romani, R. Paul Hampson, A. George Toren, and Daniel G. Landis

1996   *Data recovery investigations in the Domenigoni and Diamond Valleys.* Greenwood and Associates. Report submitted to Metropolitan Water District of Southern California, Los Angeles.

Fredrickson, David A.

1984   The North Coastal region. In *California archaeology,* by Michael J. Moratto, pp. 471–527. Orlando, Fla.: Academic Press.

Frierman, Jay D.

1987   Southern California Brown Ware. In *Historical and archaeological investigation at the Aros-Serrano Adobe, Prado Basin,* by Roberta S. Greenwood, John M. Foster, and Anne Q. Duffield, pp. 79–85. Greenwood and Associates. Report submitted to the U.S. Army Corps of Engineers, Los Angeles District.

1992   The pastoral period in Los Angeles: Life on the ranchos and in the pueblo, 1800–1850. In *Historical archaeology of nineteenth century California,* by Jay D. Frierman and Roberta S. Greenwood, pp. 1–52. Pasadena, Calif.: Castle Press.

———, editor

1982   *The Ontiveros Adobe: Early rancho life in Alta California.* Greenwood and Associates. Report submitted to the Redevelopment Agency, Santa Fe Springs, Calif.

Gebhardt, Charles L.

1962   *Historic archaeology at Vallejo's Petaluma Adobe State Historical Monument.* Report on file, California Department of Parks and Recreation, State Archaeological Collections Research Facility, West Sacramento.

Geiger, Maynard, and Clement W. Meighan

1976   *As the padres saw them: California Indian life and customs as reported by the Franciscan missionaries, 1813–1815.* Santa Barbara, Calif.: Santa Barbara Mission Archive Library.

Gibbs, George

1853a   Journal of the expedition of Colonel Redick M'Kee, United States Indian agent, through north-western California. Performed in the summer and fall of 1851. In *Information respecting the history, condition and prospects of the Indian tribes of the United States,* vol. 3, collected by Henry R. Schoolcraft, pp. 99–177. Philadelphia: J. B. Lippincott and Company.

1853b   Observations on some of the Indians dialects in northern California. In *Information respecting the history, condition and prospects of the Indian tribes of the United States,* vol. 3, collected by Henry R. Schoolcraft, pp. 420–23. Philadelphia: J. B. Lippincott and Company.

Gibson, R. O.

1976   A study of beads and ornaments from the San Buenaventura Mission Site (VEN–87). In *The changing faces of Main Street,* edited by Roberta S. Greenwood, pp. 77–166. Greenwood and Associates. Report submitted to the Redevelopment Agency, City of San Buenaventura.

Giddens, Anthony

1979   *Central problems in social theory: Action, structure, and contradiction in social analysis.* Berkeley: University of California Press.

1984   *The constitution of society.* Berkeley: University of California Press.

Gifford, Edward W.

1940   *Californian bone artifacts.* Anthropological Records, vol. 3, no. 2. Berkeley: University of California Press.

1967   *Ethnographic notes on the Southwestern Pomo.* Anthropological Records, vol. 25. Berkeley: University of California Press.

Gobalet, Kenneth

1997   Fish remains from the early 19th century Native Alaskan habitation at Fort Ross. In *The Native Alaskan Neighborhood: A multiethnic community at Colony Ross,* edited by Kent Lightfoot, Ann Schiff, and Thomas Wake, pp. 319–27. Vol. 2 of *The archaeology and ethnohistory of Fort Ross, California.* Contributions of the Archaeological Research Facility 55, University of California, Berkeley.

Godden, Geoffrey A.

1963   *British pottery and porcelain 1780–1850*. London: Baker.

1964   *Encyclopedia of British pottery and porcelain marks*. New York: Crown Publishers.

Grayson, Donald K.

1984   *Quantitative zooarchaeology: Topics in the analysis of archaeological faunas*. Orlando, Fla.: Academic Press.

Greenwood, Roberta S.

1989   The California ranchero: Fact and fancy. In *Archaeological and historical perspectives on the Spanish Borderlands West*, edited by David Hurst Thomas, pp. 451–65. Vol. 1 of *Columbian consequences*. Washington, D.C.: Smithsonian Institution Press.

——, editor

1975   *3500 years on one city block*. Greenwood and Associates. Report submitted to the Redevelopment Agency, City of San Buenaventura.

1976   *The changing faces of Main Street*. Greenwood and Associates. Report submitted to the Redevelopment Agency, City of San Buenaventura.

Greenwood, Roberta S., John M. Foster, and Anne Q. Duffield

1987   *Historical and archaeological investigation at the Aros-Serrano Adobe, Prado Basin*. Greenwood and Associates. Report submitted to the U.S. Army Corps of Engineers, Los Angeles District.

1988   *Historical and archaeological study of the Yorba-Slaughter Adobe, San Bernardino County*. Greenwood and Associates. Report submitted to the U.S. Army Corps of Engineers, Los Angeles, District.

Greenwood, Roberta S., Jay D. Frierman, and John M. Foster

1983   *The Bandini-Cota Adobe, Prado Dam, Riverside County, California*. Greenwood and Associates. Report submitted to the U.S. Army Corps of Engineers, Los Angeles District.

Gudde, Erwin G., translator

1940   Edward Vischer's first visit to California. *California Historical Society Quarterly* 19(3):6–8.

Guest, Francis F.

1979   An examination of the thesis of S. F. Cook on the forced conversion of Indians in the Alta California missions. *Southern California Quarterly* 65:1–65.

Gust, Sherri M.

1982   Faunal analysis and butchering. In *The Ontiveros Adobe: Early rancho life in Alta California*, edited by Jay D. Frierman, pp. 101–44. Greenwood and Associates. Report submitted to the Redevelopment Agency, Santa Fe Springs, Calif.

1987   Appendix 1: Analysis of faunal materials from the Aros-Serrano Adobe. In *Historical and archaeological investigation at the Aros-Serrano Adobe, Prado Basin*, by Roberta S. Greenwood, John M. Foster, and Anne Q. Duffield, pp. 119–27. Greenwood and Associates. Report submitted to the U.S. Army Corps of Engineers, Los Angeles District.

Haas, Lisbeth

1995   *Conquest and historical identities in California, 1769–1936.* Berkeley: University of California Press.

2003   Emancipation and the meaning of freedom in Mexican California. *Boletín: The Journal of the California Mission Studies Association* 20(1):11–22.

Hackel, Steven W.

1998   Land, labor, and production: The colonial economy of Spanish and Mexican California. In *Contested Eden: California before the gold rush,* edited by Ramón A. Gutiérrez and Richard J. Orsi, pp. 111–46. Berkeley: California Historical Society and the University of California Press.

Hall, Martin

2000   *Archaeology and the modern world: Colonial transcripts in South Africa and the Chesapeake.* London: Routledge.

Hastings, Lanford W.

1932   *The emigrants' guide to Oregon and California: Narratives of the Trans-Mississippi frontier.* 1845. Reprint, Princeton, N.J.: Princeton University Press.

Hastorf, Christine A.

1988   The use of paleoethnobotanical data in prehistoric studies of crop production, processing, and consumption. In *Current paleoethnobotany: Analytical methods and cultural interpretations of archaeological plant remains,* edited by Christine A. Hastorf and Virginia S. Popper, pp. 119–44. Chicago: University of Chicago Press.

1991   Gender, space, and food in prehistory. In *Engendering archaeology,* edited by Joan M. Gero and Margaret W. Conkey, pp. 132–62. London: Blackwell.

Hayden, Brian

1995   Pathways to power: Principles for creating socioeconomic inequalities. In *The foundations of social inequality,* edited by T. Douglas Price and Gary Feinman, pp. 15–86. New York: Plenum Press.

Heizer, Robert F., editor

1953   *The archaeology of the Napa region.* Anthropological Records, vol. 12, no. 6. Berkeley: University of California Press.

1978   *California.* Vol. 8 of *Handbook of North American Indians,* William Sturtevant, general editor. Washington, D.C.: Smithsonian Institution Press.

Heizer, Robert F., and Alan J. Almquist

1971   *The other Californians: Prejudice and discrimination under Spain, Mexico, and the United States to 1920.* Berkeley: University of California Press.

Heizer, Robert F., and Thomas R. Hester

1973   *The archaeology of Bamert Cave, Amador County, California.* Archaeological Research Facility, University of California, Berkeley.

Hendry, George W.

1931   The adobe brick as a historical resource. *Agricultural History* 5:110–27.

Híjar, Carlos N.

1988   Usages and customs of the Californios. In *Three memoirs of Mexican Cali-*

fornia, compiled by Thomas Savage. 1877. Translated by Vivian C. Fisher. Berkeley: Friends of the Bancroft Library.

Honeysett, Elizabeth A.

1982   Floral analysis. In *The Ontiveros Adobe: Early rancho life in Alta California*, edited by Jay D. Frierman, pp. 93–100. Greenwood and Associates. Report submitted to the Redevelopment Agency, Santa Fe Springs, Calif.

Hoopes, Chad L.

1965   *The Petaluma Adobe*. Report on file, California Department of Parks and Recreation, State Archaeological Collections Research Facility, West Sacramento.

Hoover, Robert L.

1989   Spanish-Native interaction and acculturation in the Alta California missions. In *Archaeological and historical perspectives on the Spanish Borderlands West*, edited by David Hurst Thomas, pp. 395–406. Vol. 1 of *Columbian consequences*. Washington, D.C.: Smithsonian Institution Press.

Hoover, Robert L., and Julia G. Costello

1985   *Excavations at Mission San Antonio 1976–1978*. Monograph 26, Institute of Archaeology, University of California, Los Angeles.

Hornbeck, David

1978   Land tenure and rancho expansion in Alta California. *Journal of Historical Geography* 8(4):371–90.

1989   Economic growth and change at the missions of Alta California, 1769–1846. In *Archaeological and historical perspectives on the Spanish Borderlands West*, edited by David Hurst Thomas, pp. 423–34. Vol. 1 of *Columbian consequences*. Washington, D.C.: Smithsonian Institution Press.

Hudson, LuAnn

1993   Protohistoric Pawnee lithic economy. *Plains Anthropologist* 38(146):265–77.

Hughes, Richard E.

1992   California archaeology and linguistic prehistory. *Journal of Anthropological Research* 48:317–38.

Hurtado, Albert

1988   *Indian survival on the California frontier*. New Haven, Conn.: Yale University Press.

Issler, Anne R.

1956   Notes from interview with Mrs. Alice Adams of Purvine Road, Petaluma, August 8. Copies of letters and documents concerning General Vallejo and his holdings in Sonoma County, History Room, Petaluma Regional Library, Petaluma, Calif.

Iverson, Peter

1994   *When Indians became cowboys: Native peoples and cattle ranching in the American West*. Norman: University of Oklahoma Press.

Jackson, Robert H.

1994   *Indian population decline: The missions of northwestern New Spain, 1687–1840*. Albuquerque: University of New Mexico Press.

Jackson, Robert H., and Edward Castillo

1995 *Indians, Franciscans, and Spanish colonization: The impact of the mission system on California Indians.* Albuquerque: University of New Mexico Press.

Jackson, Sheldon

1997 The British ranchero, the Scotch paisano, and the Indian wife. In *Rancho days in southern California: An anthology with new perspectives*, edited by Kenneth Pauley, pp. 239–64. Studio City, Calif.: Westerners, Los Angeles Corral.

Jackson, Thomas L.

1986 Late prehistoric obsidian exchange in central California. Ph.D. diss., Department of Anthropology, Stanford University, Stanford, Calif.

Johnson, Eric

2000 The politics of pottery: Material culture and political process among Algonquians of seventeenth-century southern New England. In *Interpretations of Native North American life: Material contributions to ethno-history*, edited by Michael S. Nassaney and Eric S. Johnson, pp. 118–45. Gainesville: University Press of Florida and the Society for Historical Archaeology.

Johnson, John

1989 The Chumash and the missions. In *Archaeological and historical perspectives on the Spanish Borderlands West*, edited by David Hurst Thomas, pp. 365–76. Vol. 1 of *Columbian consequences*. Washington, D.C.: Smithsonian Institution Press.

Johnson, Patti J.

1978 Patwin. In *California*, edited by Robert F. Heizer, pp. 350–60. Vol. 8 of *Handbook of North American Indians*, William Sturtevant, general editor. Washington, D.C.: Smithsonian Institution Press.

Jones, Olive R.

1971 Glass bottle push-ups and pontil marks. *Historical Archaeology* 5:62–73.

1986 *Cylindrical English wine and beer bottles, 1735–1850.* Ottawa: Parks Canada.

Jones, Olive R., and Catherine Sullivan

1989 *The Parks Canada glass glossary.* Revised edition. Ottawa: Parks Canada.

Karklins, Karlis

1982 Guide to the description and classification of glass beads. *Parks Canada, History and Archaeology* 59:83–117.

Kawahara, Saichi

1970 A survey of the physical setting of the Point Reyes Peninsula area, Marin County, California. In *Contributions to the archaeology of Point Reyes National Seashore: A compendium in honor of Adan E. Treganza*, edited by Robert E. Schenk, pp. 1–64. Treganza Museum Papers no. 6. San Francisco.

Kelly, Isabel

1978 Coast Miwok. In *California*, edited by Robert F. Heizer, pp. 414–25. Vol. 8 of *Handbook of North American Indians*, William Sturtevant, general editor. Washington, D.C.: Smithsonian Institution Press.

Kidd, Kenneth E., and Martha A. Kidd

1970   *A classification system for glass beads for the use of field archaeologists.* Canadian Historic Sites, Occasional Papers in Archaeology and History, vol. 1, pp. 45–89.

Klein, Richard G., and K. Cruz-Uribe

1984   *The analysis of animal bones from archaeological sites.* Chicago: University of Chicago Press.

Knack, Martha C., and Alice Littlefield

1995   Native American labor: Retrieving history, rethinking theory. In *Native Americans and wage labor: Ethnohistorical perspectives,* edited by Alice Littlefield and Martha C. Knack, pp. 3–44. Norman: University of Oklahoma Press.

Kniffen, Fred B.

1939   *Pomo geography.* University of California Publications in American Archaeology and Ethnology, vol. 36, no. 6. Berkeley: University of California Press.

Kroeber, Alfred L.

1925   *Handbook of the Indians of California.* New York: Dover Publications.

Langenwalter, Paul E., II, and Larry W. McKee

1985   Vertebrate faunal remains from the neophyte dormitory. In *Excavations at Mission San Antonio 1976–1978,* by Robert L. Hoover and Julia G. Costello, pp. 94–116. Monograph 26, Institute of Archaeology, University of California, Los Angeles.

Larkin, Thomas O.

1953   *The Larkin papers,* vol. 5. Berkeley: University of California Press.

Larson, Daniel O., John R. Johnson, and Joel C. Michaelson

1994   Missionization among the coastal Chumash of central California. *American Anthropologist* 96:263–99.

Layton, Thomas N.

1990   *Western Pomo prehistory: Excavations at Albion Head, Nightbirds' Retreat, and Three Chop Village, Mendocino County, California.* Monograph 32, Institute of Archaeology, University of California, Los Angeles.

Leacock, Eleanor B.

1980   Montagnais women and the Jesuit program for colonization. In *Women and colonization,* edited by Mona Etienne and Eleanor B. Leacock, pp. 25–42. New York: Praeger.

Leone, Mark P., and Parker B. Potter Jr.

1988   Introduction: Issues in historical archaeology. In *The recovery of meaning: Historical archaeology in the eastern United States,* edited by Mark P. Leone and Parker B. Potter Jr., pp. 1–21. Washington, D.C.: Smithsonian Institution Press.

———, editors

1999   *Historical archaeologies of capitalism.* New York: Kluwer Academic/Plenum Press.

Lightfoot, Kent G.

1995   Culture contact studies: Redefining the relationship between prehistoric and historical archaeology. *American Antiquity* 60(2):199–217.

Lightfoot, Kent G., and Antoinette Martinez

1995   Frontiers and boundaries in archaeological perspective. *Annual Review of Anthropology* 24:471–92.

1997   Interethnic relationships in the Native Alaskan Neighborhood: Consumption practices, cultural innovations, and the construction of household identities. In *The Native Alaskan Neighborhood: A multiethnic community at Colony Ross,* edited by Kent Lightfoot, Ann Schiff, and Thomas Wake, pp. 1–22. Vol. 2 of *The archaeology and ethnohistory of Fort Ross, California.* Contributions of the Archaeological Research Facility 55, University of California, Berkeley.

Lightfoot, Kent G., Antoinette Martinez, and Ann M. Schiff

1998   Daily practice and material culture in pluralistic social settings: An archaeological study of culture change and persistence from Fort Ross, California. *American Antiquity* 63(2):199–222.

Lightfoot, Kent G., Ann M. Schiff, Antoinette Martinez, Thomas A. Wake, Stephen W. Silliman, Peter R. Mills, and Lisa Holm

1997   Culture change and persistence in the daily lifeways of interethnic households. In *The Native Alaskan Neighborhood: A multiethnic community at Colony Ross,* edited by Kent Lightfoot, Ann Schiff, and Thomas Wake, pp. 355–419. Vol. 2 of *The archaeology and ethnohistory of Fort Ross, California.* Contributions of the Archaeological Research Facility 55, University of California, Berkeley.

Lightfoot, Kent G., Ann M. Schiff, and Thomas A. Wake, editors

1997   *The Native Alaskan Neighborhood: A multiethnic community at Colony Ross.* Vol. 2 of *The archaeology and ethnohistory of Fort Ross, California.* Contributions of the Archaeological Research Facility 55, University of California, Berkeley.

Lightfoot, Kent G., and William S. Simmons

1998   Culture contact in protohistoric California: Social contexts of Native and European encounters. *Journal of California and Great Basin Anthropology* 20(2):138–70.

Lightfoot, Kent G., Thomas A. Wake, and Ann M. Schiff

1991   *Introduction.* Vol. 1 of *The archaeology and ethnohistory of Fort Ross, California.* Contributions of the Archaeological Research Facility 49, University of California, Berkeley.

1993   Native responses to the Russian mercantile colony of Fort Ross, northern California. *Journal of Field Archaeology* 20:159–75.

Loeb, Edwin

1926   *Pomo folkways.* University of California Publications in American Archaeology and Ethnology, vol. 19, no. 2. Berkeley: University of California Press.

Loren, Diana DiPaolo

2001a   Manipulating bodies and emerging traditions at the Los Adaes Presidio. In *The archaeology of traditions: The Southeast before and after Columbus*, edited by Timothy R. Pauketat, pp. 58–76. Gainesville: University of Florida Press.

2001b   Social skins: Orthodoxies and practices of dressing in the early colonial lower Mississippi Valley. *Journal of Social Archaeology* 1(2):172–89.

Lorrain, Dessamae

1968   An archaeologist's guide to nineteenth century American glass. *Historical Archaeology* 2:35–44.

Lothrop, Marion L.

1926   Mariano Guadalupe Vallejo, defender of the northern frontier of California. Ph.D. diss., Department of History, University of California, Berkeley.

1932   The Indian campaigns of General M. G. Vallejo. *Quarterly: The Society of California Pioneers* 9(3):161–205.

Luby, Edward

1995   Preliminary report on the archaeological investigations in the Suñol Valley, Alameda County, California. *Proceedings of the Society for California Archaeology* 8:167–74.

Lugo, don José del Carmen

1950   Life of a rancher [1877 to Thomas Savage]. *Southern California Quarterly* 32(3):185–236.

Luscomb, Sally C.

1967   *The collector's encyclopedia of buttons.* New York: Crown Publishers.

Lyman, R. Lee

1994   Quantitative units and terminology in zooarchaeology. *American Antiquity* 59(1):36–71.

Mack, Joanne

2003   California ceramic traditions: The obscurity and the assumptions 2002. *Society for California Archaeology Newsletter* 37(1):30–33.

Majewski, Teresita, and Michael J. O'Brien

1987   The use and misuse of nineteenth-century English and American ceramics in archaeological analysis. In *Advances in archaeological method and theory*, vol. 11, edited by Michael B. Schiffer, pp. 97–209. New York: Academic Press.

Margolin, Malcolm

1989   *Monterey in 1786: The journals of Jean François de La Pérouse.* Berkeley: Heyday Books.

Marshall, Ralph P.

1982   An archaeological survey of the Ortega Vigare Adobe. *Pacific Coast Archaeological Society Quarterly* 18(1):1–61.

Martinez, Antoinette M.

1997   View from the ridge: The Kashaya Pomo in a Russian-American Company context. In *The archaeology of Russian colonialism in the north and tropical Pacific*, edited by Peter R. Mills and Antoinette Martinez, pp. 141–56. Berkeley: Kroeber Anthropological Society, University of California.

1998   An archaeological study of change and continuity in the material remains, practices, and cultural identities of Native Californian women in a nineteenth century pluralistic context. Ph.D. diss., Department of Anthropology, University of California, Berkeley.

Mason, William M.

1986   Alta California during the mission period, 1769–1835. *Masterkey* 60(2–3):4–14.

1993   Alta California's colonial and early Mexican era population, 1769–1846. In *Regions of La Raza: Changing interpretations of Mexican American regional history and culture*, edited by Antonio Ríos-Bustamante, pp. 169–87. Encino, Calif.: Floricanto Press.

Matthews, Christopher

1999   Context and interpretation: An archaeology of cultural production. *International Journal of Historical Archaeology* 3(4):261–82.

McClellan, C.

1953   Ethnography of the Wappo and Patwin. In *The archaeology of the Napa region*, edited by Robert F. Heizer, pp. 233–43. Anthropological Records, vol. 12, no. 6. Berkeley: University of California Press.

McKee, Larry

1999   Food supply and plantation social order: An archaeological view. In *"I, too, am America": Archaeological studies of African-American life*, edited by Theresa A. Singleton, pp. 218–39. Charlottesville: University Press of Virginia.

McKittrick, Myrtle M.

1944   *Vallejo: Son of California*. Portland: Binfords and Mort.

1950   Salvador Vallejo. *Quarterly of the Society of California Pioneers* 29(4):309–31.

McLendon, Sally, and Michael J. Lowy

1978   Eastern Pomo and Southeastern Pomo. In *California*, edited by Robert F. Heizer, pp. 306–23. Vol. 8 of *Handbook of North American Indians*, William Sturtevant, general editor. Washington, D.C.: Smithsonian Institution Press.

McLendon, Sally, and Robert Oswalt

1978   Pomo: Introduction. In *California*, edited by Robert F. Heizer, pp. 274–88. Vol. 8 of *Handbook of North American Indians*, William Sturtevant, general editor. Washington, D.C.: Smithsonian Institution Press.

McNally, Mary Gene

1976   Mariano Guadalupe Vallejo's relations with the Indians of California's northern frontier, 1825–1842. Master's thesis, Dominican College of San Rafael, San Rafael, Calif.

Mead, George R.

1972   *The ethnobotany of the California Indians: A compendium of the plants, their users, and their uses*. Occasional Publications in Anthropology, Ethnology Series, no. 30, pts. 1 and 2. Museum of Anthropology, University of Northern Colorado, Greeley.

Meighan, Clement W.

1985   Trade beads. In *Excavations at Mission San Antonio 1976–1978*, edited by Robert L. Hoover and Julia G. Costello, pp. 56–63. Monograph 26, Institute of Archaeology, University of California, Los Angeles.

Merriam, C. Hart

1907   Distribution and classification of the Mewan Stock of California. *American Anthropologist* 9(2):338–57.

1977   *Ethnogeographic and ethnosynonymic data from northern California tribes*. Archaeological Research Facility, University of California, Berkeley.

Meskell, Lynn

1998   An archaeology of social relations in an Egyptian village. *Journal of Archaeological Method and Theory* 5(3):209–44.

Meyer, Deborah J.

2000   Identification report no. 3107. California Department of Food and Agriculture. Letter report in possession of the author.

Miksicek, Charles H.

1987   Formation processes of the archaeobotanical record. In *Advances in archaeological method and theory*, vol. 10, edited by Michael B. Schiffer, pp. 211–47. New York: Academic Press.

Milanich, Jerald

1999   *Laboring in the fields of the Lord: Spanish missions and southeastern Indians*. Washington, D.C.: Smithsonian Institution Press.

Miller, Daniel J., and Robert N. Lea

1976   *Guide to the coastal marine fishes of California*. California Department of Fish and Game Bulletin 157.

Miller, George

1980   Classification and economic scaling of 19th century ceramics. *Historical Archaeology* 14:1–40.

1991   A revised set of CC index values for classification and economic scaling of English ceramics from 1787–1880. *Historical Archaeology* 17(2):1–25.

Milliken, Randall T.

1978   Ethno-history of the lower Napa Valley. In *Report of archaeological excavations at the River Glen Site (CA–NAP–261), Napa County, California*, pp. 2.1–2.43. Archaeological Consulting and Research Services, Santa Cruz, Calif. Report submitted to the U.S. Army Corps of Engineers, San Francisco District.

1995   *A time of little choice: The disintegration of tribal culture in the San Francisco Bay area 1769–1810*. Menlo Park, Calif.: Ballena Press.

Monroy, Douglas

1990   *Thrown among strangers: The making of Mexican culture in frontier Califor-nia.* Berkeley: University of California Press.

1998   The creation and re-creation of Californio society. In *Contested Eden: California before the gold rush,* edited by Ramón A. Gutiérrez and Richard J. Orsi, pp. 173–95. Berkeley: California Historical Society and the University of California Press.

Moore, James L.

1992   Spanish colonial stone tool use. In *Current research on the late prehistory and early history of New Mexico,* edited by Bradley Vierra, pp. 239–44. New Mexico Archaeological Council, Special Publication 1, Albuquerque.

Moratto, Michael J.

1984   *California archaeology.* Orlando, Fla.: Academic Press.

Moratto, Michael J., Adella Schroth, John M. Foster, Dennis Gallegos, Roberta S. Greenwood, Gwendolyn R. Romani, Melinda C. Romano, Laurence H. Shoup, Mark T. Swanson, and Eric C. Gibson

1994   *Archaeological investigations at five sites on the lower San Luis Rey River, San Diego County, California: Final report,* vols. 1–3. Greenwood and Associates and Infotec Research, Inc. Report submitted to the U.S. Army Corps of Engineers, Los Angeles District.

Moyle, Peter B.

1976   *Inland fishes of California.* Berkeley: University of California Press.

Mullins, Paul R.

1999   *Race and affluence: An archaeology of African America and consumer culture.* New York: Kluwer Academic/Plenum Press.

Munz, Philip A.

1968   *A California flora and supplement.* Berkeley: University of California Press.

Nassaney, Michael S.

1989   An epistemological enquiry into some archaeological and historical interpretations of 17th century Native American–European relations. In *Archaeological approaches to cultural identity,* edited by Stephen J. Shennan, pp. 76–93. London: Unwin Hyman.

Nassaney, Michael S., and Michael Volmar

2003   Lithic artifacts in seventeenth-century Native New England. In *Stone tool traditions in the contact era,* edited by Charles Cobb, pp. 78–93. Tuscaloosa: University of Alabama Press.

Newman, T. Stell

1970   A dating key for post-eighteenth-century bottles. *Historical Archaeology* 4:70–75.

O'Farrell, Jaspar

1848   Map of the land of Petaluma, confirmed 1871. Petaluma Historical Society Museum, Petaluma, Calif.

Osio, Antonio Maria

1996   *The history of Alta California: A memoir of Mexican California,* translated by Rose Marie Beebe and Robert M. Senkewicz. Madison: University of Wisconsin Press.

Padilla, Genaro
1993   *My history, not yours: The formation of Mexican American autobiography.* Madison: University of Wisconsin Press.

Pauketat, Timothy R.
2001   A new tradition in archaeology. In *The archaeology of traditions: Agency and history before and after Columbus,* edited by Timothy R. Pauketat, pp. 1–16. Gainesville: University Press of Florida.

Pauley, Kenneth, editor
1997   *Rancho days in southern California: An anthology with new perspectives.* Studio City, Calif.: Westerners, Los Angeles Corral.

Pearsall, Deborah M.
1989   *Paleoethnobotany: A handbook of procedures.* San Diego: Academic Press.

Phebus, George
1990   *Archaeological investigations in the San Pablo–Suisun region of central California.* Astoria, Ore.: Privately printed.

Phillips, George Harwood
1974   Indians and the breakdown of the Spanish mission system in California. *Ethnohistory* 21(4):291–301.

1975   *Chiefs and challengers: Indian resistance and cooperation in southern California.* Berkeley: University of California Press.

1980   Indians in Los Angeles, 1781–1875: Economic integration, social disintegration. *Pacific Historical Review* 49:427–51.

1993   *Indians and intruders in central California, 1769–1849.* Norman: University of Oklahoma Press.

Popper, Virginia S.
1988   Selecting quantitative measurements in paleoethnobotany. In *Current paleoethnobotany: Analytical methods and cultural interpretations of archaeological plant remains,* edited by Christine A. Hastorf and Virginia S. Popper, pp. 53–71. Chicago: University of Chicago Press.

Powers, Stephen
1976   *Tribes of California.* 1877. Reprint, Berkeley: University of California Press.

Rawls, James
1984   *Indians of California: The changing image.* Norman: University of Oklahoma Press.

Reitz, Elizabeth J., Tyson Gibbs, and Ted A. Rathbun
1985   Archaeological evidence for subsistence on coastal plantations. In *The archaeology of slavery and plantation life,* edited by Theresa A. Singleton, pp. 163–91. New York: Academic Press.

Reitz, Elizabeth J., and Elizabeth S. Wing
1999   *Zooarchaeology.* Cambridge Manuals in Archaeology. Cambridge: Cambridge University Press.

Revere, Joseph Warren

1849   *A tour of duty in California.* New York: C. S. Francis and Company.

Richman, Irving B.

1965   *California under Spain and Mexico 1535–1847.* New York: Cooper Square Publishers.

Ringrose, T. J.

1993   Bone counts and statistics: A critique. *Journal of Archaeological Science* 20:121–57.

Robinson, Alfred

1891   *Life in California during a residence of several years in that territory.* San Francisco: William Doxey.

Rogers, Daniel, and Samuel M. Wilson, editors

1993   *Ethnohistory and archaeology: Approaches to postcontact change in the Americas.* New York: Plenum Press.

Rosenus, Alan

1995   *General M. G. Vallejo and the advent of the Americans: A biography.* Albuquerque: University of New Mexico Press.

Ross, Lester A.

1989   Analysis of glass beads from Santa Ana Inés Mission. In *Santa Ana Inés Mission excavations, 1986–1988,* edited by Julia Costello, pp. 149–61. Salinas, Calif.: Coyote Press.

1990   Trade beads from Hudson's Bay Company Fort Vancouver (1829–60). *Beads* 2:29–67.

1997   Glass and ceramic trade beads from the Native Alaskan Neighborhood. In *The Native Alaskan Neighborhood: A multiethnic community at Colony Ross,* edited by Kent Lightfoot, Ann Schiff, and Thomas Wake, pp. 179–212. Vol. 2 of *The archaeology and ethnohistory of Fort Ross, California.* Contributions of the Archaeological Research Facility 55, University of California, Berkeley.

Rubertone, Patricia

1989   Archaeology, colonialism, and 17th-century Native America: Towards an alternative interpretation. In *Conflict in the archaeology of living traditions,* edited by Robert Layton, pp. 32–45. London: Unwin Hyman.

2000   The historical archaeology of Native Americans. *Annual Review of Anthropology* 2:425–46.

2001   *Grave undertakings: An archaeology of Roger Williams and the Narragansett Indians.* Washington, D.C.: Smithsonian Institution Press.

Sahlins, Marshall

1985   *Islands of history.* Chicago: University of Chicago Press.

Sainsbury, John A.

1975   Indian labor in early Rhode Island. *New England Quarterly* 48:378–93.

Saitta, Dean J.

1997   Power, labor, and the dynamics of change in Chacoan political economy. *American Antiquity* 62(1):7–26.

Salvatore, Ricardo

1991   Modes of labor control in cattle-ranching economies: California, southern
        Brazil, and Argentina, 1820–1860. *Journal of Economic History* 51(2):441–
        51.

Sanchez, Nellie Van de Grift

1929   *Spanish Arcadia*. San Francisco: Powell Publishing Company.

——, translator

1930   Isadora Filomena: My years with Chief Solano. 1874. *Touring Topics* 22:39,
        52.

Sánchez, Federico A.

1986   Rancho life in Alta California. *Masterkey* 60(2–3):16–25.

1993   Rancho life in Alta California. In *Regions of La Raza: Changing interpreta-
        tions of Mexican American regional history and culture,* edited by Antonio
        Ríos-Bustamante, pp. 213–35. Encino, Calif.: Floricanto Press.

Sandels, Gustav M. Waseurtz af

1880   Visit of the "King's Orphan" to California in 1842–3. From *Upham's Notes*
        and *San José Pioneer,* Bancroft Library, University of California, Berkeley.

Schulz, Peter D., Betty J. Rivers, Mark M. Hales, Charles A. Litzinger, and Eliza-
        beth A. McKee

1980   *The bottles of Old Sacramento: A study of nineteenth-century glass and ce-
        ramic retail containers,* pt. 1. California Archeological Reports no. 20, De-
        partment of Parks and Recreation, Sacramento.

Schuyler, Robert L.

1978   Indian-Euro-American interaction: Archeological evidence from non-In-
        dian sites. In *California,* edited by Robert F. Heizer, pp. 69–79. Vol. 8 of
        Handbook of North American Indians, William Sturtevant, general editor.
        Washington, D.C.: Smithsonian Institution Press.

Scott, James C.

1985   *Weapons of the weak: Everyday forms of peasant resistance.* New Haven,
        Conn.: Yale University Press.

1990   *Domination and the arts of resistance: Hidden transcripts.* New Haven, Conn.:
        Yale University Press.

Shackel, Paul A.

2000   Craft to wage labor: Agency and resistance in American historical archae-
        ology. In *Agency and archaeology,* edited by Marcia-Anne Dobres and John
        E. Robb, pp. 232–46. London: Routledge.

Sherman, William L.

1979   *Forced Native labor in sixteenth century Central America.* Lincoln: Univer-
        sity of Nebraska Press.

Shoup, Laurence H., and Randall T. Milliken

1999   *Inigo of Rancho Posolmi: The life and times of a Mission Indian.* Menlo
        Park, Calif.: Ballena Press.

Silliman, Stephen

1997   European origins and Native destinations: Historical artifacts from the

Native Alaskan Village and Fort Ross Beach sites. In *The Native Alaskan Neighborhood: A multiethnic community at Colony Ross*, edited by Kent Lightfoot, Ann Schiff, and Thomas Wake, pp. 136–78. Vol. 2 of *The archaeology and ethnohistory of Fort Ross, California*. Contributions of the Archaeological Research Facility 55, University of California, Berkeley.

1999 *Beneath historic floors: Archaeological investigations of the Petaluma Adobe Seismic Retrofit Project.* Report submitted to California Department of Parks and Recreation, State Archaeological Collections Research Facility, West Sacramento.

2000a Colonial worlds, indigenous practices: The archaeology of labor on a 19th-century California rancho. Ph.D. diss., University of California, Berkeley.

2000b Obsidian studies in the archaeology of 19th-century California. *Society for California Archaeology Newsletter* 34(1):1, 26–29.

2001a Agency, practical politics, and the archaeology of culture contact. *Journal of Social Archaeology* 1(2):190–209.

2001b Theoretical perspectives on labor and colonialism: Reconsidering the California missions. *Journal of Anthropological Archaeology* 20:379–407.

2002 *Streamlined cultural resources: The Adobe Creek Archaeological Site Stabilization Project, Petaluma Adobe State Historic Park, Sonoma County, California.* Report submitted to California Department of Parks and Recreation, State Archaeological Collections Research Facility, West Sacramento.

2003a Contact or colonialism? Interpreting indigenous people in North American historical archaeology. Paper presented at the 5th World Archaeological Congress, June 21–26, Washington, D.C.

2003b Using a rock in a hard place: Native American lithic practices in colonial California. In *Stone tool traditions in the contact era*, edited by Charles Cobb, pp. 127–50. Tuscaloosa: University of Alabama Press.

2004 Social and physical landscapes of contact. In *North American archaeology*, edited by Timothy Pauketat and Diana DiPaolo Loren. Malden, Mass.: Blackwell Publishing, forthcoming.

n.d. Beyond prehistory: Energy-dispersive X-ray fluorescence sourcing and hydration dating of historical obsidian artifacts and their implications for obsidian studies. Manuscript in possession of the author.

Silliman, Stephen W., Paul Farnsworth, and Kent G. Lightfoot

2000 Magnetometer prospecting in historical archaeology: Evaluating survey options at a 19th-century rancho site in California. *Historical Archaeology* 34(2):89–109.

Simmons, Marc, and Frank Turley

1980 *Southwestern colonial ironwork: The Spanish blacksmithing tradition from Texas to California.* Albuquerque: Museum of New Mexico Press.

Simons, Dwight

1997 Bird remains from the Fort Ross Beach and Native Alaskan Village sites. In *The Native Alaskan Neighborhood: A multiethnic community at Colony Ross*, edited by Kent Lightfoot, Ann Schiff, and Thomas Wake, pp. 310–18. Vol.

2 of *The archaeology and ethnohistory of Fort Ross, California*. Contributions of the Archaeological Research Facility 55, University of California, Berkeley.

Simpson, George

1847   *An overland journey round the world during the years 1841 and 1842*. Philadelphia: Lea and Blanchard.

Singleton, Theresa A.

1985   Archaeological implications for changing labor conditions. In *The archaeology of slavery and plantation life*, edited by Theresa A. Singleton, pp. 291–304. Orlando, Fla.: Academic Press.

Skowronek, Russell K.

1998   Sifting the evidence: Perceptions of life at the Ohlone (Costanoan) Missions of Alta California. *Ethnohistory* 45(4):675–708.

Skowronek, Russell K., M. James Blackman, Ronald L. Bishop, Sarah Ginn, and Manuel García Heras

2001   Chemical characterization of earthenware on the Alta California frontier. In *Proceedings of the 3rd International Symposium on Nuclear and Related Techniques*. Havana, Cuba.

Smilie, Robert S.

1975   *The Sonoma Mission, San Francisco Solano de Sonoma: The founding, ruin, and restoration of California's 21st mission*. Fresno, Calif.: Valley Publishers.

Spicer, Edward

1961   Types of contact and processes of change. In *Perspectives in American Indian culture change*, edited by Edward Spicer, pp. 517–44. Chicago: University of Chicago Press.

Sprague, Roderick

1985   Glass trade beads: A progress report. *Historical Archaeology* 19(2):87–105.

Stephenson, Terry E.

1963   *Don Bernardo Yorba*. Los Angeles: Glen Dawson.

Sussman, Lynne

1977   Changes in pearlware dinnerware, 1780–1830. *Historical Archaeology* 11:105–11.

Tays, George

1937   Mariano Guadalupe Vallejo and Sonoma–A biography and a history. *California Historical Society Quarterly* 16:99–121, 216–54, 348–72.

1938   Mariano Guadalupe Vallejo and Sonoma–A biography and a history. *California Historical Society Quarterly* 17:50–73, 141–67, 219–42.

Thomas, Brian

1998   Power and community: The archaeology of slavery at the Hermitage Plantation. *American Antiquity* 63(4):531–52.

Thomas, David Hurst, editor

1989   *Archaeological and historical perspectives on the Spanish Borderlands West*. Vol. 1 of *Columbian consequences*. Washington, D.C.: Smithsonian Institution Press.

1990   *Archaeological and historical perspectives on the Spanish Borderlands East.* Vol. 2 of *Columbian consequences.* Washington, D.C.: Smithsonian Institution Press.

1991   *The Spanish Borderlands in Pan-American perspective.* Vol. 3 of *Columbian consequences.* Washington, D.C.: Smithsonian Institution Press.

Treganza, Adan E.

1958   *Archaeological investigation of the Vallejo Adobe, Petaluma Adobe State Park Historical Monument.* Report on file, California Department of Parks and Recreation, State Archaeological Collections Research Facility, West Sacramento.

Tuomey, Honoria

1926   *History of Sonoma County, California.* 2 vols. San Francisco: S. J. Clarke Publishing Company.

United States District Court

1852   Land case no. 321, Northern District. United States District Court Land Case Files 1852–92, Bancroft Library, University of California, Berkeley.

Upton, Dell

1996   Ethnicity, authenticity, and invented traditions. *Historical Archaeology* 30(2):1–7.

Vallejo, Guadalupe

1890   Ranch and mission days in Alta California. *Century Magazine* 41(2):183–92.

Vallejo, Mariano Guadalupe

1874a   Letter from Mariano G. Vallejo, June 4, 1835. In Documentos para la historia de California, 1769–1850, compiled by Mariano G. Vallejo, 1874. BANC MSS C–B 3:37, Bancroft Library, University of California, Berkeley.

1874b   Contract between Mariano G. Vallejo and H. Petit, March 22, 1848. In Documentos para la historia de California, 1769–1850, compiled by Mariano G. Vallejo, 1874. BANC MSS C–B 12:336, Bancroft Library, University of California, Berkeley.

1874c   Letter from Leandro Luso to Mariano G. Vallejo, September 21, 1852. In Documentos para la historia de California, 1769–1850, compiled by Mariano G. Vallejo, 1874. BANC MSS C–B 13:204, Bancroft Library, University of California, Berkeley.

1874d   Letter from J. Payton to Mariano G. Vallejo, October 26, 1853. In Documentos para la historia de California, 1769–1850, compiled by Mariano G. Vallejo, 1874. BANC MSS C–B 13:318, Bancroft Library, University of California, Berkeley.

1875a   Recuerdos históricos y personales tocante a la Alta California: Histórica política del país. Vol. 1. Translated by Earl Hewitt. BANC MSS C–D 17, Bancroft Library, University of California, Berkeley.

1875b   Recuerdos históricos y personales tocante a la Alta California: Histórica política del país. Vol. 2. Translated by Earl Hewitt. BANC MSS C–D 18, Bancroft Library, University of California, Berkeley.

1875c   Recuerdos históricos y personales tocante a la Alta California: Histórica política del país. Vol. 3. Translated by Earl Hewitt. BANC MSS C–D 19, Bancroft Library, University of California, Berkeley.

1875d   Recuerdos históricos y personales tocante a la Alta California: Histórica política del país. Vol. 4. Translated by Earl Hewitt. BANC MSS C–D 20, Bancroft Library, University of California, Berkeley.

1875e   Recuerdos históricos y personales tocante a la Alta California: Histórica política del país. Vol. 5. Translated by Earl Hewitt. BANC MSS C–D 21, Bancroft Library, University of California, Berkeley.

1876   History of Sonoma County from the earliest settlement to the American occupation, delivered in Santa Rosa July 1, 1876. *Sonoma Democrat*, vol. 2, July 8.

1941   *The Old Adobe. A letter from General M. G. Vallejo* [1889, to N. L. Denman]. San Francisco: Duncan H. Olmstead.

Vallejo, Napoleón Primo

1890   General Vallejo: Some reminiscences and incidents about him. BANC MSS 76/79c, box 3, Correspondence and Papers of Napoleón Vallejo, Bancroft Library, University of California, Berkeley.

n.d.a   During convalescence. BANC MSS 76/79c, box 3, Bancroft Library, University of California, Berkeley.

n.d.b   Oro fino (gold dust). BANC MSS 76/79c, box 3, Bancroft Library, University of California, Berkeley.

Vallejo, Platon Mariano Guadalupe

1914   Memoirs of the Vallejos. *San Francisco Bulletin*, January 26–February 16. Bancroft Library, University of California, Berkeley.

Vallejo, Salvador

1874   Notas históricas sobre California: Sonoma, California. 1874. BANC MSS C–D 22, Bancroft Library, University of California, Berkeley.

Voss, Barbara L.

2000   Colonial sex: Archaeology, structured space, and sexuality in Alta California's Spanish-colonial missions. In *Archaeologies of sexuality*, edited by Robert Schmidt and Barbara L. Voss, pp. 35–61. London: Routledge.

2002   The archaeology of El Presidio de San Francisco: Culture contact, gender, and ethnicity in a Spanish-colonial military community. Ph.D. diss., University of California, Berkeley.

2003   Culture contact and colonial practices: Archaeological traces of daily life in early San Francisco. *Boletín: The Journal of the California Mission Studies Association* 20(1):63–77.

Wake, Thomas A.

1997a   Bone artifacts and tool production in the Native Alaskan Neighborhood. In *The Native Alaskan Neighborhood: A multiethnic community at Colony Ross*, edited by Kent Lightfoot, Ann Schiff, and Thomas Wake, pp. 248–78. Vol. 2 of *The archaeology and ethnohistory of Fort Ross, California*. Contributions of the Archaeological Research Facility 55, University of California, Berkeley.

1997b   Mammal remains from the Native Alaskan Neighborhood. In *The Native Alaskan Neighborhood: A multiethnic community at Colony Ross*, edited by Kent Lightfoot, Ann Schiff, and Thomas Wake, pp. 279–309. Vol. 2 of *The archaeology and ethnohistory of Fort Ross, California*. Contributions of the Archaeological Research Facility 55, University of California, Berkeley.

Wallace, William J.
1959   Historical research pertaining to the original Hugo Reid adobe house. *Lasca Leaves* 9(1):14–23.

Wallace, William J., and Edith Taylor Wallace
1958   Indian artifacts from the Hugo Reid Adobe. *Lasca Leaves* 8(4):74–80.

Ward, James
1878a   Extracts from the diary of an early Californian. *Argonaut*, August 10, pt. 2.
1878b   Extracts from the diary of an early Californian. *Argonaut*, August 24, pt. 5.

Weber, David J.
1992   *The Spanish frontier in North America*. New Haven, Conn.: Yale University Press.

Webster, Gary S.
1990   Labor control and emergent stratification in prehistoric Europe. *Current Anthropology* 31:337–66.

West, G. James
1989   Early historic vegetation change in Alta California: The fossil evidence. In *Archaeological and historical perspectives on the Spanish Borderlands West*, edited by David Hurst Thomas, pp. 333–48. Vol. 1 of *Columbian consequences*. Washington, D.C.: Smithsonian Institution Press.

White, John R.
1977   Aboriginal artifacts on non-traditional material: Six specimens from Fort Ross, California. *Northwest Anthropological Research Notes* 11:240–47.
1978   Bottle nomenclature: A glossary of landmark terminology for the archaeologist. *Historical Archaeology* 12:58–67.

Wilkes, Charles
1845   *Narrative of the United States Exploring Expedition during the years 1838, 1839, 1840, 1841, 1842*. Vol. 5. Philadelphia: Lea and Blanchard.

Wilkie, Laurie
1996   Glass-knapping at a Louisiana plantation: African-American tools? *Historical Archaeology* 30(4):37–49.

Wilkie, Laurie, and Paul Farnsworth
1999   Trade and the construction of Bahamian identity: A multiscalar exploration. *International Journal of Historical Archaeology* 3(4):283–320.

Wohlgemuth, Eric
1994   *Macrofloral remains from CA–Son–159 and CA–Son–1695*. Report on file, Northwest Information Center, Sonoma State University, Rohnert Park.
1996   Resource intensification in prehistoric central California: Evidence from archaeobotanical data. *Journal of California and Great Basin Anthropology* 18(1):81–103.

Wolf, Eric R.

1982   *Europe and the people without history.* Berkeley: University of California Press.

Wurst, LouAnn

1999   Internalizing class in historical archaeology. *Historical Archaeology* 33(1):7–21.

Wyckoff, Martin A.

1984   *United States military buttons of the land services 1787–1902: A guide and classificatory system.* Bloomington, Ill.: McLean County Historical Society.

Wylie, Alison

1992   Invented lands/discovered pasts: The westward expansion of myth and history. *Historical Archaeology* 27(4):1–19.

Young, Amy L.

1997   Task and gang labor: Work patterns at a Kentucky plantation. *North American Archaeologist* 18(1):41–66.

Zeitlin, Judith F.

1989   Ranchers and Indians on the southern Isthmus of Tehuantepec: Economic change and survival in colonial Mexico. *Hispanic American Historical Review* 69:23–60.

Index

bird-bone tubes, 142–44, 187, 198
birds, 162, 163, 182
blacksmithing, 53, 102
blankets, 13, 22, 23, 53, 55, 59, 69, 73, 165, 188, 190, 192, 196
Boggs, William M., 46, 52, 53, 67, 161, 167, 173
bone artifacts, xvii, 42, 142–44, 152, 177, 187, 198, 212n6; incised, 98, 142, 144, 187
bones: animal, xv, xvii, 33, 85, 154, 177, 185; bird, 158, 162–64; fish, 54, 94, 101, 105, 158, 159, 163, 164
bottles: alcohol, 126–29, 131, 151, 190, 191; ceramic, 137, 140; glass, xvii, 33, 37, 82, 85, 86, 101, 102, 126–31, 136, 141, 151, 187, 189–91, 197, 198, 203
bridles, 53, 124, 189
Brown, Charles, 56, 197
Bryant, Edwin, 46, 124, 153, 174
buckles, 87, 101, 116, 123, 124, 152, 211n4
burial, xi, 187, 188
butchery, 124, 156, 157, 159–61, 168, 189, 190, 193–97
Butron, Manuel, 18
buttons, 86, 87, 98, 116–18, 122, 124, 142

Cainamero, 65, 210n9
Californio, 20, 29, 40, 54, 56, 72, 140, 159, 165, 174, 188, 201
cans, 119
capitalism, 10, 132
Carriger, Nicolas, 65
Carrillo, Julio, 59, 61, 73, 124
Carrillo, María Ygnacia López de, 50, 66, 71, 72, 74, 202
Casa Grande. See Sonoma, Vallejo home in
CA–Son–2294, 82, 97, 141
cattle, 3, 25, 27, 40, 49, 56, 59, 61, 67–69, 76, 78, 153, 154, 162, 181, 188,

189, 193–96, 211n13; archaeological recovery of remains of, 94, 101, 159–61, 175, 179, 213n1 (chap. 6); arrangements for between Vallejo and Native people, 20, 28, 30, 55, 63, 65, 73, 180; branding of, 59, 189
ceramics, xvii, 20, 33–36, 39, 85, 86, 90, 93, 94, 98, 101, 102, 125, 132–41, 151, 152, 159, 178, 184, 190, 191, 198, 202, 203, 208n3 (chap. 2); availability of, 10, 142; Brown Ware, 34–37, 134; classification of, 132–34, 212n5; creamware, 133, 134; galera, 134; hallmarks on, 135–36; ironstone, 135, 136, 211n5; majolica, 134, 140, 141; mocha, 134; modification of, 135, 141, 191; pearlware, 133, 134; porcelain, 133–35, 140, 191; production of, 34, 35, 42, 132–34, 138–40; refined earthenware, 133–36, 140, 141; stoneware, 133–38, 140, 141, 191; transfer-print, 133–35, 141; white-ware, 133–35, 211n5; yellowware, 134, 142
charcoal, 86, 87, 90–95, 98, 157, 170, 183
charmstones, 42, 187
chert, 42, 85, 98, 106, 111–15, 185, 187; Franciscan Complex, 115
chickens, 158, 162, 180
Chief Marín, 64
Chief Solano, 45, 46, 49, 57, 60, 61, 64, 65, 163, 209n3
children, 3, 26, 41, 59, 69; Vallejo family, 40, 70, 78
choice, 10, 23, 30, 31, 35, 38, 72, 74, 99, 116, 151, 152, 175, 176, 184, 195, 198
classification of artifacts, 102, 113, 132, 134, 145, 212n8
Clear Lake, 46, 66, 186
cleavers, 151, 161, 189, 190, 194
clothing, 74, 116, 149, 164, 165, 175,

epidemics, 56, 60, 61, 67

ethnographic accounts, xiv, 8, 36, 41–44, 62, 79, 105, 143, 149, 150, 163, 170, 172, 181, 182, 186, 195, 200, 201

Estudillo, José Antonio, 37

excavation, xiv, 7, 54, 99–102, 151, 174, 180, 183, 189, 191, 194, 202, 211n1 (chap. 5); of Areas A and B, 82–95, 134, 138, 212n8; of Block, 103, 106, 107, 110–12, 121–23, 133, 135, 138, 142, 143, 148, 158, 160, 162, 166, 167, 169, 180, 212n6; description of, 82–93, 96–98, 134, 157, 211n2 (chap. 4); inside Petaluma Adobe, 81, 140; methods of, xvii, 39, 84, 157; of other sites, 33, 34, 134, 137, 172, 173, 212n7; previous, at Petaluma, xiii, 53; screening of, 84–87, 90, 114; surface testing during, 82, 83, 131

Farris, Glenn J., 150, 173

faunal: data, 155–59, 165, 173, 180, 205; remains, 86, 87, 90–95, 98, 142, 151, 156, 159, 163, 167; resources, 42, 142

Features: A, 87, 98, 157, 169, 170, 180, 213n7; B, 91, 98, 104, 119, 157, 166, 169, 170, 180; C, 91, 98, 157, 170, 180; D, 91, 92, 95, 98, 134, 157, 166, 170; E, 93–95, 98, 142, 143, 157, 166, 170, 180; F, 93–95, 98, 157, 170

felsite, 106, 107, 113–15

files, 87, 122, 124, 184

Filomena, Isadora, 57

fire-cracked rock, 84, 85, 91, 92, 94, 95, 98, 123, 151, 179, 182

fishing, 23, 41, 43, 75, 105, 163, 164, 175, 178, 182, 208n4

Fitch, Carlos, 174

Fitch, William, 68, 69, 213n2

flotation, 85, 86, 90, 157, 169

Fort Ross. See Colony Ross

frontier: colonial, 5, 10, 20, 40, 49;

northern, 4, 15, 25, 29, 47–49, 55, 72, 78, 125, 202

fuel, 155, 168, 170, 172

fugitivism, 60, 71

gender, xi, xv, xviii, 7, 8, 10, 30, 40–42, 100, 105, 132, 155, 184, 185, 188, 195–198, 204; and division of labor, 59, 69; identities, 10, 80, 102, 188, 192

geophysical survey, xiv, 82–84, 89, 93, 97

Gibbs, George, 27, 46, 64, 66, 74

glass, 39, 86, 90, 93, 94, 98, 118, 124–31, 159, 178, 184, 187, 189, 191, 198, 202; window, 129, 131; worked, 86, 90, 98, 101, 129–31, 151, 198

goats, 37, 159, 161

gopher, 84, 94, 95

gradiometer, 82, 92

grass, 41, 101, 166, 170, 172, 175, 181, 183, 193, 198, 213n7; as building material, 21, 25, 43

Greenwood, Roberta, xiii, xvi, 36, 80, 81, 204

ground stone, xvii, 34, 37, 42, 85, 86, 90, 91, 94, 98, 101–4, 151, 152, 159, 179, 183

Gutiérrez, Padre José, 48

haciendas, xii, 11, 22, 50, 204

Hawaiians, 54

heat treatment, 112, 113

herding, 67, 69, 124, 167, 188–90, 193–96, 201; Native, 23, 28, 55, 180; sizes of herds, 22, 67, 68, 181

hides, 13, 18, 51, 69, 139, 194; cattle, 22, 40, 53, 68, 158–61, 181, 188, 189; deer, 53, 161

Híjar, Carlos, 54, 69

historical anthropology, 30, 199, 200

hooks, 41, 42, 116, 122, 124

Hoopes, Chad L., 67, 73, 177, 178, 214n5

horses, 61, 69, 76, 165, 181, 189, 193,

195; bones of, 165, 167; stealing of, 49, 56, 200

hot rocks, 123, 171, 182, 183

houses, indigenous, 33, 36, 43, 75, 76, 80, 97

Hubbert, Presley, 37

hunter-gatherers, 11, 138, 153, 208n4

hunting, 23, 30, 41, 43, 60, 75, 123, 125, 154, 162, 164, 165, 169, 182, 192, 195, 203

Hurtado, Albert, 27, 58

identity, xii, xviii, 3, 8, 15, 16, 21, 44, 61, 66, 152–55, 192, 205; and daily practice, 9; and food, 176, 181, 193; and material culture, 36, 38, 80, 81, 99, 101, 102, 191–93; Californio, 20, 40, 207n1 (preface); laborer, xiv, 10, 31, 70, 188, 191–96, 198, 205; studies of, 7, 10, 179

indebtedness, 6, 28, 38, 55, 71

indigenous peoples, 21, 35, 49, 97, 101, 132, 154; inequality of, xvi, 3, 8, 10, 24, 43, 153; practices and experiences of, xvi, 3, 5, 6, 9, 30, 31, 35, 56–59, 81, 142, 152, 154, 175–78, 184, 199, 203, 205

Iverson, Peter, 195

kettle, 119, 122, 123, 151, 182, 189

knives, 100, 107, 119, 151, 161, 185, 189, 190, 194, 195

labor, xi, xv, xvi, xviii, 6, 72, 153, 197; agreements, 28, 30, 31, 57, 65, 169, 180; colonial, xv, xvi, 8, 9, 12, 16, 21, 38, 40, 66, 78, 79, 99, 139, 189, 193–96, 202, 205; duties or roles of, 30, 49, 51, 60, 68, 69, 76, 124, 149, 176, 185, 188, 192–98, 201, 205; forced, 27, 29, 56, 57, 65, 70, 72, 177; mission, 18, 24, 59; Native, xiv, 4, 5, 8, 11–16, 21–31, 35–38, 40, 54–56, 58–61, 64, 68, 74, 79, 80, 82, 174, 178, 188, 191, 195, 203, 209n5;

organization of, xiv, 23–27, 44, 54, 55, 66–71, 75, 159, 188–92, 196, 202, 214n5; payment or compensation for, 6, 22, 26, 27, 29, 50, 53, 66, 72–74, 124, 131, 142, 149, 152, 154, 175, 179; rancho, 11, 14, 22–31, 38, 56, 59, 60, 69, 72, 76, 79–81, 176, 178, 184–86, 189, 198, 202, 205; recruitment of, 13, 25, 28–31, 49, 55, 197, 203; regimes, xii, 5, 22, 24, 38, 58, 124, 139, 154, 178, 185, 188, 197, 199, 202; seasonal, 4, 22, 25, 27, 51, 58–60, 68, 71, 80, 97, 154, 172, 173, 176, 182, 186, 190; scheduling of, 14, 59, 69, 80, 154, 179, 181, 196, 197, 214n5; shortage of, 61, 67; skilled, 54, 139; theoretical perspectives on, 7–11, 16, 17, 31, 155, 185, 195, 199; treatment of, 23, 26, 31, 71–73, 177

language, 44, 64–66

Libantiloyomi, 63, 209n7

Licatiut, 63, 64, 182, 210n8

Lightfoot, Kent, 36, 94

lithic: artifacts, 33, 37, 86, 90, 106, 93–96, 102–14, 131, 151, 159, 178, 184–87; cores, 42, 43, 107, 110–14, 131, 160; debitage, 96, 102, 105, 107, 112–14, 208n3 (chap. 3), 211n2 (chap. 5); flakes, 110–15, 131, 185, 187, 194, 211n2 (chap. 5); scrapers, 185; shatter, angular, 110–13, 211n2 (chap. 5); technology, 34, 43, 104, 107, 112–14, 151, 184–88, 192, 197, 198, 202, 211n2 (chap. 5)

livestock, xi, 7, 11, 12, 18, 21, 22, 25, 27, 54, 68–70, 140, 154, 172, 176, 180, 181, 189, 192, 195, 201, 202; raids, 21

Los Angeles, xiii, 25, 28, 29, 35, 156

magnesite, 43, 188

majordomo, 52, 55, 67, 70, 71, 76, 124

map, historic, 53, 54, 97

marriage, 8, 66, 188, 203

oral history, xiv, 6, 32, 204
overseer, 22, 31, 51, 78, 160, 174, 184, 189, 192. *See* majordomo

peonage, 23, 26, 28, 38, 71, 73
Petaluma, 27, 42, 48, 49, 53, 56, 62, 66, 162, 170, 211n13
Petaluma (Native group), 63, 208n1 (chap. 3), 209n2, 209n7, 210n8
Petaluma Adobe, 21, 22, 45, 46, 50–55, 58, 69, 76, 82, 98, 101, 123, 125, 140, 159, 164, 165, 167, 173, 176, 177, 181, 182, 188–92, 196, 201, 209n2, 209n7; description of, 22, 50–53; excavations at, 53, 147, 165
Petaluma Adobe State Historic Park, xii, 81
Petaluma River, 50, 63, 68, 115, 162
Phillips, George Harwood, 28, 200
pigs, 165, 180
pinole, 73, 169–71, 181–83, 210n12
pipe, 86, 87, 98, 133, 138, 139, 142
plant remains, xvii, 33, 85, 86, 90, 94, 98, 155, 168–75, 177, 179; absence of, 173; ubiquity of, 157, 169, 170, 172
plants, grown on North Bay ranchos, 53, 174; popular Native, 41, 42, 104, 170, 172, 175, 181, 183, 198, 210n10
plantation, 10, 26, 72, 154, 196, 197
plowing, 25, 59, 94, 174, 193, 196
politics: indigenous, xi, 44, 62, 65, 116, 201; nineteenth-century, 15, 18, 20, 21, 24, 27–29, 40, 44, 47–50, 55–57, 64, 66, 70, 201, 204, 207n1 (preface); of history, xi, xviii, 4, 5, 26, 178, 204; social, 5, 10, 30, 58, 100–102, 116, 153, 154, 176, 179, 184, 185, 192, 198, 199, 205
Pomo, 77, 92, 163, 186; Eastern, 66; Southeastern, 66; Southern, 63, 65, 209n7, 210n9
postsecularization, 20, 55, 58, 62, 66
precontact, 23, 32, 36, 105, 152, 184,

205; deposits, 34, 84, 96, 115, 197; patterns in Petaluma area, xvi, 41–44, 95, 115, 138, 143, 170, 171, 175, 186, 187; patterns in southern California, 34, 132
prehistory, 7, 10, 34, 36, 95, 96, 204
presidio, 17, 18, 47, 49, 171–75, 212n7
Presidio de San Francisco, 45, 47, 49; archaeological study of, 140, 171–75, 212n7
prisoner, 4, 26, 27, 56, 65, 70, 71
projectile points, 34, 42, 96, 107, 109, 114, 115, 131, 151, 179, 185, 187

quartz, 106, 107, 113, 114
Quijas, Father José Lorenzo, 48, 49

rabbit, 41, 156, 158, 164, 175, 182, 198
ranchero, xiii, 20–39, 58, 61, 68, 72–74, 81, 124, 154, 161, 167, 182, 188, 190, 202–3
ranchos, xi–xiii, xvi, xviii, 7–9, 11–13, 15–25, 30, 33–39, 40, 44, 49, 50, 53, 54, 67–69, 73–75, 80–82, 100, 161archaeological research on, 94, 134, 159, 201; comparison of to other institutions, 70, 154, 196, 197, 202, 205; incorporation of into indigenous cycles, 28, 55, 58; list of, 35; period, 94, 98, 148, 150, 169, 186, 200, 204; provisioning of, xvii, 6, 23, 29, 66, 72–75, 79, 80, 124, 142, 152, 154, 159, 160, 169, 175, 176, 179–83, 188, 190, 196, 198, 203, 205. See also *haciendas*; labor: rancho
Ranchos: Cañon de Santa Ana, 24; Los Cerritos, 25, 35; San Jacinto Viejo, 37; San Joaquin, 35; Santa Ana del Chino, 25; Santiago de Santa Ana, 35; Soscol, 21; Suñol, 37
refuse, 9, 33, 39, 83, 91, 94–99, 113, 123, 131, 138–41, 150, 168–71, 174, 180–83, 185, 194

205; stone, xv, xvii, 36, 39, 41–43, 54, 82, 85, 91, 94, 98, 102–16, 125, 126, 132, 151, 152, 161, 177, 179, 183, 193–98, 202, 205, 208n3 (chap. 3)

Torres, Manuel, 207n1 (chap. 1)

trade, 22, 29, 30, 53, 105, 131, 139, 140, 144, 145, 149, 152, 164, 173, 188, 190, 203; goods, 25, 43, 55, 80, 190; hide and tallow, 20, 53, 159; Native, 43, 60, 150, 182, 186, 197, 198, 203

trees and shrubs, 41, 166, 170, 172, 175, 181, 197, 213n2 (chap. 6)

trenches: descriptions of, 83–94, 157; contents of, 88, 89, 103, 106, 107, 110–12, 118–23, 126, 129, 130, 133, 134, 138, 143, 148, 158, 159, 160, 162, 166–71, 180, 212n6

Vallejo, Francisca Benicia Carrillo de, 3–6, 45, 60, 70, 71, 192, 193, 207n1 (chap. 1)

Vallejo, Mariano Guadalupe, xii, 4, 7, 14, 28, 55, 62, 77, 138, 140, 151, 176, 191, 213n2 (chap. 6); biography of, xiii, 14, 45, 46, 48, 49; and control of Rancho Petaluma, xiii, 22–26, 48–50, 53–63, 66–81, 124, 125, 150, 151, 159, 161, 173–76, 180–84, 190, 194–98, 211n13, 213n1 (chap. 6); home life of, 22, 51, 52, 55, 58, 60, 72, 79; military career of, 15, 20, 29, 44, 48–50, 55–57, 64, 65, 70, 125; political life of, 15, 40, 44, 48, 57, 64, 74, 201; and relations with Native groups, 57, 65, 78, 190, 203, 209n3, 209n5, 210n9; and relations with Russians, 22, 48, 50,

60, 203, 209n3; statements about, 26, 57, 59, 67, 71, 74, 160, 177, 197

Vallejo, Napoleón, 73, 149, 151, 163, 183, 210n12

Vallejo, Platon, 55, 60, 183

Vallejo, Salvador, 40, 46, 49, 50, 56, 67, 165, 202

vaquero, 25, 53, 58, 59, 67, 69, 72, 78, 124, 167, 189, 195

Verdugo, José María, 18

Vischer, Edward, 46, 75, 76, 182

Wappo, 63–66, 150, 186, 210n9

Ward, James, 46, 66, 76

waterfowl, 43, 125, 162, 197

weapons: ammunition, 87, 120, 123, 125, 151; arrows, 41, 42, 107, 151, 186; firearms, 120, 121, 123–25, 162

weaving, 51, 53, 68, 69, 192, 196

wheat, 22, 53, 54, 59, 68, 76, 104, 153, 168, 169, 173–76, 181, 183, 197, 210n10; archaeological recovery of, 101, 166, 168, 169, 172, 179

Wilkes, Charles, 3–6, 26, 46, 57

wine, 25, 126, 129, 131, 178

women (Native), 26, 30, 35, 41, 42, 53, 68, 69, 77, 105, 124, 163, 171, 175, 181, 182, 192–98; statements about, 40, 65, 70, 183

World Systems Theory, 10

Ynitia, Camillo, 45, 46, 57, 58, 63

Yolotoi, 45, 65

Yorba: Bernardo, 22, 24, 25, 31, 32; Juan Antonio, 35; ranchos, 202

Yount, George, 50, 202

Zampay, 45, 65